The real war on
INFLATION
has not begun

A discussion and analysis of all the purported
causes of this period (1937 to present) of inflation
and the long-range solution to it

By

Robert S. Morrison, Chairman & Chief Executive Officer
Molded Fiber Glass Companies
1315 W. 47th Street
Ashtabula, Ohio 44004

Analyses by

W. Angus Ray, Retired President
Northeastern Ohio National Bank
(Now AmeriTrust Company of Northeastern Ohio, N.A.)
Ashtabula, Ohio 44004

Western Reserve Press, Inc.
P.O. Box 675
Ashtabula, Ohio 44004
(216) 993-6886

First Edition—May, 1982
Copyright, 1982, by Robert S. Morrison
Library of Congress Card Number 82050571
ISBN Number 912400–25–0
Printed by: Kingsport Press, Kingsport, TN

The Inflation Battle Is Just Beginning*
by Seymour Zucker

With unemployment hitting a six-year high and more and more economic sign-posts pointing to a sharp recession, economists are already beginning to talk about a sustained slowdown in the inflation rate. And some, especially those who have their eyes glued to the money supply numbers, are even saying that the U.S. has entered an era of disinflation. Indeed, in contrast to the double-digit price rises recorded earlier this year, the November consumer price index is expected to show an annualized increase of less than 4%—below the comfortable 4.8% rate registered in October. The critical question for both policymakers and business people is whether this sharp deceleration of inflation is part of a long-run trend or is simply a short-run aberration.

One way to answer that question is to separate the markets for goods and services into two broad categories. And viewed from the perspective of how prices are determined in these markets, it appears that the nature of the recent slowing of inflation is more temporary than lasting. Sir John R. Hicks, Britain's first Nobelist in economics, calls these markets "flexprice" and "fixprice." In flexprice markets, prices are set mostly by the ebb and flow of supply and demand. These markets include most farm commodities, industrial commodities, and financial assets. Flexprices fluctuate widely, and a slowdown in economic activity depresses demand enough to bring about sharp declines. The prices of such industrial commodities as lumber and copper and steel scrap, for example, are down about 25% since the beginning of the year, and prices may drop even further as the recession deepens. On the consumer front, farm prices—especially of meat—have been under sharp pressure. If, on the other hand, the economy recovers from recession next year, as most forecasters expect, prices in the flexmarkets will inevitably rebound, perhaps sharply, as they did in the recovery period following the deep 1974–75 recession.

Overlapping forces. In contrast, the key characteristic of fixprice markets—which are predominant in the U.S.—is that they are largely insulated from the forces of supply and demand. Companies set prices in these markets to reflect their production costs. Prices tend to change slowly, whether up or down. And they can go lower and stay lower only if production costs do the same.

Certain production costs in the fixprice sector are determined in flexprice markets. For example, steel scrap, an industrial commodity, feeds the auto industry. How do companies respond when the price of a flexprice commodity crucial to their production process tumbles? If the price decline is viewed as only temporary, the tendency to reduce prices of finished goods will not be very strong. If, however, costs stay low for an extended period, companies begin to consider

* Reprinted from the December 21, 1981 issue of *Business Week* by special permission, (c) 1981 by McGraw-Hill, Inc., New York, N.Y. 10020. All rights reserved. The author, Seymour Zucker, is Senior Editor and Chief Economist of *Business Week*.

them normal, and they adjust the price of their products accordingly.

Because recessions in the U.S. have generally been short, and because most companies depend on flexprice commodities, the prices of finished goods rarely fall to reflect what are judged to be only temporary drops in input costs. It is therefore little wonder that attempts to halt inflation with recessions have ended in failure.

To be sure, as recession bites deeper and inventories build, business starts to offer products at distress prices. Indeed, such distress sales have been part of the "good news" in the CPIs in recent months, especially the decline in new-car prices. But these price dips will prove to be short-lived as production is brought into line with sales.

The wages impact. By far the most significant expense for companies that sell in fixprice markets is labor, which accounts for almost two-thirds of total production costs. Wage rates are not determined in the flexprice market by supply-and-demand forces; they are more like fixprice products. Thus, labor costs move relatively slowly, and again history shows that the impact of recessions on wages has been limited.

But there is one bright spot on the longer-run inflation horizon. This time the combination of recession and sharply stepped-up international competition has apparently induced labor to curtail its wage demands from an increase of about 11% a year to about 8%. If this trend continues—and it is a big if—reduced demands will begin to enter companies' longer-run cost calculations and subsequently translate into lower prices. Such gains in the fight against inflation will be a long time coming, however. In the meantime, business people and Administration officials who expect a lasting cut in inflation to come quickly may be sadly disappointed. The battle against inflation is just beginning.

Henry C. Wallich, Member, Board of Governors of the Federal Reserve System, told the American Economic Association on December 28, 1981,

"We are now looking ahead to the outcome of wage bargaining between a few large unions and a few large corporations or industries. The inflation outlook for all the rest of the economy, vastly larger in the aggregate than these contenders, seems to hang on the outcome of those isolated struggles. We are reenacting a scene from the Middle Ages, when wars between armies were decided by the single combat of their champions. There must be a better way of dealing with inflation, and we had better find it."

STATEMENT by Alfred E. Kahn, Professor of Economics at Cornell University, and formerly President Carter's "Inflation Fighter" in the New York Times.

Inflation we continue to experience is predominantly a consequence of a continuing stubborn increase in wages.—Wages account for 75 percent of our national income, and as long as they keep going up at a 9 percent rate, while productivity goes up little or not at all, an 8 or 9 percent continuing inflation rate is inescapable. Continuing wage increases are directly responsible for mounting unemployment.

Contents

Contents

Contents

Index of Charts

Index of Tables

A Forewarning

In 1945–46 I was president of the Ashtabula County Auto Dealers Association and a director of the Ohio Auto Dealers Association. (I was the Ashtabula Ford dealer from late 1937 to early 1948). It was obvious to me that large compensation increases obtained by the United Auto Workers from the auto companies would result in ever-increasing prices for cars and trucks.

Being president and director gave me no power and, of course, no salary but it did give me an opportunity to express my views and fears. The U.A.W. struck General Motors on November 12, 1945 demanding 25¢ an hour and some costly fringes. This averaged about a 20% increase. What the U.A.W. would get from General Motors it would subsequently get from Ford and all others in the auto industry.

I tried to get the auto dealers associations to take a stand against a wage settlement that resulted in an increase in the price of cars. I proposed that dealers go on record that they would not handle cars if prices went up. I made this proposal in a meeting of the Ohio Auto Dealers Association and over the phone to the National Auto Dealers Association in Washington. I told them that unless these inflationary cost increases were nipped in the bud, they would continue ever after and eventually do great harm to the industry and the auto dealers.

One director, who was an Oldsmobile dealer, said to

me, "Morrison, you can live on your hardware (service) business. I've got to have cars. The hell with the price." A Washington official of the National Auto Dealers Association called me and politely told me to shut up. The local dealers did not argue with me, but neither did they support me.

I doubt if my proposal would have been effective even if supported by the N.A.D.A. and other dealer organizations, but if the movement had obtained some publicity it might have influenced the size of the increase, and caused people to realize that wage increases followed by price increases guaranteed inflation.

After a devastating 113-day strike, General Motors settled for 18½¢ an hour. Up went the price of cars. Postwar inflation (instead of normal post-war deflation), took off with a flying start.

In February, 1982, the U.A.W. and Ford, and later General Motors, renegotiated their existing contracts. This was hailed by superficial observors of evidence that unions (in general) were becoming more reasonable and had actually willingly accepted cuts in wages. Nothing of the kind.

Under the renegotiated contracts, the U.A.W. will receive increases of 6.4% a year in place of 8.7% a year under the old contract. Further, the companies have given up some rights to shut down losing operations and to place orders for parts with foreign suppliers. These conceptions will cost the companies money and provide more job security for union members.

To make the U.S. auto companies competitive with foreign competition, wages, salaries, and fringes need to be cut 25% or more, which still leaves U.A.W. members paid far more than the average American factory worker. These so-called concessions only slightly slow down the rate of inflation, not stop it.

Preface

War, said Georges Clemenceau, is too important to be left to the generals.

It is now evident that economics is too important to be left to the economists.

Economics is the science dealing with the production, distribution and consumption of wealth. Those who assert that they alone are qualified to speak on the subject—professional economists—have little or no real experience with these matters. No wonder Peter Drucker advises, "Don't put the fate of your business in the delusions of economists."

Economists are at the mercy of the theories to which they have committed themselves. Typically, Milton Friedman told me that he had read my theories and did not agree with them—so there was no use talking further.

John Neville Keynes, the father of John Maynard Keynes, once said that comparing a professional economist to a businessman-economist was like comparing an astronomer to an astrologer. But when we look at the fruits of what the professional economists have done it's apparent that comparing the professional to the businessman is more like comparing a witch doctor to a general practitioner.

Who has more experience with—and interest in—the production and distribution of wealth than a businessman? I am prepared to admit that professional economists are used to consuming wealth.

So—without apology—here are some analyses and solutions created by a "general practitioner" of economics: a businessman. Much of what I say may shock you. I ask you to consider it on its merits.

Acknowledgments

When Angus Ray retired early . . . in 1981 . . . as President of the Northeastern Ohio National Bank, (now AmeriTrust Company of Northeastern Ohio, N.A.), I was just getting started on the manuscript for this book. I asked him to help collect statistics, read articles, and prepare analyses of many of the factors influencing inflation. The major part of the analysis consists of his work, as well as some of the charts and tables in the body of the text.

Professor William Peterson, Director of the Center for Economic Education for the University of Tennessee at Chattanooga, contacted me last fall suggesting that I get together with Professor Simon Whitney of Scarsdale, N.Y., whose theories on the cause of inflation generally coincided with mine, and who was planning a book on the subject. Peterson has been a great sounding board for my ideas over the years. Professor Whitney and I met. We agreed on the major cause of inflation but not on its solution. He felt that my blaming the perpetrators of compensation-cost-push inflation was too strong. We decided to go our separate ways. Over the time I have been writing this manuscript I have submitted chapters in it to Professor Whitney, who has read them and sent back to me cogent comments, suggestions, and criticisms. Ed Stevens and Betty Maynard of the Cleveland Federal Reserve Bank have been very helpful and constructive.

Several years ago I met with Seymour Zucker and William Wolman, senior editors and economic writers for Business Week. We were all concerned about inflation and what steps would have to be taken to stop it. I was pleased to read Zucker's discussion in the December 21, 1981 issue of Business Week entitled, *The Inflation Battle Is Just Beginning.* I obtained permission from McGraw-Hill to reprint it. He speaks of a *battle;* I speak of a *war* against inflation. He says the battle *is just beginning;* I say it *has not begun.* A mere difference is semantics. We agree on its cause.

William Gottlieb of Morrison/Gottlieb in New York is the P/R agency who handles Molded Fiber Glass Companies. Jack Tarrant has professionally edited other books for me as well as this one.

Sharon DeFazio has retyped this manuscript many times as I expanded, refined, and corrected my ideas. They all had important hands in putting this manuscript together and making it clear.

Definitions

Listing definitions at the beginning of this book instead of in the glossary or appendix at its end serves three purposes. First, many readers may be unfamiliar with the meaning—in an economic context—of some words and phrases. Second, I have taken liberties with other words and phrases, limiting or expanding their scope to make their use in the text more exact. Third, the usually accepted meanings of some terms, such as GNP and cost-of-living, are inaccurate and lead to erroneous assumptions and conclusions.

INFLATION Before a discussion on any subject begins, the subject should be defined. While recent usage of the word "inflation" seems to indicate a rising price level, past usages and dictionary definitions have sometimes considered inflation to be a rapid expansion in the supply of paper money which in turn causes rising prices.

For this study, inflation will be defined as follows: *A continuing and general increase in the prices of raw materials, products, services, real estate, intangibles, wages, taxes, and/or items for which money is paid.* In this discussion the word will occasionally be used to describe continuous rising prices of any item, such as land or doctor bills, with the item so identified.

ADMINISTERED PRICES   Prices set for his product by a producer of goods or services arrived at by summing up all costs, i.e.: raw materials, labor input, taxes, administrative, overhead, etc., and adding the profit he expects to earn.

ADULTS   People over 26 years old.

CASH FLOW   The change in cash position of a business resulting from the following factors:

PLUS FACTORS
After-tax earnings, depreciation charges, sale of assets, borrowings, increases in liabilities, and equity investment.

MINUS FACTORS
After-tax losses, increases in non-cash assets, repayment of debt, decreases in equity investment, dividends.

CHILDREN   Those under 16 years old.

COMPANY   Any business for profit, whether incorporated, partnership, or proprietorship, regardless of type of activity, except professions.

CONSUMERS   People who spend their own money for goods and services.

CONSUMER PRICE INDEX   An index prepared by the Bureau of Labor Statistics reflecting retail price changes of selected goods and services used by typical families. This index is often erroneously referred to as a Cost-of-Living Index, which it is not, since it does not include taxes and it is unduly influenced by fluctuations in such items as housing and interest costs. The CPI currently uses 1967 prices for its base figure of 100.

CONTAX PLAN   A plan which will stop our continuing inflation.

DEFLATION   The opposite of inflation.

DEMAND   The amount of a product or service which the market will absorb at a given price. Demand is "elastic" when a lower price results in more sales; a higher price less sales. Example: luxury items such as jewelry. Demand is "inelastic" when price changes have little effect on sales volume. Example: table salt.

DEPRECIATION   Normally a decrease in value of a fixed asset due to wear and tear in use and gradual obsolescence. In accounting and tax returns depreciation is a non-cash charge against earnings which does not necessarily match the actual depreciation of such assets. The word depreciation also applies to a decline in the value of a currency, which happens during inflation.

ELASTIC DEMAND   (See DEMAND)

ELASTIC SUPPLY   (See SUPPLY)

THE ESTABLISHMENT   The present economic-social-political system in the United States.

FISCAL POLICY   The actions of Government in the areas of taxing and spending that influence the economy.

GROSS NATIONAL PRODUCT (GNP)   The official title is Gross National Product and Expenditures. GNP is generally considered to be a summary of total production of final goods and services, both private and public, measured in money, at annual rates. On the contrary, it is a total of the estimates of personal consumption expenditures for durable goods, non-durable goods, and services; gross private domestic investment; business inventory changes; net exports; and government purchases of goods and services. The relationship between production and expenditures is not constant. The change in business inventories hopefully adjusts for this change. The value of services which are not directly purchased is considered to be the input in the form of wages, salaries, and similar costs, since there is no way to estimate their market value. As services become an increasing proportion of GNP&E, the accuracy of its total as an estimate of the total real national production is lessened.

GOVERNMENT Unless specifically limited, this includes all forms of tax-supported activity, including local, county, state and federal governments, tax-supported schools and other institutions, and government-operated businesses, whether subsidized or self-supporting.

IMPLICIT PRICE DEFLATOR The U.S. Department of Commerce has developed a number of indexes called "deflators" to measure price changes in "constant dollars" by converting them to prices in a base year. This corrects for variations in the purchasing power of the dollar.

One widely used index is called Implicit Price Deflators for Gross National Product, currently using 1972 as its base year. It includes information on personal consumption expenditures for durable and non-durable goods and for services, private domestic investment, exports and imports of goods and services and government expenditures for goods and services.

The deflator index is actually a better measure of inflation than the CPI, because it is broader-based, while the CPI reflects only changes in retail prices. Since its 1972 base year, the GNP Deflator has increased 25% less than the Consumer Price Index.

INELASTIC DEMAND (See DEMAND)

INELASTIC SUPPLY (See SUPPLY)

INSTITUTIONAL FIELD Privately managed activities, such as hospitals, private schools and colleges, usually not for profit, or in which a large percentage of the individual operations are not for profit.

JOB EVALUATION The determination of the relative compensation for each class of jobs in an organization, based on physical, mental, and other requirements of the individual and the importance of proper job performance to the organization.

MARGINAL PRODUCER In theory, a producer whose gross income from products and services sold just equals his total costs of production. A producer who makes no profit on an average throughout a year or other complete cycle of production. A marginal producer might also be considered one who makes less return on his equity than if he had it invested in government bonds.

MILITANTS Individuals who seek to openly force their desires or aims on others, on institutions, and on society in general through the use of force and such tactics as blocking access to, occupying, or damaging property, injuring persons, or other illegal acts. The line between the militant and the criminal is often fuzzy. For this discussion, a criminal may be defined as one who seeks personal gain through illegal acts, while a militant acts for a group cause which may or may not benefit him directly.

MOB Any group of more than one person which illegally, unethically, immorally, or selfishly forces or attempts or threatens to force its demands, whether economic, political, or social, onto others, including individuals, companies, institutions, and governments. Also included are groups whose actions interfere illegally with the personal and property rights of others. Mob action is usually instigated by persons employing inflammatory emotional rhetoric to induce others to further their interests. These inciters may be militants, criminals, or members of special interest groups seeking economic advantages.

MONETARY POLICY The actions of officials of the Federal Reserve System to maintain the stability of the national currency by increasing or decreasing the supply of money and credit. Methods of control include changing bank reserve requirements, open-market buying and selling of Government securities, changing bank rediscount rates and federal funds rates, and using moral suasion to prevent overheating of the economy. Excess money supply is believed by many to be an important cause of the present inflation.

MONEY SUPPLY   Funds quickly available for spending or investing. This could be called a generic definition of a subject made increasingly complicated by increasing sophistication in financial markets. The measure watched most closely is M-1, which includes currency in circulation, bank demand deposits, and other checkable deposits at banks and savings institutions. The broader measures, M2 and M3, include, in addition to time deposits, savings accounts, and money market funds, such esoteric items as overnight Eurodollar borrowings, bank repurchase agreements, large-denomination negotiable certificates of deposit, etc.

OLIGOPOLY   A small group of large companies which together dominate an industry and have among themselves effective control over the price of a product or service. New companies are usually discouraged from entering the industry by the large amount of technical knowledge or the size of investment required.

PERCENTAGE CHANGE OF AN INDEX   Throughout the text comparisons between an index for one year and a subsequent year will be made by showing a percentage change. The formula used for calculating percentage changes in an index is:

$$\frac{\text{Current Index}}{\text{Previous Period Index}} - 1.00 \times 100 = \text{Percent change}$$

Examples:
$$\frac{90}{80} = 1.125 - 1.00 = .125 \times 100 = 12.5\% \text{ increase}$$

$$\frac{72}{80} = .090 - 1.00 = -.10 \times 100 = 10\% \text{ decrease}$$

POLITICIANS   Some people consider the word politician derogatory. I do not. Politics is an honorable and very necessary part of life. A politician is a person who is a candidate for, or holder of, an elective government office, or a person who has an office, either elective or appointive, in a political party or who is quite active and influential in a political party. Unfortunately the realities of political life make it difficult for politicians to hold to the highest levels of consistency in policies and viewpoints, ethics, and associates.

PRIVATE INDUSTRY   This term encompasses all private economic activities, whether goods producing or service producing. Such activities may be conducted by corporations, partnerships, proprietorships, institutions, and non-profit organizations. It does not include local, state, and federal government operations of any type, whether tax-supported or self-supporting.

PRODUCTIVITY   Productivity is, in its simplest term, the amount of product or service produced by the individual worker in a given time.

Government statisticians, economists, and others like to speak of productivity increases as if they were a national wave pervading all areas and economic activities evenly and steadily. This misconception will be discussed at length in the text.

PROFITS   In this study "profits" will mean the net income of a business after all expenses, including managerial salaries and taxes (including income taxes) are paid.

RETIREES   People who have voluntarily or involuntarily completed their full-time working careers and who are living on income from, or principal of, privately-owned assets, annuities, pensions, and social security; or who are supported by relatives, friends, or non-welfare institutions. In this discussion, it is assumed that a retiree has no power to increase his income through his personal efforts. Speculative income from reinvestment of assets might be possible, but it is not considered a "power" since the risk is great and net result likely to be zero or less.

SUPPLY   For this study, the quantity of goods or services available to meet market demand. If an increase in price creates an increase in supply, the supply is considered elastic. Example: mining of lower-grade ore when mineral prices rise. Since increasing the supply of an item may take some time, the supply of such an item may be temporarily inelastic.

Supply is inelastic when it remains relatively constant in spite of price increases. Examples: animal hides from the meat-packing industry and slag from steel production.

TAXPAYERS   All people who pay taxes, directly and/ or indirectly. Not considered taxpayers are those who receive from the government more in welfare payments, subsidies, pensions (not including Social Security), food and other goods and services, gifts and other non-earned income, than they earn from their own efforts and their property.

UNEARNED INCOME   A popular misnomer for income from savings or investments. The term imputes a stigma to the virtue of contributing to the economic base.

VALUE ADDED BY MANUFACTURE   The difference between the total sales of a manufacturing company and the total amount paid for raw materials, components, products, supplies, containers, fuels, purchased electricity, and contract work, plus or minus net change in finished goods and work-in-process inventories.

WAGES   In this discussion the word "wages" will include all types of compensation for personal services, including hourly wages, incentive and other wages, salaries, commissions, bonuses, fees, contracts, feather-bedding payments, tips, and fringe benefits, unless a limiting word, such as "hourly," is used in conjunction with "wages." From an employer's point of view, wages include all labor costs. The employee considers wages as what he receives. In most of the discussions in this book, wages and labor costs will be synonymous.

WELFARERS   People who receive more than 50% of their total income from government welfare payments of all types and/or private charities. Social Security recipients are not considered welfarers unless the recipient did not, or his spouse did not, make any previous compulsory or voluntary contributions to the Social Security fund.

YOUNG PEOPLE   Those from 16 through 26 years of age.

Introduction

WHY THIS BOOK?

Much has been written and said about the present period of inflation. Many experiments have been tried to slow down inflation, but none have been successful, nor will they be. Nothing that has been proposed will be. Business recessions and bumper crops will slow down the rate of inflation but are temporary abberations in the long-term upward trend of prices.

Tremendous damage to the U.S. economy has been done by faulty and fruitless efforts to stop inflation. Inflation can be *stopped* by the right policies and legislation. This book tells you how it can be done. It will not be easy. It will be a long war, not a short battle. To stop inflation permanently a great majority of Americans will have to have the courage to stand up and be counted.

The book presents a sound and practical solution to inflation . . . the only long-term solution. The chances of its being adopted in the near term are slight. It challenges the firmly entrenched, though erroneous, theories about the causes and cure for inflation. In some form, eventually, the principles set forth in this book must be adopted. Whether they will be adopted under our present representative form of government is very questionable.

For the reader to understand the thrust of this book, he must know more about me and why I wrote it. I have been a loner, an iconoclast, all my life. My father was a merchant in Ashtabula, Ohio, who married late (at 45) and died early (at 56). I was small and somewhat younger than my schoolmates, and to make matters worse, I skipped the 6th grade in school on the recommendation of the school teachers, putting me in with a group both physically and socially ahead of me. I had no conflicts with anyone, but also no close associations. This did not bother me. In fact, I was hardly conscious of it. It set a pattern which has continued ever since. I have felt no compulsion to conform, but also no compulsion to be different just for the sake of being different.

I have frequently questioned the views and actions of the majority. If I agree with them, I keep quiet. If I disagree with their views and actions and believe that I can or should do something about it, I at least publicly explain what the proper views should be.

For more than a half century I have done this, in live talks as well as in all news media.

In early 1931 I wrote a paper explaining why a serious depression was ahead, when all other forecasters predicted the recession would be over in 3 to 6 months. In 1937, after the steel and auto wage settlements were announced, I predicted permanent inflation. Most people thought that after the unions got their big wage increase (17–20%) they would be satisfied, but I did not. I had been forewarned by a man by the name of Tym, who I had met in 1932. Tym had been the finance minister of Ukrainia in 1917–1919 and barely escaped when the Bolsheviks took over in 1919. In the summer of 1934 he and I were discussing the Roosevelt administration's efforts to cure the depression. F.D.R. had started playing up to the union bosses. Tym said that giving more power to the unions was very dangerous. He said that no matter how much power and money they were given they would always want more, until they had taken over all power.

I majored in economics (with honors) at Oberlin College, graduating in 1930. When I finished the first year at Harvard Business School in 1931 I did economic and market research for two Milwaukee firms. When the 1933 bank holiday and the depression resulted in my being out of a job in June, 1933, I returned home.

I considered continuing in economic and marketing research, but jobs were scarce in 1933. Further, I noticed that when I worked for others my propensity for expressing my own views on a subject when the boss' views differed from mine could make advancement as an employee difficult. Since then I have been in business for myself.

I learned the facts of retail business life as a Ford dealer from late 1937 to early 1948. During this period I handled a number of successful industrial development projects for our community. One project, a pulp molding plant, did not succeed. I took it over personally. After many trials, errors, and losses, I converted it to a fiber glass plastic molding plant. I have been in the fiber glass plastic business ever since.

The total cumulative volume of sales of the Molded Fiber Glass Companies under my management through the end of 1981 has been over $700,000,000. Current volume is running around $50,000,000 a year. At one time I owned 100% of the present operations, but have transferred most ownership, but not control, to the next two generations. I believe, but cannot prove, that these operations are the largest dollar volume producers of fiber glass reinforced plastic in the world, and the total over the years is the largest. We have a number of new products and processes coming along which should not only keep us in first place, but also widen the gap ahead of second place. In 1973 I was elected a charter member of the Plastics Hall of Fame, the only active molder to be elected.

Great-but how does this experience qualify me to be an expert on economics and inflation? First, it combines the theoretical economics training I obtained at Oberlin and Harvard with the practical experience of the marketplace, both as a manufacturer and a retailer. The professional economist has the theories, but has not had marketplace and production shop experience. I also have had first-hand experience dealing with unions, with more than normal success.

Second, in the 72 years of my existence (born 11/19/09) more good things, more bad things, more production, more destruction, more prosperity, more depression, more wasting of natural assets, more casualties, greater reduction of deaths from disease, and greater increase in population have occurred than in any other previous period in history. First-hand contact, knowledge, and experience over this particular time period should give a close observer an opportunity to check out economic theories in the real world. Some are right, some are wrong, and some are vague enough to be considered either right or wrong, depending on the viewpoint of the speaker.

Third, over the years I have personally computed the prices of thousands of products MFG makes and sells and have developed pricing formulae and price computation sheets for others to use. I have also been on the receiving end of tens of thousands of price increases on everything the Molded Fiber Glass Companies buy, and

I know what causes prices to go up. MFG also reports monthly prices on certain products to the U.S. Bureau of Labor Statistics for its Producer Price Index (PPI).

I have watched prices go up steadily every since 1937 and have watched the Federal government either do nothing about these price increases or, directly or indirectly, do the wrong things, which result in prices going up even faster. I have watched, and been a victim of, Federal Reserve attempts to stop inflation which have been both futile and destructive.

I had several letters to and from Ronald Reagan prior to his starting to campaign for the presidency. I thought I was making some progress with him, but when he stated, at a speech in Erie in 1979, that the sole causes of this period of inflation were government deficits and too much money in circulation I realized he did not understand how to stop inflation. His strong stand against the Air Traffic Controllers union had my enthusiastic approval, even though it has caused some inconvenience and delays in our MFC plane flight schedules. (We have two small twin-engine planes.)

However, his recent kowtowing to the union bosses, headed by Lane Kirkland, (December, 1981) and his stand against SB 613, The Hobbs Act, which would make picket line violence and similar actions a Federal offense, shows very clearly that Reagan will not take the steps necessary to stop inflation. If Reagan will not take a stand on compensation-cost-push inflation who among all the candidates for President who possibly could get elected will? Remember, to accomplish this both the Senate and the House must originate and/or approve such legislation before it gets to the President's desk. More about this situation in late chapters in this book.

Shortly after World War II a friend and I were talking. He had been born before the turn of the century. He said he was happy because now that the war was over, prices would fall back to their pre-war levels. I told him that prices would not drop back, as they had done after all previous U.S. wars, but would keep on going up, year after year. I had forgotten this conversation, but a few years ago he recalled it for me.

He then asked me how I could have been so sure in 1946 that we would have continued permanent inflation. The answer to his question is between the covers of this book. However, just answering his question would not justify the effort and expense of writing a book, nor could I ask for the reader's individual attention. It is not enough to make a valid prediction, or to analyze what has gone wrong. What this country desperately needs is a plan to make things go right. That is the real thrust of this book.

A person usually writes a book to earn money, or to improve his status in his profession or business, or to see his name in print, or to improve his political position, or to give himself something to do in retirement. I have none of those motives.

So, why am I writing this book? *The greatest, most productive, freest, country and economy in the world is in very serious danger of being destroyed by a man-caused inflation.*

Men were smart enough, and brave enough, to establish this country, but now are neither smart enough to see the main cause of this inflation, nor brave enough to speak out about it if they do see it. Inflation has become a way of life and business, with a few people and businesses benefiting from it, some just getting along with it, and a great many suffering severely from it. Attempts so far to stop it have been both futile and destructive.

Why? Because too many people, those in high political office, high banking circles, and high academic life do not fully understand what has caused this forty-five year period of inflation, 1937-to-date, and are trying to stop inflation by the wrong methods; by very destructive methods that will not effectively stop inflation, but will cause, if carried to the extremes contemplated by some, not only wide-spread depression but also wide-spread bankruptcy of both private and public businesses and institutions. Even then the major force causing this inflation will not have been eliminated.

Ever since leaving school I have been actively reading, writing, and talking about economics and business. (Economics: the science that deals with the production, distribution, and consumption of wealth) I have not been willing to let this subject be dominated by theoretical academic economists with no experience in the real world in production, distribution, and consumption. A person with years of economic training and continued interest in economics and widespread business experience should have a far better knowledge of real economics than they.

People who read this book may come to the conclusion that I was born and have been ever since a rock-ribbed super-conservative Republican. In the early 1930's I considered myself a Democrat, believing in free trade, states' rights, a limited federal government, and the little man.

However, in 1933 and after, I watched with dismay the attempts the administration made to overcome the depression, with most every attempt contrary to economic principles and every attempt increasing the power and domination of the Federal government. Gradually the complexion of the Democratic party changed. It had always been a coalition of various minority groups, including a so-called labor group, with no one group dominating it. In the 1930's the labor union group emerged as the most powerful, and the other groups, except the southern Democrats, tagged along with the labor group, giving it domination of the Democratic party. At that point I became a mugwump and finally a Republican.

How did I get started writing a book on inflation in 1970? From 1948 to 1970 I had been deeply involved in the fiberglass-reinforced plastic business, with little time for much else. I had formed the Molded Fiber Glass Body Company in 1953 to make parts for the Chevrolet Corvette body. My businesses were always undercapitalized, and since they were growing, they needed more funds than could be generated internally. Ashtabula had three small banks with limited lending power. In 1960 the three of them together could lend to one borrower about $500,000. Business volume grew slowly at first, so MFG could get along just borrowing from local banks.

In the early 1960's business grew rapidly, new plants had to be constructed, and more borrowed funds were needed. We first went to a Cleveland bank, but had the misfortune of being assigned a very cautious loan officer who had never made a bad loan in his life and was about to retire. He wanted to keep his record intact. One of our new major projects did not get going as rapidly and smoothly as we had projected, which usually happens. He started to tell me how to run my business, and strongly recommended I retrench. I refused.

In those days big banks wanted big customers and considered customers my size as marginal; expendable when money got tight. Our business kept on growing but I could get no more money from this bank. With help from a supplier, I switched over to a Pittsburgh bank.

It is a long story, told in detail in my *Handbook for Manufacturing Entrepreneurs,* but MFG got caught twice in Federal Reserve attempts to stop inflation by forcing commercial banks to reduce their commercial loans, once in 1965–66, and again in 1969–70. Sales volume had jumped from $10 million in 1960 to $40 million in 1970. In late 1969 MFG was finishing up a new plant and tooling up for the largest job in its history. I went to the bank for more money, and was told they not only would not lend MFG more money, but would reduce our credit limit by one million. They blamed the Federal Reserve but there was more to that story than that. MFG was an expendable account.

A large company had been romancing me for a couple of years about acquiring the MFG Body Company. I felt that trying to switch to another bank under the Federal Reserve restriction would be a waste of time, so I agreed to the merger, which was effected April 8, 1970.

I was not in favor of the merger. I said I could work out of our troubles in six months if MFG had another million dollars. The MFG statement justified it. Net equity of the Molded Fiber Glass Body Company was $8,004,000, net long-term debt $2,642,000, net short-term debt, less than $2,000,000. Start-up costs on new jobs were high, but the overall operation was profitable and had been ever since it started.

What happened to the acquired operations? Over the years I guesstimate it has lost $40,000,000 pre-tax. The Ashtabula operation, when I relinquished it, employed about 1,000 people. In 1981 it employed about 200 people. A successful growing company providing jobs and opportunities in Northeastern Ohio has been turned into a shambles because the Federal Reserve, under McChesney Martin, tried to stop inflation by trying to reduce commercial bank loans, and thus the money supply. This policy results in putting the squeeze on young, growing, but financially weak, companies.

How many thousand times has this been repeated throughout the United States? In 1965–66, 1969–70, and particularly 1980–81? Big companies still could get loans. (see page 44 Chapter 3). If the Fed's efforts at stopping inflation by tightening the money supply had been successful one might excuse the ruthlessness of their policy, but letting myopic theoretical economists try and try again with a policy that never has worked and never will work has caused inestimable destruction. This shows how badly people in power and economists need to be educated about both inflation and the science of production, distribution, and consumption of wealth.

So far I have not told how I started writing a book on inflation. On April 22, 1970 an economist and a senior vice president of the Federal Reserve Bank of Cleveland came to Ashtabula. The local banks invited their directors and Ashtabula industrialists to a meeting and cocktail party that afternoon. The economist gave a talk, with charts, on inflation. He explained how the Fed had tightened the money supply. He said, "Now we have inflation under control." When they got through their talks they asked for comments and questions from the floor audience.

I told him that the Fed had not even tackled, and he had not discussed, the major cause of this period of inflation. He asked me what my ideas on the subject were. I told him I was not prepared to discuss the causes and solution to inflation from the floor, but I would put my thoughts down on paper and bring them to him for his comments.

I expected to write a 35 to 40 page thesis, but the more I dug into the available literature and current articles in newspapers and magazines on inflation, the more I realized that every suspected cause of inflation needed to be analyzed, since many of these so-called causes were more the *results* of inflation than the causes. I also needed to discuss in detail the solution to inflation, and how it could be effected. This discussion became longer and longer and resulted in a book, which I titled, *The Contax Plan.* Contax stands for Consumer-Taxpayer.

When I wrote *The Contax Plan* I felt a new political party would be needed to get it adopted, The Contax Party. The platform of this new party would be that the government should be operated for the benefit of all consumers and taxpayers, and that all legislation should be so evaluated. Over the last five decades far too many laws and administrative regulations and even court decisions have unjustifiably favored some special group while completely ignoring the amorphous majority of consumers and taxpayers.

I considered the idea but made no effort to form a Contax Party. I am not suggesting it now. The Reagan administration should be given all opportunity to put its programs into effect, but its expectation that controlling the money supply and cutting government expenses and taxes will stop inflation will turn out to be wrong. *Cutting government expenses and taxes are both very constructive, regardless of inflation,* but attempting to stop inflation by controlling the money supply is an exercise in futility. I wrote a second book, *Inflation Can Be Stopped,* in 1973, an elaboration of certain key points in the Contax Plan.

Why have I written a book now, after already having written two on the same subject? For several reasons, the first of which I have already explained:

Practically no one is talking about the major cause of this inflation.

I have read hundreds of statements of how inflation can be stopped, but none have attacked the real cause of our present inflation. The cause is obvious, but talking about it is avoided, just as telling a person he has cancer was twenty-five years ago.

Second, somebody has to have the guts to call a spade a spade, so I'm it.

Third, I have developed some additional ideas and data not included in previous writings and discussions on this subject.

Fourth, I am not getting any younger.

Fifth, several big MFG projects on which a lot of MFG and some personal money and much time has been gambled appear to be working out successfully, and MFG's biggest headache has been eliminated. I now have some time to devote to the war on inflation.

Sixth, I am in good enough health to go out again to campaign to stop inflation.

Seventh, I believe thinking people are beginning to realize that present plans and programs to stop inflation will not be successful.

Eighth, my conscience would bother me the rest of my life if I did not make one last serious effort to stop inflation.

CHAPTER 1

What Is Inflation? When Did Our Present Inflation Start?

Inflation is a continuing and general increase in the price or tax paid for raw materials, products, commodities, real estate, wages, private and public services, rentals, interest, other intangibles, and other items for which money is paid.

This is not the dictionary definition; nor the definition you will hear from the classical economists. What I have just written is the *real life* definition. The conventional definitions misstate the problem—and, in doing so, fatally flaw efforts to find a cure.

Dictionaries describe inflation as a sharp increase in the money supply resulting in a rapid increase in prices. This confuses cause and effect. The definition would be accurate if it had just said "a rapid increase in prices." An increase in the money supply is not *THE* cause of this inflation. There are several causes, but just one *major* cause of our present inflation.

The major cause of inflation will be discussed at length. But let me state it here in brief. *The paramount element in the price of just about any product or service (and this emphatically includes government service) is labor cost.* For many years we have been afflicted with a situation in which the free market for labor has been abolished. Instead we have powerful and invulnerable monopolies which set the cost of labor at an artificially ever-increasing high price. *We all pay that price.*

It's a matter of common sense. Think about people you know of who are being paid a lot more than they are worth—because of a union contract or because they have a safe government job or are a member of a group that can unilaterally set their own compensation. When you look with shock at your bill at the supermarket checkout counter, or the sticker price of a new car, remember those overpaid people. *You are paying their salaries.*

That's the real root of inflation. That's what this book is about. That's why some of the recommendations you find in these pages will strike you as tough and sweeping.

We'll get to them. Right now let's begin with an examination of the background and nature of our present inflation.

Over the centuries civilization has existed, inflation has erupted frequently, usually in a single country or area with its own problems. The Roman Empire was racked by inflation during the time of Nero. Accurate data on ancient inflations is not available. Chart I shows consumer prices in England from 1275 to 1975 A.D. and illustrates various types of inflation.

In 1334 a bubonic plague carried by fleas started in the Mid-East and was brought back to Europe by the Crusaders. It reached England shortly before 1350. About ⅓ of the population died from it. Prices jumped sharply. The supply of food, fuel and clothing was inadequate. Production workers were scarce and some farms lost their entire work force. It took almost a generation before prices settled back to the pre-1350 A.D. level.

2

CHART I

INFLATION IS NOT NEW - - - BUT IT CAN BE DIFFERENT. THIS HISTORICAL CHART OF ENGLISH INFLATION SHOWS THAT, FOR MOST OF THE 700 YEARS IT CHRONICLES, WAR, FAMINE, PESTILENCE AND DEATH RANK IN THE FOREFRONT OF CAUSES. ANY OF THESE APOCALYPSEN HORSEMAN SERVED TO REDUCE THE SUPPLY OF LABOR AND TO RAISE ITS COST, AS WELL AS THE PRICE OF LABOR'S PRODUCTS. HISTORICALLY, INFLATIONS HAVE BEEN SELF-CORRECTING, THIS BOOK SHOWS WHY TODAY'S INFLATION HAS NOT.

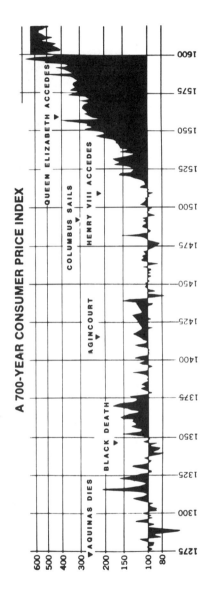

A 700-YEAR CONSUMER PRICE INDEX

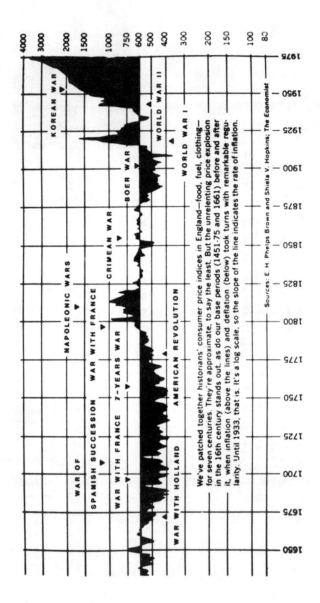

We've patched together historians' consumer price indices in England—food, fuel, clothing—for seven centuries. They're approximate, to say the least. But the unrelenting price explosion in the 16th century stands out, as do our base periods (1451-75 and 1661) before and after it, when inflation (above the lines) and deflation (below) took turns with remarkable regularity. Until 1933, that is. It's a log scale, so the slope of the line indicates the rate of inflation.

Sources: E. H. Phelps Brown and Sheila V. Hopkins; The Economist

4

The second period occurred after the Battle of Agincourt in 1415 when King Henry V and his long bows decimated the French Army and took over France, with the result that farm production suffered in England and taxes increased. Prices did not subside until 1440. For about seventy-five years prices were steady.

These first two inflationary periods were self-correcting but about 1515 gold from the New World started coming back into Europe. Prior to then gold was a very scarce commodity in Europe and a little of it bought a lot. With no noticeable increase in the production of goods and services to match the increase in gold, prices were driven up to a level 500–600% above the 1500 level. This was a permanent level, not self-correcting.

During the 110 years it took (1515 to 1625) for prices to advance 500% there were short self-correcting periods in which prices increased sharply above the long-term trend and then settled back. 1515–35, 1545–1570, and 1590–1605. Henry VIII's wars and extravagances, and internal squabbles after his death before Elizabeth became queen were largely responsible.

Once the new price levels were established, and the power of English kings curtailed, no major periods of inflation occurred until a combination of the French and Indian War, the American Revolution, and the Napoleonic Wars pushed prices up 150% in 55 years.

Prices collapsed with the cessation of hostilities, but not to their 1760 level until 1885. World War I resulted in very sharp price increases and almost as sharp price decreases.

This was the last of the self-correcting periods of English inflation. Prices started moving up several years before World War II started and have been moving up ever since. Prices stuttered a little bit after World War II but did not fall back as they had after previous major wars. A new cause of permanent inflation has obviously developed.

I have used English economic history because it is longer than U.S. history and the same forces at work in this country have been at work in Great Britain.

The essence of this book is that our present period of inflation—engulfing the United States, England and much of the world—is *not* self-correcting. It is not only worse than inflations of the past. It is different: more malignant and more enigmatic.

To find out why, let's review some of the basics of the subject, and the yardsticks commonly used to measure inflation.

Chart II shows the Bureau of Labor Statistics Consumer Price Index (C.P.I.) from 1800 to 1974 and the Producer Price Index from 1890 to 1974. To have shown them through 1981 would have resulted in the vertical coordinates of the charts being reduced by 50% and making the graphic presentation of points in this discussion less clear. See Chart II and supplement showing the C.P.I. from 1974 through 1981.

What is this C.P.I. based on? Many years ago the Bureau of Labor Statistics (BLS) estimated what a typical blue-collar urban family of four would spend on its various requirements, food, clothing, shelter, transportation, medical costs, entertainment, education, incidentals, everything but taxes, such as income and social security, and started collecting prices monthly on these items. From time to time the BLS changes the components, or their relative percentages. When they do this, changes are made in the base year also. Thus the C.P.I. is not a continuous index of the prices of certain components over a long period of time.

Before 1978 the Consumer Price Index covered urban wage earners and clerical workers. A new index C.P.I.-U

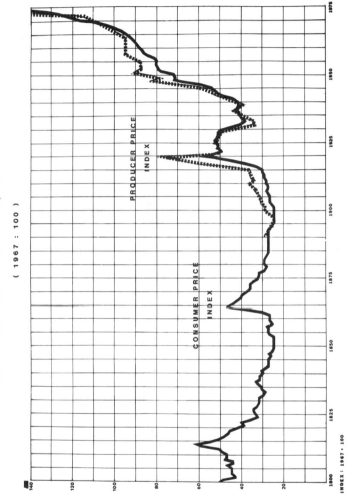

CHART II

CONSUMER PRICE INDEX, 1800 – 1974,
AND PRODUCER PRICE INDEX, 1890 – 1974

(1967 : 100)

PRODUCER PRICE
INDEX

CONSUMER PRICE
INDEX

SOURCE = BUREAU OF LABOR STATISTICS

INDEX : 1967 · 100

7

SUPPLEMENT TO CHART II
CONSUMER AND PRODUCER PRICE INDEXES—1974 THROUGH 1981

	Consumer Price Index	% Increase Year to Year	Producer Price Index	
1974	147.7		147.5	
1975	161.2	9.1	163.4	10.8
1976	170.5	5.8	170.6	4.4
1977	181.5	6.5	181.7	6.5
1978	195.4	7.7	195.9	7.8
1979	217.4	11.3	217.7	11.1
1980	246.8	13.5	247.0	13.5
1981	271.6	10.0	270.0	9.3

—covering all urban consumers—has been published monthly since January 1978. It is intended to gradually take the place of the previous C.P.I.-W. At this writing both indexes are still being published.

There is another consumer index that is not widely used or known, the Implicit Price Deflator for Personal Consumption Expenditures. This overcomes some of the deficiencies of the C.P.I. but also introduces some of its own.

The Producer Price Index (P.P.I.), (formerly the Wholesale Price Index), measures prices at various stages of manufacture from raw material to finished product. Electricity is one component. All other components are tangible. The P.P.I. is not a good measure of inflation because it is more volatile than the C.P.I. and includes no service industry prices, many of which have advanced more rapidly than tangible products.

The Implicit Price Deflator for Gross National Product theoretically could be considered the best measure of inflation because it includes both products and services. However, it is based on calculations of G.N.P., not sampling, as is done for the C.P.I. With all its faults, the C.P.I. is probably the least objectionable index.

8

What has caused the present period of inflation? It's a long story, told in Chapters 7 & 8. It actually started in the late 1890's, but for the purpose of this discussion its starting point will be considered to be early 1937. World War I, its aftermath, and the Great Depression of 1929–41 so affected prices and production that the upward trend of prices since the 1890's is not as clearly seen as since early 1937.

The forces that started this present period of inflation were felt in just a few industries first, both in the late 1890's and 1937. These earlier forces were almost completely wiped out in the 1929–33 period, but were reestablished by law in the mid-1930's.

After World War II, U.S. prices did not settle back to prewar levels as they did after the Revolutionary War, the War of 1812, the Civil War, and World War I. With minor interruptions in 1949 and 1954, prices have advanced at an accelerating pace ever since. A new power had been spawned in the Depression which guarantees permanent inflation. It will not be overcome by cutting the money supply, balancing the budget, or the discovery of enough oil to make the U.S. independent of foreign oil.

In the Sixteenth Century Spain was the most powerful nation in the world, with its great wealth from the New World. Gross mismanagement, fierce internal squabbles, and superior military skills of other nations gradually eroded the power of Spain until it is no longer influential, and the standard of living of its people the lowest in the European Free World. With proper management and foresight, the gold received by Spain could have become a long-term blessing, not the short-term fiasco that led to Spain's downfall. With proper management, foresight, and understanding of economic principles, the United States could have emerged from the 1929–1933 Depression and World War II a permanently-strong, economically and politically, world leader. Where are we heading now? Disaster.

ANALYSIS 1

Why Inflation Is Beginning to Hurt

The following chart shows that the U.S. public has been living with inflation since the mid-1930's. It also shows why most people have treated it more as an annoyance than as a danger; incomes have more than kept up with the price increases for the majority of the public. So long as one could continue to live better year after year, why worry? True, those who could remember the 1930's and '40's were appalled at paying $3.50 for a motion picture, ten times the 35¢ they paid in their younger days, but only those living on fixed incomes had a real problem.

In about mid-1979, however, the squeeze began. For the first time, income began to lag behind prices. A look at the right-hand side of the chart shows income in 1972 dollars leveling off, indicating a decline in purchasing power. Except for a brief dip during the 1974–75 recession, this is the first such experience in thirty years.

It hurts now. Unless we take positive steps to eliminate the cause of this inflation, it will hurt much more in the future.

CHART III

THE DAY OF RECKONING

PERSONAL DISPOSABLE (AFTER TAX) PER CAPITA INCOME
IN CURRENT DOLLARS VS. 1972 (CONSTANT) DOLLARS

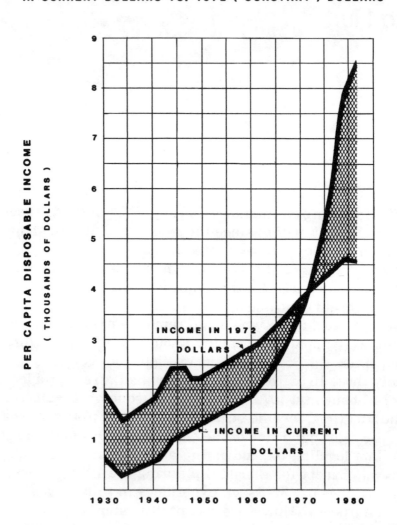

SOURCE : ECONOMIC REPORT OF THE PRESIDENT, JANUARY, 1981

CHAPTER 2

What Causes Prices to Move Up or Down?

If demand goes up, the price will go up; and vice versa. That is classic economic theory, dating back to Adam Smith's *Wealth of Nations* (1776). We all know the corollary: if (all other things being equal) supply goes up, the price will go down. If supply goes down, the price rises.

The great balance-wheel in the theory of supply and demand, the self-righting mechanism that makes Adam Smith's proposition a thing of beauty, is the concept of what happens when you take the theory one step further. If prices go up, demand will go down or supplies will go up; or both will happen. This brings prices back down. When prices go down, demand rises. This reduces the supply and brings the price back up.

This is a neat, symmetrical theoretical mechanism. However, for Adam Smith's theory to operate freely and promptly, both supply and demand must be elastic. The test of elasticity is whether demand for a product increases when the price declines and declines when the price increases. Beef is a good example. Most Americans prefer steak to chicken. They will eat more beef when its price is low enough; but they switch to chicken when the price of beef goes up.

In similar fashion, supply of a product is considered elastic when it increases when the price goes up and decreases when the price goes down.

If demand and supply were invariably elastic, the maintenance of economic health would be simple. But they are not.

Take the example of gasoline. The demand for gasoline appears to be relatively inelastic. So when the supply is short the price may be driven quite high. Conversely, if the demand is inelastic and low and there is an excess of supply, the price may drop quite low. An example of this is what happens with recreational products in the off-season.

Over the 200 years since Adam Smith published his book, a number of complicating factors have developed. Their cumulative effect causes the law of supply and demand to operate differently from the way it did when Smith postulated it.

To a growing extent, prices are *administered.*

WHAT ARE ADMINISTERED PRICES?

They are computed by the supplier, based on his costs, his profit margin, and competition within his industry. Costs include raw materials, components, supplies, direct labor costs, fuel and electricity, taxes, depreciation, tools, transportation, insurance, interest, payroll, and scores of other items. Allocating these costs as accurately as possible, the manufacturer costs out each item he produces.

To this he adds a profit margin to arrive at his selling price. This profit margin is determined by one or more methods. One is return on investment, which should range at least a few points above the prime interest rate to compensate for the risk taken in investing his capital. A second method often used in determining profit margin is return on sales. When a manufacturer is making a wide variety of products, it is easier to compute return on sales than return on investment, because different machines and equipment with wide differences in cost may be used in making the various products.

A third method is based on *value added by manufacture.* Some products go through many operations, machines, and hands as they move from receiving dock to shipping dock. Others in the same plant go through only one operation. It may take weeks or months for the former product to go from receiving to shipping, and less than a day for the latter. The percentage profit margin on the former product should be considerably higher than on the latter.

The most important factor in pricing is competition. Unless the manufacturer is making a product that no one else makes or makes one for which substitutes cannot easily be used in place of his product, he has to price his product close to the price of competitive products delivered to the customer.

It is likely that his competitors will have about the same costs as he does, so under a fairly well balanced demand and supply condition, competitors' prices will be about the same as his prices. Uninformed people think similar prices mean collusion. Wrong. If costs are going up, Company A will announce a new price schedule. If this new price schedule appears reasonable, other companies in the industry will change their prices accordingly. However, if Company B, a large producer, does not agree with the new price schedule—and holds increases to a smaller amount or leaves prices unchanged—the rest of the industry will not go along with the increases posted by Company A. They are likely to change their price schedules to agree with Company B's schedule.

In most industries, especially those having a large number of small companies, competitive prices vary fairly widely. Some companies exist by offering lower prices than competitors. However, they may not be as dependable as the higher-priced competitors are in meeting deliveries or quality requirements.

Over the past 45 years prices in general have gone up steadily. However, in particular instances there have been price declines.

The biggest reason for price declines is increases in productivity that exceed the increases in materials and labor and other costs that have occurred at the same time. The various ways productivity can be increased are discussed in Chapter 9. In some products such as computers and other complex electronic equipment, prices have gone down sharply in relation to the capacity or services provided by the equipment.

In more cases productivity increases have resulted in the price of the product or service not going up as rapidly as prices in general. If there has been no increase in productivity, the price of the product or service will go up about as rapidly as prices in general, or as rapidly as costs go up. If the persons producing the product or service have the power to increase their own compensation more rapidly than the price level in general increases, the price of the product or service will go up more rapidly. If the company producing the product or service cannot or does not increase its price as rapidly as its costs go up, its profit per dollar of sales will decline.

The only way the standard of living of people in general can increase permanently is through increases in productivity or the discovery of some new natural resource. Increases in dollar compensation for one group may increase the standard of living of that group, but only by decreasing the standard of living of all other people who directly or indirectly buy and/or use the product or service produced by the first group. Giving people or letting people have the power to force their own compensation demands on their employers, who in turn must increase the price or tax paid for the product or service they provide, is permitting legalized robbery. Everyone should share in the benefits of productivity increases, and no one should have the power to force others to pay him more for his labor than a free market pricing system would justify.

While productivity increases are the major cause of price declines, there are other temporary reasons for price declines. If business activity in general slows down, some prices will go down, which results in a slower increase in overall prices. This will encourage wishful thinkers, especially government officials, to believe they have really attacked the cause of inflation. When business activity improves the rate of inflation will increase again.

Not all prices move up or down at the same time. Some price declines may be caused by a sharp drop in the cost of raw materials—which means that the materials in question are reacting to the operation of the law of supply and demand in another area.

Such price variations are not always visible. They may come as discounts off the posted price, not publicly announced but offered to major customers. When demand improves or the raw material price goes up, the discounts are dropped.

If there is relatively permanent over-capacity throughout an industry, manufacturers will try to take business away from competitors by under-pricing them. This can result in some or all of the producers being unable to make a profit. If the industry has a high fixed capital investment in equipment that cannot be adapted to other uses, production may be carried on for years by companies which are operating continuously at a small loss. They will stop production only when the facilities and equipment are technically obsolete or worn out.

If there is excess demand in relation to supply within an industry, and if production cannot be increased rapidly, manufacturers are able to add on a higher profit margin than justified by a fair return on investment or value added by manufacture. If they do so they will make higher immediate profits. However, this will make it quite attractive for others in the industry to expand capacity and for new competitors to come in. Often such expansion, particularly in capital-intensive industries, results in over-capacity and a depressed level of profits for decades, until demand catches up with supply and old facilities wear out or become obsolete.

This happened in the petrochemical industry in the 1950s and 60s. In the early 1950s the chemical companies were making excellent profit margins on petrochemicals, while the oil producers were showing poor profit margins on petroleum products. The oil companies had plenty of cash so they jumped into petrochemical production with new efficient plants. Price of some petrochemicals dropped as much as 75%, and chemical stocks fell in esteem on Wall Street. No one made much profit until demand caught up with supply in the mid-1970s.

Another classical economic theory about pricing is the theory that prices are set by the costs of the marginal producer. This has some merit. Not every producer of a product is equally efficient. The least efficient producer who can stay in business at the existing product price is called the marginal producer. His costs are about equal to his selling price, so he shows neither profit nor loss.

He will lose more money if he stops producing the product, so he keeps on. The profit of the more efficient producers is the difference between their costs and the marginal cost. The most efficient producer is practically guaranteed a profit.

If the price level drops because demand drops, the marginal producer stops making the product and the next least efficient producer becomes the marginal producer. If prices go up (and costs stay the same), because demand increases, the marginal producer becomes profitable and a new marginal producer goes into production, attracted by the higher price.

Under this theory it is necessary for the price to increase to get the previously submarginal or new producer to go into production.

This somewhat archaic theory operates on the concept of diminishing returns; costs go up as volume of production goes up. This is generally true of extractive industries such as agriculture, mining, fishing, and forestry— assuming there is no change in technology or equipment. In most mechanized manufacturing industries production costs go down as demand and production volume increase. The higher volume justifies use of more elaborate tooling and fixturing, faster and larger equipment, product research and improvement, and greater technical and management expertise. The most efficient producer can increase production more easily and quickly than the marginal producer, so marginal producers are forced out of business and the industry becomes dominated by a few large producers. A study of the auto industry over the past 80 years illustrates this pattern.

The elimination of marginal producers and the concentration of production in a few large companies does not necessarily result in higher prices, less competition, poorer products, or a slower rate of product development and improvement. Larger companies will tend to have higher overheads per dollar of output, but lower costs for purchased materials and components and lower man-hours per unit of output. They can spread high tooling costs over a much larger unit volume and can justify investment in high production labor-saving tooling, which the small volume producer cannot do.

In spite of the advantages enjoyed by the large producer, there is plenty of room in the U.S. economy for small-volume producers. Some industries well-suited to smaller companies are:

Custom stampers and fabricators of metal
Custom rubber and plastic molders
Tool and die shops
Custom printers
Custom foundries
Custom machine shops and machine builders
Other custom and specialty work
Highly technical specialized low volume equipment
Highly-styled clothing
Highly-styled furniture and furnishings.

Usually these companies are owner-managed, with the owner being his own best salesman and technical expert. Their pricing systems usually are not as sophisticated as those of larger companies. Practically all custom manufacturers quote each job separately rather than working from a price list.

The line between compensation of the owner-manager and company profits is indistinct. This can result in the company's price quotations varying widely, depending on how busy and profitable the company is. If it is quite busy, quotations on new jobs may be high. If business is slow and the manager is anxious to keep his workforce intact, he may bid a job at little or no profit. In general the well managed, technically competent, small company in the right industry can provide an excellent living for its owner-manager, a good future for its key personnel, and fair prices and good quality and service for its customers.

People who are not familiar with how prices are determined often believe a company can set any price it desires. While it is true that a company might temporarily price its product or service way above its cost of production, sooner or later competition, or substitute products and services, will catch up with it and force prices down. If the demand for the product or service is quite elastic, the company may make more money at lower prices and higher volume, and keep competition from being attracted.

Many people believe that the profit per manufacturing sales dollar runs between 25% and 35%. The fact is that it averages around 5% after income taxes in prosperous years and is much lower in slow years. (See Chart IV). In distribution of food and similar items, profit per sales dollar will run between 1% and 2%.

People also do not realize the fierce competition that exists in most lines of business activity. They do not realize that sooner or later, if costs of production go down, prices will go down and everyone will benefit. Many believe that business profits are so large that cost increases can be absorbed without price increases.

We have been discussing ideas about prices which have to do primarily with what happens in the marketplace. Now let's broaden the discussion to include other factors often cited by economists as being influential in moving prices up or down.

We begin with a most influential school of economic thought called the *monetarists*.

Monetarists believe that an excessive increase in the

CHART IV

AFTER-TAX PROFIT OF ALL MANUFACTURERS

AS PERCENT OF SALES AND OF NATIONAL INCOME

(SELECTED YEARS 1950-1980)

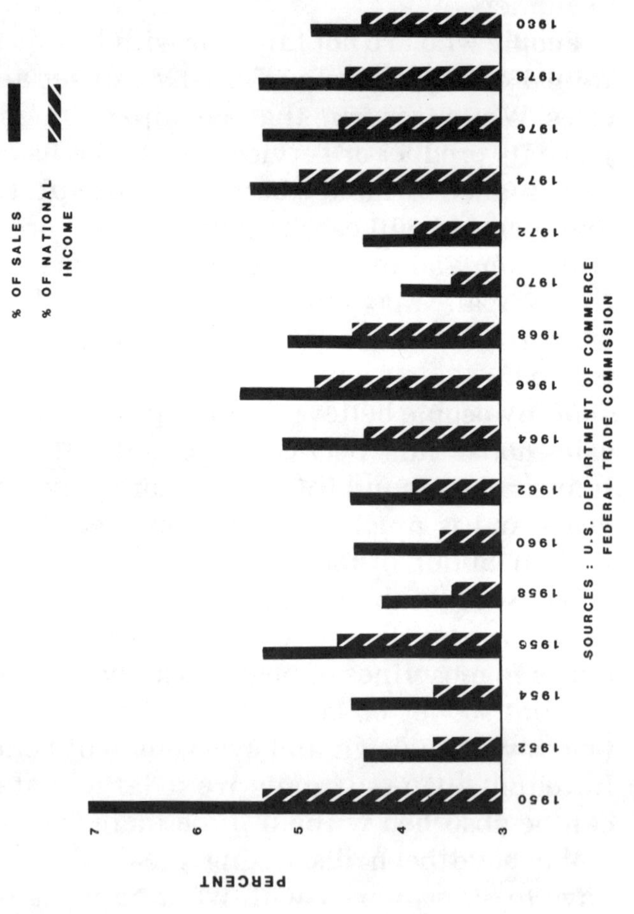

% OF SALES

% OF NATIONAL
INCOME

PERCENT

7

6

5

4

3

1950 1952 1954 1955 1958 1960 1962 1964 1966 1968 1970 1972 1974 1976 1978 1980

SOURCES : U.S. DEPARTMENT OF COMMERCE
FEDERAL TRADE COMMISSION

22

money supply causes prices to go up. They also reason that if the money supply is decreased, business activity will go down, demand will go down, and prices will go down. (This line of reasoning is based on the theory advanced by Adam Smith discussed at the opening of this chapter.) They fail to realize that the prices (or tax) paid for most products and services are administered prices, not open-market prices. What is meant by open-market prices, and how are open-market prices set? Brokers meet in a large room, usually in a major city often near the source of the commodities, but not necessarily so. Some brokers want to buy commodities, others have commodities to sell. The selling broker calls out the quantity and price of the commodity he wants to sell. If a buyer wants to buy at that price, he calls out his agreement to buy and the transaction is quickly completed. If no one wants to buy at the price the seller asks, buyers will make offers at lower prices. If the seller decides to take the lower price, he calls out his acceptance and the transaction is completed.

What types of products are bought, sold, and priced by open-market bid-and-asked transactions? Commodities such as wheat, corn, oats, rye, barley, beef, pork, chicken, cattle, hogs, copper, coffee, cocoa, sugar, eggs, fats, oils, cotton, hides, rubber, and soybeans.

The quality of the commodity has to be consistent so the buyer knows what he is getting. Neither the selling broker nor the buying broker usually see the commodity. The selling broker gives the buying broker a piece of paper entitling the buyer to delivery of a specific quantity of the commodity. Settlement in cash is usually made daily.

Bid-and-asked quotations, and completed transactions, are usually displayed on an illuminated board so all buyers and sellers are kept up to the minute on prices. Some commodity exchanges will handle several different commodities, often in an extremely large room which has posts for each different commodity. The brokers specializing in a commodity will gather around the proper post. Some exchanges will handle only one or a few similar commodities.

Prices can change many times a day. No one person or group has much control over prices. Adam Smith's law of supply and demand is in full sway. Daily prices may fluctuate from way below the marginal cost of production to far above it, but in the long run prices must equal or exceed the costs of the marginal producer. If the cost of agricultural machinery, or seed and fertilizer, or farm labor, or real estate taxes go up, the price of the crop will have to increase. If prices are far above the marginal costs of production, farmers will plant more, the supply will increase, and next year's price will be lower.

If prices are low and consistently unsatisfactory, suppliers may decide to cut down production, by not planting as large a crop or breeding as many animals. There are usually thousands of suppliers for most commodities, so the decision to curtail production is far from unanimous. Because of wide differences in productivity between one farm and another, some producers will earn a profit on a commodity at $2.00 a unit, while others will have to receive $3.00 a unit before a profit is shown. The theory of the marginal producer is clearly illustrated in agriculture. The law of diminishing returns applies to all types of agriculture. Consequently, costs of production for practically all farmers, even the most efficient ones, go up on a unit basis if they push their output beyond the point of diminishing returns.

What makes the monetarists' efforts to stop inflation so futile is that the prices of most products and services are determined by costs, not by free-market action. In manufacturing the greater the unit production, the lower the unit cost. While competition will keep such prices from going too high, costs, including both direct and indirect (overhead), will keep the prices from dropping very much, regardless of a monetary squeeze.

The monetarists also fail to realize that there is no mechanism for changing such prices through a bid-and-asked transaction. The producer sets his price and the buyers either pay that price or do not buy. If the producer is not getting enough orders at the price he had established he may announce a lower price schedule, or under present day inflation, he may not increase his prices as much as his costs increase. No one involved in the pricing of products or services automatically adjusts his prices as the money supply goes up or down.

In this discussion of what causes prices to move up and down, several causes have been listed:

1. Changes in supply
2. Changes in demand
3. Changes in cost
4. Competition
5. The marginal producer
6. The law of diminishing returns
7. The money supply

Monopolies have not been discussed in this chapter. Business monopolies are outlawed, except in public utilities whose prices and charges are controlled by government boards. However, over the years, *labor monopolies* have been established in most major activities employing people. The growth of these monopolies and their effect on prices and inflation are discussed in a subsequent chapter. By increasing the labor cost per unit of production these monopolies eliminate the availability of products and services at the previous price. A new price (or tax) covering the increased costs is forced on the producers by these higher costs.

If the demand for the product or service is inelastic, the labor monopoly is effective in obtaining increased income for most, if not all, of its members. If the demand is very elastic, the increased compensation demands which result in higher prices for the product reduce the demand for the product or service, and thus a large number of the members of the labor monopoly lose their jobs. The monopoly disintegrates, unless held together by violence and biased government laws and court decisions. The auto industry is a prime example of monopoly labor pricing ruining an industry.

In recent years the most effective labor monopolies have been those of public employees, even though strikes and violence by public employees are illegal. The need for public services is constant (completely inelastic) and there are no substitutes, no stockpiling, no importing, and no reservoirs of people available to perform such services. Taxes are in effect a price paid for the services supplied and certainly are an important part of the cost of living. They will be discussed in a later chapter.

Demand-Pull Inflation, Or
"Too Many Dollars Chasing Too Few Goods"

The above quotation is about the most asinine statement made about this 45-year period of inflation. Except for war-caused shortages (World War II and slightly in the Korean and Vietnam Wars), O.P.E.C. oil monopolies, art works, contrived monopolies, and prime real estate in the sunbelt areas, this nation has been able to produce more of everything, both products and services, than we have been able to consume. For example, I have been running a manufacturing business in a growing industry for 34 years and have practically always had idle capacity. Only with short seasonal peaks like two months or so have the plants operated at full capacity.

In 1937–38 production and sales of autos, steel, and construction materials dropped 45%, 46%, and 30% respectively, yet prices went up 10–12%. It was the first outstanding example of stagflation. We have had many periods of stagflation including now (Spring, 1982). Since then prices of most everything have gone up, up, up whether demand is high, medium, or low, in spite of Adam Smith's postulates. The rate of price increase is influenced in some cases by the demand, particularly products and services with elastic demand, or products in which a free market commodity makes up a major share of its selling price. In a major percentage of products and services, changes in demand, especially on the downside, have had no effect on the rate of price increase.

In many situations an increase in demand results in a lower price, as explained on page 19. Total costs go down as production goes up. Increased demand often attracts new producers, as in the petrochemical industry, page 18, with the result that prices go down and the consumer gets more and better plastic products for his dollar.

There is no question that in historical periods of inflation, such as listed on page 34 inflation was caused by too much paper money, but not in this long period of inflation. Oversimplified statements such as, too many dollars chasing too few goods, just prevent most people from searching for and finding the real cause of inflation.

CHAPTER **3**

Excess Money Supply

The Money Supply—Is It a Cause of Inflation? Or Is Controlling It a Cure for Inflation?

This is a long chapter with many dry statistics. Those who find statistics and technical discussions not only boring but hard to follow may, if they wish, read the following summary before deciding whether they want to read the entire chapter.

This chapter makes the following points:

1. Contrary to popular belief, the U.S. government does not print money for its own account and use that money to pay its bills. If its expenditures exceed its receipts, it must borrow money and pay current market interest rates on it.
2. The Federal Reserve has very little control over the money supply.
3. The Federal Reserve can strongly influence interest rates if business activity is high.
4. The historical correlation between money supply and the rate of inflation in the United States is poor.
5. Inflation forces business and consumers to increase their borrowings.
6. In practically all other countries where price in-

creases and increases in the money supply coincided, the governments have printed paper money to pay their bills, or have issued securities which were in the main purchased directly by the central banks. These banks were not independent of the governments. The Federal Reserve is independent of the U.S. government and makes its own decisions. It does not have to buy government bonds.

7. Borrowings by the government, business, and consumers will be paid off as rapidly as the debtor has the funds to do so.

8. The demand for money depends far more on the potential use for it than on the interest rate.

9. Increases in the money supply have been only a minor factor in this 45-year period of inflation.

10. It is very difficult to decrease the money supply if business activity is high.

11. To offset tight money and high interest rates, people, businesses, and banks have adopted practices that increase the rate of turnover (velocity) of money by carrying lower average balances in demand accounts, accelerated collections, electronic transfer of funds, post office lock boxes, central office financing of outlying divisions and subsidiaries, etc. These reduce the demand for money.

12. Decreases in the money supply that can be accomplished by Fed action do little to slow down inflation.

13. Attempts to decrease the money supply by tightening credit and raising interest rates are very unfair and destructive to small businessmen, farmers, home buyers, and savings institutions, while accomplishing very little in the battle against inflation.

14. Forcing interest rates high to attempt to stop infla-

tion makes investing in new equities very unattractive to the investor who can get 15% or more on his money without the risk of a new enterprise. This reduces competition, productivity increases, and jobs, while increasing inflation.

15. If business activity and demand for loans are low, the Federal Reserve can do little to increase the money supply. Trying to do so is like pushing on a string.

16. The government and the Federal Reserve should give up trying to stop inflation through control of the money supply and interest rates and face the real cause of this inflation.

What is meant by Money Supply? There are several ways of measuring money supply, but the one most used currently is called M1. M1 measures currency in circulation, but not in vaults of commercial banks, plus demand deposits and other checkable deposits at banks and thrift institutions. It is assumed that these types of deposits are active and may be put to use at any time. It is assumed further that time deposits and other interest-earning deposits, certificates, etc., are not active enough to be effective components of the money supply.

How is the M1 total obtained? The Federal Reserve gets weekly reports from all but the very smallest commercial banks, savings institutions, credit unions and any other organizations that provide checkable deposit accounts for their depositors, whether interest-bearing (NOW accounts) or regular demand deposits. All checkable deposits and cash in circulation are added together to obtain M1. If a bank's figures are not in on time, the Fed will phone it for them. The first figures announced are called preliminary and occasionally are changed slightly the following week.

M1 is an interesting statistic, but changes in the way banks obtain money, in the management of liabilities, not assets, and other structural banking changes make it a measure of a gradually evolving banking condition. The target does not stand still.

How is the money supply increased in the United States?

There are three ways the money supply is increased: the production of gold by domestic mines increases the money supply. Even some of the silver production increases the money supply minutely. In the 19th century silver was an important part of the money supply. Gold production has been a minor factor in increasing the U.S. money supply during practically all of the 20th century. It was not produced rapidly enough to keep up with the increasing needs for money due to the tremendous increase in production and business activity in this country.

The money supply has been increased in the 20th century primarily through the commercial banks, with the assistance of the Federal Reserve banks. The procedure is as follows:

Commercial banks increase the money supply through their loan operations. Practically all commercial borrowers carry a checking account with the bank. When the bank lends money to a commercial borrower, it usually does not give him cash, but rather makes a deposit to the borrower's account. The borrower issues checks against his account and draws his balance down. Usually there is an agreement, often oral, that the borrower will keep a minimum balance—say 10% of the amount of the loan—in his account.

Some of the checks the borrower issues to his creditors will likely be redeposited in the same bank to the credit of other accounts. This is particularly true of local businesses in major cities. At the same time, the checks drawn by the original borrower will permit his creditors to make deposits to their accounts in other banks and then draw checks against these deposits. Some of these checks may be deposited in the original borrower's bank, especially if it is a large bank with many branches. It may take more than one generation of checks to creditors for some or most of the funds loaned to the original borrower to get back to his bank, but the net result is that the bank's loans to its commercial customers usually draw down the bank's total deposit balances only 20–40% as much as the amount of the loans made. Let's say the bank's customer borrows $200,000, and leaves one-fourth of it in his account. His bank can lend, after reserve requirements of, say 15%, $42,500 of the $50,000 left on deposit. The bank or banks that receive the other $150,000, can lend $127,500 of their new deposits. This increases overall bank loans by: the original $200,000, plus the new loans of $42,500 + $127,500 = $170,000, for a total of $370,000. Then . . . the banks that end up with the deposits generated by the new loans totaling $170,000, can lend, after reserves, $144,500. By this time, the original $200,000 loan has amassed $514,500 in bank assets . . . and the process continues until the resultant amounts are too small for banks to bother lending. This "multiplier effect" can readily expand the money supply.

So, when business loans are expanding throughout the country, deposits and the money supply expand, the Federal Reserve having practically nothing to do with it. If a bank's reserves fall below the minimum required by the Federal Reserve, it can temporarily borrow reserves from another bank which has excess reserves, or it can go to the Federal Reserve and borrow from it.

The Federal Reserve itself can increase the money supply by buying government bonds on the open market and permitting the level of commercial bank borrowing from the Federal Reserve to rise permanently.

When borrowers from banks pay off their loans and commercial banks pay off their indebtedness to the Federal Reserve, and governments operate on a surplus and retire some of their indebtedness, the money supply is decreased rapidly. The "multiplier effect" works in reverse.

Contrary to popular belief, the U.S. government does not print money for its own account and use it to pay its bills. What money it needs above the income it receives from taxes, fees, duties, royalties, etc., must be borrowed in the open market. Whether or not these borrowings increase the money supply depends on the lenders. The government cannot sell its securities direct to the Federal Reserve Banks. The Federal Reserve can buy U.S. government securities from a previous owner, so the restriction that the Fed cannot buy government securities direct can be circumvented, but the government cannot compel the Federal Reserve to buy its bonds.

The governors of the Fed and the open market committee are free to make their own decisions. The government has charged the Federal Reserve with the responsibility for trying to maintain the value of U.S. currency. The Federal Reserve does this by attempting to control the money supply and interest rates. The record over the years indicates the Fed has very little real effective power to maintain the value of U.S. currency and little control over the money supply. It has, however, considerable influence on interest rates.

The belief that increases in the money supply have caused the present period of inflation, is widely held by economists, central bankers, and many government officials. Why should they hold this belief?

Over the centuries inflation has occurred in many

countries. Some of the most virulent inflations were or still are:

Germany—1920-23
Hungary—1948
Argentina—1949 till now
Brazil—1957 till now
France—Late 18th and early 19th century
Europe—1500-1600
Confederate States of America—1861-1865
Roman Empire—Various times
United States—1861-65
The Colonies—1776-1783

The primary cause of most of these inflations was the inability of the governments to raise enough money through taxes and borrowings to pay their bills. To meet their debts, nations either directly printed fiat paper money (unbacked by coin or sound debt securities), debased their coins, or issued government bonds and forced the central bank to purchase them by issuing credits to the government's account at the bank. All of these methods increased demand without a corresponding increase in the supply of goods and services.

Thus prices were bid up, roughly in proportion to the unbacked increase in money.

As prices went up, the government kept creating more money or issuing more bonds to pay its bills, which were getting larger and larger in terms of the currency. The value of the currency continued to decline until in most past cases it became practically worthless.

Price increases in many countries have resulted from unfavorable balances of foreign trade, particularly since O.P.E.C. began to increase petroleum prices. For example Brazil must import almost all of its oil. It is paid for with paper cruizeros, which end up abroad. The recipients do not want to buy enough Brazilian exports to use up their cruizeros, so they want to get rid of the cruizeros as soon as possible. They convert this money into marks, yen, francs, pounds, or dollars, to buy other goods and services. Selling cruizeros puts downward pressure on their value, which makes recipients even more anxious to sell cruizeros. As their value goes down, up goes Brazilian inflation.

Over the centuries many countries issued fiat currency, backed only by the government's promise and ability to pay, with practically always the same result, a rapidly devaluing currency. This spectacle of big increases in fiat money followed by rapid increases in the price level was so common that dictionaries and economic textbooks incorrectly defined inflation as a rapid increase in the money supply, causing a sharp increase in the price level.

The dictionary definition completely ignores increases in the price level caused by shortages, crop failures, wars, increased costs of production, declining productivity, and a number of other factors. Unfortunately, most people believe that the dictionary definition of a word is forever fixed and immutable. Dictionaries are constantly changing and expanding the meaning of words as public usage changes. Even the meaning of "money supply" was changed recently as banks and savings institutions increased their fierce competition for deposits.

Let's look at the history of U.S. money supply, government borrowings, deficits, and price levels. The U.S. financed much of the Civil War (1861–65) expenses through the issue of Greenbacks, which were backed only by the government's promise to pay. These Greenbacks dropped rapidly in value until the Civil War ended. Then the government retired them at 100¢ on the dollar. This is one of the few times when holders of a fiat currency did not lose. The Revolutionary War Continentals became worthless, as did the Confederate Civil War currency. Chart II shows the C.P.I. during most of this period.

In World War I the U.S. government made great efforts to hold down consumer purchasing power and inflation by selling War Savings Stamps and Liberty Bonds. Income tax rates and other federal taxes were boosted tremendously, but since income taxes were paid about one year after earned and levied, and fiscal years ended on June 30, a deficit of $9 billion was incurred for the year ending June 30, 1918 and $13 billion for year ending June 30, 1919. How much of the war did the Federal Reserve and commercial banks finance?

At the end of 1918 the Federal Reserve Banks held $239 million of U.S. government securities; at the end of 1919, $300 million. In three years from the end of 1916 to the end of 1919 member banks increased their holdings about $2.7 billion from $1+ billion to close to $4 billion. With a cumulative government deficit of $23¼ billion, the U.S. banking system financed about 11% of the World War I deficit. Over $20 billion of Liberty Bonds, War Savings Stamps, and other government securities were bought by individuals, businesses, funds, institutions, and state and local governments. Such purchases did not increase net purchasing power or the money supply, because the buyers of the securities gave up as much purchasing power as the seller (the government) gained.

War-time shortages of goods and services were primarily responsible for the increase in prices between Jan. 1917 and mid-1919. The net increase in the money supply from the end of 1916 to the end of 1919 was $10.1 billion, an increase of 39.2%. During the same period wholesale prices increased 62.1%, consumer prices 58.4%. Gross National Product in current dollars increased 58.5%, while in constant dollars it increased 7% including military items. The money supply was reluctantly forced to increase with the increase in prices, not vice versa.

Total compensation for hourly industrial workers and farm hands increased close to 100% in current dollars, 15% in real dollars. Great effort was placed on increasing the production of food, to feed the Allies as well as ourselves. Over 50% of U.S. citizens lived on farms, where productivity was very low as compared to present-day agriculture. Farm wages almost doubled to keep workers "down on the farm" rather than going to the cities or enlisting.

Compensation increases plus war-caused shortages in raw materials and finished products—along with some speculation (1919-20)—caused a sharp post-war increase in the Wholesale Price Index (now Producer Price Index–P.P.I.) and the Consumer Price Index (C.P.I.). Even after prices had receded between mid-1920 and 1922 they were still 40% higher than in 1915. The C.P.I. dropped 16.3% between 1920 and 1922, where the P.P.I. dropped 36.8% between 1920 and 1921. These price levels held until late 1929. What happened to money supply, G.N.P., and business activity between 1920 and 1929? The money supply increased 43%. Business activity increased 55%, G.N.P. 43%.

Then the stock market collapsed suddenly, and business activity reluctantly followed, reaching bottom in early 1933. What happened to prices, the money supply, G.N.P., and the index of business activity? The C.P.I. dropped 24.6%. The P.P.I. dropped 32%. The money supply decreased 23.6%, G.N.P. decreased 46.1%, business activity dropped 52.3%.

The problem in comparing changes in the money supply to changes in a price index results from the fact that population continues to increase, whether prices go up, down, or stay the same.

Why the small decrease in money supply between 1929 and 1932 when there was a bigger drop in G.N.P. and business activity? Borrowers had great difficulty paying off or reducing loans during that period, and owners of cash were hesitant to invest in noncash assets. Turnover of the money supply was low. While private demand deposits dropped over 25% from the end of 1929 through 1933, currency in circulation increased by 21%, indicating people were holding more cash at home. This "hot" money had little effect on consumer demand and the C.P.I.

Between 1920 and 1930 the federal government operated at a surplus every year, reducing its debt from $25,482 million to $16,185 million, a total of $9,297 million, or 36%. In 1931 government receipts dropped about 25% from 1930, and in 1932 the drop from 1930 was over 50%. Federal deficits were incurred every year from 1931 on to 1946. Between 1929 and 1941 the money supply increased 85%. G.N.P. increased 38%, business activity 22%. By the end of 1941 the cumulative deficit was $25.6 billion, yet the P.P.I. was 14% below 1929 and the C.P.I. 9.2% below.

The entire 1920–1940 period shows no correlation between changes in the money supply and prices, or government deficits and prices. The money supply correlated very poorly with changes in business activity, going down far more slowly between 1929 and 1933 than business activity, and increasing in 1938, a very slow year, over 1937, a strong year, while business activity dropped 39% from 1937 peak to 1938 bottom. The continuing deficit through 1941 appeared to have little effect on prices.

During the years 1942 through 1945 the federal government ran a deficit of $176.3 billion. The Federal Reserve banks increased their holdings of government securities $22 billion. Commercial banks increased their holdings $75 billion, partially because the demand for industrial, commercial, and consumer loans was down. Bank deposits increased $80 billion. Others, individuals, corporations, state and local governments, institutions, trusts, savings banks, life insurance companies, and the federal government itself increased their holdings of government securities $109 billion. While commercial banks increased their holdings $75 billion, their borrowings from the Fed increased $329 million, so it cannot be claimed that the Fed supplied the government funds indirectly through the commercial banks.

What happened to the money supply during World War II? It increased 108%. Prices increased 22%. G.N.P. in current dollars increased 70%. In constant dollars 35%. Again the correlation between money supply and business activity, and money supply and prices was not very good.

After World War II prices did not drop sharply, as they had done after World War I, the Civil War, the War of 1812, and the Revolutionary War. One of the reasons was that price controls had kept prices from rising as rapidly as they had in major previous wars. This does not explain the rapid increases in post-World War II prices; 34% in three years. Part of the reason was demand-pull inflation, particularly in autos and construction. It took three years, 1946, '47, and '48 before this pent-up demand was reasonably satisfied. This still was not the major cause of these price increases. The major cause will be discussed and analyzed in a subsequent chapter.

Business activity slowed slightly in early 1949 but picked up in March 1950 before the Korean War started.

Even though price controls were applied shortly after the war started in June, 1950, prices went up 11% in 1951–'52–'53. The C.P.I. hestitated a moment in 1954, dropping from 80.5 to 80.2 (1967 = 100), and then resumed its upward march without any interruption ever since. By November 1981, it had reached 280.7, or 3.5 times the 1954 level.

During the post-World War II period many events have seriously affected business and prices: the Korean War; various Israeli-Arab wars; the Vietnam War; the Arab oil embargo and subsequent O.P.E.C. action; conflicts in Africa and Asia; gradual shortages of minerals, forest products, fishery products; the rapid adoption and expansion of social welfare programs; the increasing role of governments in economic affairs; and the tremendous increase in the power of organized minorities to obtain their selfish aims at the expense of consumers and taxpayers.

In spite of all these influences, there are people in high places who believe increases in the money supply are the main, if not the only, cause of this period of inflation. To create a continuing inflationary pressure, the money supply would have to be increased in such a way as to permanently expand total purchasing power in relation to total output of goods and services.

Are loans which temporarily increase the purchasing power of the recipient inflationary? If the lender is not a commercial bank or the Federal Reserve, the loan is not inflationary as long as the lender gives up as much purchasing power as the borrower receives. As the borrower pays off his loan, he loses purchasing power as the lender gains it. It makes no difference if the borrower is John Doe or the U.S. government.

Some people claim, without examining the facts, that the Federal Reserve and the commercial banks, by buying government securities, have financed most of this 1936–81 period of inflation and government deficits, also a historical cause of inflation.

However, a study of the government bonds held by both the Federal Reserve and all commercial banks in the country as compared to all other owners of government securities shows:

TABLE 1
OWNERSHIP OF FEDERAL GOVERNMENT SECURITIES
BILLIONS

		Owned By				
		Fed.	Fed.	Comm.		
Total	Total	Govt.	Res.	Banks	Private	C.P.I.
End of 1946	$259.1	27.4	23.3	74.5	133.8	58.5
October 1980	929.8	192.5	121.3	104.7	511.3	258.4
% Increase	258.9	602.6	420.6	40.5	282.1	341.7
Dollar increase	670.7	165.1	98.0	30.2	377.5	
% of Total Loans						
(End of 1946)	100	10.6	9.0	28.8	51.6	
(End of 1980)	100	20.7	13.0	11.3	55.0	

The Federal Reserve and the commercial banks combined have not increased the money supply to an inflationary extent by buying government bonds. They have not, as some economists say, "validated the inflation" by excessive purchases of government bonds. Let's examine how a commercial bank can temporarily add to the money supply.

If a commercial bank buys a government bond, it pays for it with a check drawn on its own account, thus reducing the amount it can lend to a customer or invest in another security. Purchasing power is reduced accordingly. The bank can use the bond as security for a short-term loan from the Federal Reserve at its discount window, but it is discouraged from doing so by the Fed. Each loan is made on the merit of the securities pledged. The bank cannot borrow from the Fed on an unsecured basis. It can borrow overnight federal funds from another bank without security.

Commercial banks have reduced their relative holdings of government and municipal bonds because loans, including loans to other banks in the federal funds market, are more profitable. Since most loans are of short duration, interest rates can be adjusted upward more rapidly.

Other investors are in a quandary. Common stocks have not increased in market value very much in the last decade or more, so after allowing for inflation they have actually dropped substantially in value. Dividend yields as a percent of market value are generally lower than bonds, so the investor does not have an inflation-proof, income-producing type of investment.

The federal government does not have the direct power to increase the money supply, and the Federal Reserve and the commercial banks have not increased the money supply through the purchase of government bonds nearly as much as the increase in the C.P.I.

There is no automatic way in which a certain amount of new money is put into the monetary system, even though the Federal Reserve talks as if it could intentionally increase the money supply by a target percentage.

Inflation has greatly increased the need for money to handle the same physical volume of business. This has resulted in private industry borrowings of all types increasing rapidly in recent years. Banks that used to carry loans at 50–60% of their total assets now are loaning out 70–80% of their total assets and have had to resort to various ways of obtaining money to expand their loaning ability.

Banks used to be able to attract sufficient funds in the

form of no-interest demand deposits and low-interest savings accounts to cover their demands for loans. Now, with interest rates four to five times as high as they were several years ago, banks have had to resort to certificates of deposit and other high interest-paying deposits to obtain sufficient money to meet demand for loans. Savings institutions are particularly hard hit because they make long-term loans at fixed interest rates and obtain their funds from depositors who can withdraw their deposits at any time.

Now many banks and some savings institutions are refusing to make fixed interest loans, either short- or long-term. The interest rate paid is fixed to prime, such as 1% above prime. They have been able to get funds from depositors at slightly below prime.

The Federal Reserve at times tries to discourage the lending of money by banks. The theory is that reducing loans will reduce the money supply, which in turn will reduce inflation. It expects that high interest rates will discourage borrowers. On the other hand, with the interest-rate squeeze described above, a bank is now looking for borrowers who will pay prime and above. With higher overheads than ever before, it needs more loans, not less.

A bank exists to make good loans. It has long-term customers who carry substantial balances in their accounts most of the time, and may from time to time borrow from the bank. These customers are just as important to the bank as is a large customer of a manufacturing concern. While the Federal Reserve may believe that it is in the national interest for banks to reduce their commercial loans, each bank is going to run its own business and make loans to good customers when the customer wants the money, not when the Fed says he should have the money.

What effect did the Federal Reserve 1969–1970 effort

to reduce bank loans have? Let's look at total and commercial and industrial bank loans:

Outstanding Loans	Total	Com. & Ind.
End of 1968	$258.2 billion	$ 95.9 billion
1969	279.4 billion	105.7 billion
1970	292.0 billion	110.0 billion
1971	320.9 billion	116.2 billion

Business activity (B-W index) slowed from 110.0 in December 1969 to 104.2 in December 1970, which may account for the smaller increase in 1970 over 1969. Obviously, the banks as a whole did not reduce their commercial and industrial loans, nor did the effort of the Federal Reserve to hold down inflation in 1969–70 accomplish anything. The C.P.I. went up faster in 1969 and 1970 (5.4% and 5.7%) than in any time since 1951. (The Korean War)

So, when business is expanding and good customers want money, banks have to expand their loans and increase the money supply.

On the other hand, if business in general is contracting and businessmen are paying down their loans, the money supply decreases. The bank may actually have more cash in its vault, but far less deposits and loans. Cash in the bank's vault, which actually may consist of deposits at the Federal Reserve or other banks, as well as money, is not included in M1, or any other measure of the money supply, even if the banks may have cash sticking out their ears.

Under such circumstances banks are eager to make loans. They may offer lower interest rates and even make loans to applicants they might have turned down when business activity was higher. The term "Money Supply" is really a misnomer as far as the banks themselves are concerned. They have more money to lend when the so-called Money Supply is low than when it is high, in spite of the multiplier factor.

The Federal Reserve, in its misguided attempts to stop inflation or stimulate business, often tries to increase or decrease the money supply. It cannot give money away to increase the supply, nor take it away to decrease the money supply. As pointed out before, when people, businesses, institutions, etc., borrow more money from the banks the money supply is increased, and when they pay the loans back the money supply is decreased.

How can the Federal Reserve keep borrowers from borrowing more money? First, by raising interest rates. There are several ways the Fed can raise interest rates. It can increase its discount rate, or the federal funds rate, (the rate at which banks borrow from each other to bring up their reserves to the required level), or can reduce commercial bank lendable funds by selling securities it owns in the open market. If commercial banks buy these securities, their cash is reduced as they pay for them, so they can lend less. They can, however, take these securities to the Fed discount window and borrow as much as 100% of their face value (subject to negotiation) from the Fed. They thus replace their reserves, or their cash in vault, and have in effect lost little of their borrowing power. Commercial banks over the years have decreased their holdings of governments, so Fed sales of governments to banks are not huge successes.

Another way the Federal Reserve can reduce the total lending ability of its member banks is by increasing the reserve requirements which banks must carry against deposits. Member banks, however, are not all loaned out to the same extent, so increasing reserve requirements may affect one bank profoundly but have little effect on another bank. Many large national banks have changed over to state banks to avoid onerous reserve requirements.

In these various ways The Federal Reserve can raise interest rates and put downward pressure on the money supply. But banks operate to make a profit, and their biggest source of income is loans, so they are going to make, and have made, loans in almost ever-increasing totals to their good customers. In 1980 and 1981 it was shown that the demand for short-term money is relatively inelastic. If a business needs money, it will borrow it at almost any rate of interest, while if it does not need money, a low rate of interest will not increase the demand for short-term money. The demand for long-term money is much more affected by interest rates, especially for consumer financing of large-ticket purchases, such as houses and automobiles.

What can the Fed do to increase the money supply? If the money supply has been tightened by previous Fed actions, it can relax such actions. If the money supply is declining because business activity is declining and businesses and consumers are retiring loans faster than they are taking on new loans, the Fed can do little to increase the money supply. It can buy securities in the open market, thus putting money into the vaults of commercial banks or in the hands of the sellers of the securities, who in turn will either reinvest in other securities or deposit the proceeds in the bank. Unless the banks have an increasing demand for loans, no increase in the money supply will result.

Lower short-term interest rates resulting from reversing previous actions by the Fed will do little to increase the money supply. Lower long-term interest rates may gradually increase the money supply if businesses and consumers have use for the money. If they do not, the move will have little effect. Under such circumstances the Fed's attempts to increase the money supply are practically futile.

The demand for money depends primarily on the opportunity to use it, not on its cost. If a business needs money to carry raw materials, work-in-process, finished goods, and accounts receivable, and to pay payrolls and accounts payable, and is not able to obtain that money, its loss is considerably greater than the difference between 5% and 20% per annum interest. It will try hard to increase turnover, reduce inventories, and stretch payables, but it will not stop borrowing short-term money because of cost.

The turnover on long-term loans is slow (probably less than 10% a year). Most older existing loans are at fixed interest rates. Therefore an increase in long-term interest rates immediately affects only a small percentage of such loans. If interest rates on some long-term loans are tied to prime, the borrower is stuck with whatever rate the formula calls for. He usually borrowed the long-term money to buy fixed assets and is not able to pay off the loan in advance. Use of the fixed assets earns the money to pay off the loan over the term of the loan.

High long-term interest rates tend to discourage new borrowers, particularly home buyers, but the extra cost of money, after tax, is offset by the belief (so far substantiated by fact) that the price of the asset purchased by the borrowed funds will go up faster than the differential in interest rates. Consequently, high long-term interest rates are not as great a deterrent to borrowing as they would otherwise be.

Lenders, unless they are tax-exempt institutions and funds, have to pay income tax on interest received. If inflation is 12% per annum and the taxpayer is in the

50% tax bracket, he would have to receive 32% interest per annum to net 4% interest after inflation and federal income tax. Corporations can deduct interest payments, but not dividend payments. A corporation needs just enough equity to establish its credit with its suppliers and provide a cushion against temporary business losses. Its capital needs beyond that can be more economically supplied by long-term debt for fixed assets and short-term debt for seasonal and cyclical fluctuations in working capital requirements.

The situations described above illustrate why trying to reduce business activity and inflation by raising interest rates and tightening the money supply has not been effective. Further, some businesses and individuals have been forced into bankruptcy by excessive interest costs and tight money. The attempt to stop inflation by raising interest rates and tightening the money supply is like tightening a noose around a man's neck to squeeze a cancer of the colon out of him. Raising interest rates and tightening the money supply affects different types of business differently. Those who supply products and services with quite inelastic demand are little affected, while those with very elastic demand, or weak financial structures, are seriously affected. Regardless of whether it is effective in trying to hold down inflation or not, it is very inequitable, selective, and harmful to our economy.

The current preoccupation of the Federal Reserve, bankers, economists, and Wall St. with week-to-week changes in the money supply is ridiculous, but it is like the weather. It gives these people something to talk about. The big flap and stock market collapse that followed the announcement of a 4.2 billion increase in the money supply for the week ending April 22, 1981 is a prime example of such hysteria. The following week M1 dropped 3.6 billion, but the damage was done. All interest rates had shot up, some to an all-time high.

Some comments made by a Governor of the Federal Reserve System on April 22, 1981 are interesting and informative on this subject. He points out that individual banks now have many ways, in addition to regular demand and time deposits, to increase their liabilities and obtain funds to lend:

"Twenty-five years ago,—when liquid assets were drawn down, banks turned away nonlocal borrowers and nondepositors, halted credit flows to particular industries, and in other ways tightened nonprice credit terms."—"Innovations (sale of CD's etc.) and regulatory changes have, by and large, eliminated the periodic reductions in credit availability that accompanied an increase in monetary restraint. As a result, monetary policy now transmits its effects to the real economy largely through fluctuations in interest rates. Monetary restraint still works, but in different ways and perhaps more gradually.—It—now requires a higher level of real interest rates than it did before—. I once thought that this shift (in bank liability management)—was an unmixed blessing.—It improved the efficiency of money and capital markets, affording savers and investors great opportunities to lend and borrow at or near market rates. I no longer take so sanguine a view."

"—High interest rates hit the housing market,—small businesses, and particularly farmers, as badly or worse—now than they did 20 years ago."

"Since 1974, innovation in payment practices have led to a substantial decline in the amount of money needed to finance a given level of GNP.—"

Is expansion of the money supply (M1) inflationary?

If demand is increased without a corresponding increase in products and services, and the increase in demand is obtained through borrowed money which is never paid back, or fiat money, it is inflationary. If one person's demand is increased by borrowing from another person whose demand is decreased by the amount he loaned, this is not inflationary.

To the extent that federal government securities are bought, directly or indirectly, by commercial banks, the increase in these loans from year to year is partly inflationary, probably to the extent of 60 to 70% of the amount of the increase. This depends on the individual bank's situation. The increase, from year to year, of Federal Reserve holdings of government bonds is inflationary.

The total increase from year to year of holdings of government securities by the Fed and the commercial banks averaged $3.7 billion a year from 1946 through 1980. In the years 1970–1980 the increase averaged $11.3 billion a year. With an annual 1970–80 increase of $163.4 billion in G.N.P. at current dollars it does not appear that the $11.3 billion increase in Fed and commercial bank holdings of government bonds could have affected prices to any extent.

To support their claim that increases in the money supply are the main cause of inflation, monetarists cite the fairly close correlation between increases in commercial bank loans as a whole compared to the increase in current G.N.P. Between 1946 and 1980 current G.N.P. increased 1152% from $209.8 billion to $2627.4 billion. Bank loans increased 2728% from 31.1 billion to $899.4 billion. Between 1970 and 1980 current G.N.P. increased 165%, bank loans 208%. The base in 1970 was much larger, which accounts for the smaller percentage as compared to 1946.

Why did businesses and people increase their borrowings so greatly? They did not borrow because they wanted to, they borrowed because they had to. Businesses borrowed to buy the essentials needed to keep them operating and because it was far cheaper to borrow than to raise equity capital with 50% or higher total corporate income taxes. With up to 70% personal income tax and high capital gains taxes, finding investors with equity money was generally difficult. Insufficient depreciation rates also added to business long-term debt vs. equity. Over the last decade and more, businesses have increased their debt seven times as fast as they have been able to increase their net worth.

One reason that business borrowings expand so rapidly is that whatever the business purchases, inventories or fixed assets, will cost more later, so they buy ahead of need. Inflation feeds on itself.

With yearly escalations in their income people have been willing to take on larger installment and mortgage debts than current income can conveniently handle, counting on the income increases over the years to lighten the load. They have gradually reduced savings, realizing that their money depreciates, while durable fixed assets will generally increase in value after allowance for depreciation.

Another factor which has sharply increased bank loans has been the great increase in leasing of cars and durable goods rather than buying or going without. Leasing eliminates the necessity of a substantial down payment or disposition of the old car or asset at the end of the lease. The lessors borrow from banks on the security of the asset leased and the lease itself.

It is obvious from the data and analyses revealed in this chapter that changes in the money supply occur without good correlation to price indexes, business activity, or G.N.P. The present banking system accommodates wide variances in money supply without corresponding changes in other factors.

The unavoidable conclusion is that bank loans, which also result in deposits and money supply, have been forced up by inflation, by increases in real G.N.P., by higher standards of living, by unwise tax policies, by O.P.E.C., by other shortages, by government regulations, by government deficits, and by the primary cause of inflation. Increases in the private money supply *are not a cause* of inflation, but *are the result* of inflation.

The many abortive attempts that have been made over the years to slow down inflation by trying to control the money supply and raising interest rates have proven the futility and destructiveness of such efforts. Continued attempts will be even more destructive.

CHAPTER 4

Do Government Deficits Cause Inflation

Or Are They a Result of Inflation?

At a Public Policy Week meeting of the American Enterprise Association, December, 1981, William Niskanen, a member of the President's Council of Economic Advisors, stated:

> "Deficits arc not inflationary unless the Fed finances them by creating new money. Public policy can prevent that by seeing to it that the deficits are financed by borrowing from the private sector."

Whether or not government deficits are inflationary depends upon how the deficits are financed. If the deficits are financed by means of the central bank directly or indirectly issuing currency or credit to the government, or by the government printing unbacked paper money, such deficit financing is inflationary. If the government finances its deficits through the sale of its interest bearing securities to the general public, businesses and financial institutions, pension funds, trusts, and others, such deficit financing is not inflationary, because it reduces the purchasing power of the investors in these government securities an amount equal to the deficit so financed.

If it sells its securities abroad and uses the proceeds

to buy an equal amount of imports, the loan is not inflationary. If the proceeds are used to balance its budget and pay internal creditors, the loan is inflationary.

For many years there have been two schools of thought on the cause and cure of inflation. The monetarists believe that excess money supply causes inflation. A dissenting group believes that government deficits cause inflation. Some believe that a combination of proper monetary and fiscal policies will stop inflation. All are 10% right.

The previous chapter discussed the money supply theory of inflation. This chapter will discuss the *deficit* theory of inflation. Many of the analyses discussed in the previous chapter are applicable to this chapter. The major difference between the monetarists and the fiscal policy (deficits and surpluses) theorists is that each believe that if their particular cause is brought under control, without regard to the other, inflation will be stopped. In other words, they believe if deficits were eliminated inflation would be stopped without having to tighten the money supply, or vice versa.

Practically all of the governments listed in the previous chapter as having greatly expanded their money supply without backing it with gold or other collateral were running at a deficit. They did not, and usually could not, sell enough securities to fund their deficits, so they or their central banks issued fiat money. The deficit and the increase in the money supply went hand in hand. Both were usually caused by an unusual demand on the government, in most cases because of war. In the case of Germany in 1920–23 reparations for World War I damage and Allied expenditures, loss of colonial markets, and depression caused the deficits.

The economies of most of these countries were upset by a war or reparations and loss of colonial markets so the tax income of the governments was greatly reduced. Victors usually were able to absorb the deficits with subsequent surpluses without repudiation of debt, but losers often were unable to pay off the debt or retire the fiat money issued to finance the war.

Let's review the 20th century history of U.S. surpluses and deficits.

In World War I the U.S. incurred a deficit of $23,248 million through June 30, 1919. Consumer prices (C.P.I.) went up 83%, but dropped 17% in 1920–21. As described in Chapter 3, World War I was financed almost entirely by sales of government securities, war bonds, thrift stamps, etc., to the general public and private industry and institutions.

Eleven years (1920 through 1930) of surpluses followed, totalling $8,360 million. Prices were practically the same in 1930 as in 1922. The budget surpluses had no apparent effect on prices. Between 1930 and 1941 we had eleven straight years of deficits, totalling $39,626 million. In spite of these huge peace-time deficits, prices were 12% lower in 1941 than in 1930. These deficits had no apparent effect on prices. During the four years of World War II the government ran at a deficit of $194,396 million. Prices were frozen internally, but prices of commodities and products set on international markets had to be increased to enable U.S. customers to buy. Some service industry prices went up. The effects of all the various influences on prices during World War II are hard to determine. Prices during the period of actual warfare increased 29%, but in the following three years prices increased 34%. During these years the government operated at a surplus of $16,466 million. In 1956, '57 and '58 the surplus totalled $11,600 million. Prices increased 8%. In 1969 the government had a surplus of $7,115 million yet prices advanced 5.3%.

A comparison of the cumulative government deficit from the beginning of 1947 to the end of 1960 shows that prices (C.P.I.) went up 51.6%. The cumulative total government deficit was $996 million, which was less than $\frac{1}{10}$% of total government outlays during that time. Certainly federal government deficits were not the cause, even a minor cause, of the 1947–60 price increases.

Deficits have occurred every year since then, some quite huge. Prices increased 141% from mid-1969 to March, 1981. The price increase in some years has been much greater than in others, but there has been little correlation between the size of the price increase and the size of the budget deficit. Annual deficits were as high as $66 billion (1976) with a price increase of 6%, and as low as $4.7 billion (1974), with a price increase of 9%.

Many other factors influenced both the deficits and prices since 1970, but the poor correlation between surpluses or deficits since World War I indicates that deficits do not immediately cause prices to change.

Nevertheless people think deficits cause inflation. They believe that the Federal Reserve banks and the commercial banks together have financed most of the government deficit by buying government securities. Not so; *it should be repeated here that, contrary to popular belief, the U.S. government does not print paper money and give it to itself to pay its bills.* It has to borrow money on the open market if its expenditures exceed its income from taxes and other sources. The Federal Reserve cannot directly purchase government securities from the government and the government cannot force the Fed to buy its securities second hand in the open market.

Table 1 shows the ownership of government securities. Commercial banks sharply decreased their relative holdings of governments in proportion to other assets. The

Federal Reserve increased its percentage holdings of governments from a small base in 1946. The two combined owned only 24.8% of the total in October 1980 as compared to 38.1% in 1946. Private buyers and federal government agencies themselves have been the big buyers.

When individuals or organizations other than Federal Reserve banks or commercial banks buy securities of any sort, they lose as much purchasing power as the borrower receives. Consequently, over 75% of the increase in government debt from 1946 to October 1980 was in no sense inflationary.

The Federal Reserve buys government securities from a dealer or commercial bank. It does not buy them from individuals or corporate owners. The bank has an account at the Fed. The dealer deposits the Fed's check at his bank, which the bank sends to its F.R. bank.

The Fed credits the bank's account at the Fed. The bank often does not withdraw this amount from the Fed, so the Fed in effect has acquired the securities without putting up any cash for them. The bank now has additional reserves at the Fed against which it can make loans, theoretically, up to several times the amount of the new credit.

The selling dealer most likely will turn around and reinvest the funds he received from the sale in other securities, either government or private. This may or may not result in withdrawing from the bank all or most of the money he received from the sale of the government securities and which had been previously deposited at his bank. The seller of the new securities will very likely deposit the proceeds at his bank, which may or may not be the buyer's bank. If a seller is a foreigner and carries his account at a foreign bank, the money will very likely be taken out of the U.S. banking system.

Money invested in long-term securities, either government or private, will likely stay invested for many years. Money invested in short-term securities may often be money that has been set aside for a relatively immediate need such as paying taxes, pension funds, or other items. In the case of individuals, the sale of short-term government securities may result in additional consumer purchasing power, but the prior setting aside of money for the purchase of these government securities has resulted in an equivalent reduction of purchasing power. In the case of corporations or institutions, the proceeds more likely will go to retire existing debt or to purchase fixed assets.

The purchase of government securities in the open market by the Federal Reserve normally increases the money supply. Conversely the sale of government securities in the open market reduces the money supply because sooner or later the money paid to the Fed for the securities will be withdrawn from a commercial bank, usually in the form of a reduction in the bank's account at the Federal Reserve.

The profit motive has little to do with the Federal Reserve either buying or selling securities. 90% of Federal Reserve profits are turned over to the U.S. government yearly, after adequate reserves are set up and some provision made for increase in capital. It is likely that when the Fed wants to sell securities to tighten the money supply the price of securities has already been depressed by high interest rates. If it wants to buy securities to increase the money supply and stimulate business, it is likely that interest rates are lower and bond prices are higher.

Whether or not the purchase of securities by the Fed has an inflationary effect depends to a great extent on what the seller of the securities does with the proceeds and whether the purchase by the Fed enables the government to increase its debt an equivalent amount. The seller is going to put that money to work someplace. Temporarily it might be sterilized by being in the bank's vault or in excess bank reserves. This is most likely to happen when business activity is low. The Fed's purpose in buying these securities is to put such money to work. It may or may not accomplish this result.

When the Fed offers securities for sale, no one has to buy them. Presumably, if the demand for government securities is thin, the Federal Reserve Open Market Committee will not put more securities on the market than it can absorb without breaking the price.

The commercial banks are not likely to buy them if they have demand for loans that use up all of their available reserves. Some banks not only lend up to their available reserves but deliberately overloan and borrow federal funds from other banks. These funds are borrowed for one day. Each Wednesday all member banks must settle their reserve position at the Fed for the previous 6 days of the week. This way a bank, even though it pays a high rate in federal funds, can make a substantial profit, because the return on loans is generally higher than the penalty for inadequate reserves. Consequently, the Fed's power to reduce the money supply by selling securities is less than absolute.

Where does the money come from to buy government securities? Not from commercial banks. Only a relatively small amount of it comes from the Federal Reserve. Individuals and businesses are deeply in debt and are borrowing money at rates generally much higher than those paid on government securities. Even so, there are many individuals and businesses with surplus money they can and do invest in government securities. They do not, however, make up the major market in government securities.

The amount of money in management funds and other investment trusts, insurance companies, private pension funds, public pension funds, state funds, such as workmens' compensation and unemployment compensation, trusts, institutions, endowments, and profit sharing funds is at an all-time high and growing continuously. Most of the managers of such funds are reluctant to put much of their money in equities and real estate mortgages. They prefer to invest in liquid fixed face value securities of the highest quality. The % increase in holdings of such securities since 1946 is far greater for this group than for any other, over 700%. The Federal government is also a good customer for its own securities, increasing its holdings 602.6% by October 1980 from the end of 1946.

The purchase of U.S. government securities by foreign investors, foreign banks, including central banks, and other foreign funds has increased substantially over the last number of years. Interest rates on U.S. government securities have been attractive and while the average U.S. citizen may question the solvency of the U.S. government, in comparison with most other governments it is still extremely highly regarded financially. On a short-term basis, the purchase of U.S. securities by foreigners increases the money supply and might be considered inflationary to a minor extent. The amount of O.P.E.C. country funds invested in U.S. securities probably runs over a hundred billion dollars.

Sales of government securities to internal funds is not inflationary. In the case of the social security fund the amount it has to invest has been taken away from employers and employees. Many of the other funds have been employer supported and the money contributed to them would have otherwise been available to the employer.

In conclusion, historically government deficits have

been a major cause of inflation. Great national catastrophes or extravagances have caused the deficits. While the Federal government in the last several decades has been extravagant, its extravagance as a percentage of national income, after deducting the transfer payments from employers and employees to social security recipients, *has not been a tremendous and growing share of national income.* Such deficits cannot be blamed as a major cause of this period of inflation.

The analysis that follows shows graphically, with explanatory comments, government's share of GNP and total government spending in recent years.

ANALYSIS 2

Government's Share

Illinois' Everett Dirksen, the Silver-Haired Sage of the Senate, said of the Federal budget, "A billion here, a billion there . . . pretty soon you're talking about real money."

The accompanying charts show the share of our Gross National Product (GNP) used by Federal and by State and local governments from 1929 through 1980. The first chart by no means covers *all* expenditures of the Federal government. The Gross National Product may be briefly described as the dollar value of goods and services produced in the country. It does not include Federal "transfer" payments, such as monies paid to Social Security recipients, Federal pensioners, beneficiaries of Aid to Dependent Children, etc. It also excludes grants-in-aid to State and local governments, interest on the Federal debt, and various subsidies. These items are included in the second chart, which shows Federal expenditures in total dollars from 1958 through 1980.

To gain an idea of the growth of governmental expenditures for goods and services alone, consider the follow-

CHART V

GOVERNMENT PURCHASES OF GOODS AND SERVICES AS PERCENTAGE OF GROSS NATIONAL PRODUCT

(WORLD WAR II YEARS OMITTED)

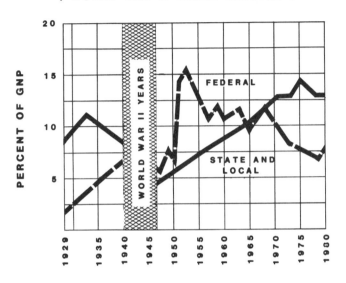

SOURCE : U.S. DEPARTMENT OF COMMERCE

ing: in 1929, the GNP was 103.4 billion dollars; the Federal government spent 1.4 billion of this, State and local governments, 7.4 billion. By 1980, the GNP has grown to over 2.6 trillion dollars, Federal expenditures to 198.9 billion. State and local to 335.8 billion.

You will notice that the World War II years are eliminated from the chart. The effect of a full wartime economy, with Federal purchases of goods and services absorbing up to 42.5% of GNP unreasonably distorts the figures.

Senator Dirksen's tongue-in-cheek reference to governmental spending raises an interesting question: just how

CHART VI

FEDERAL GOVERNMENT EXPENDITURES BY CATEGORY
1958 - 1980

(BILLIONS OF DOLLARS)

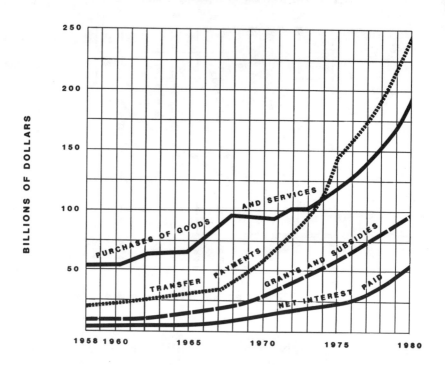

SOURCES : U.S. DEPARTMENT OF COMMERCE AND
OFFICE OF MANAGEMENT AND BUDGET

much is a billion dollars . . . a trillion dollars? For a billion, two examples:

1. a million dollars is a stack of $1,000 bills 12 inches high; a billion dollars is a stack of $1,000 bills 453 feet, 6½ inches higher than The Washington Monument;

2. approximately one billion minutes have passed since the Zealots died on Masada in 73 A.D.

And a trillion dollars? Multiply a billion by 1,000.

As Senator Dirksen said, this is "real money." As the first chart indicates, the percent spent by the Federal

CHART VII

NATIONAL DEBT AS A PERCENT OF
GROSS NATIONAL PRODUCT

(DOLLAR FIGURES ADJUSTED TO 1972 LEVELS)

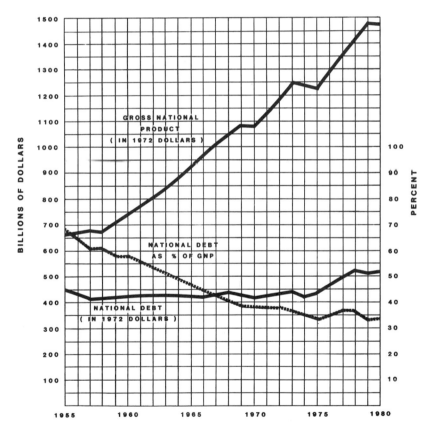

SOURCE: U.S. DEPARTMENT OF COMMERCE

government for goods and services alone is about the same as in 1949, but State and local spending shows a fairly steady percentage uptrend since 1947.

The Federal government's expenditure for goods and services . . . which covers salaries as well as goods purchased . . . is sizeable—almost 200 billion dollars, however, it amounts to only about ⅓ of the 601 billion spent in 1980. Our second chart shows the other principal categories of Federal spending. It is evident that the fastest growth in dollars has been in the catch-all category labeled "Transfer Payments," which includes outlays for pensions and Social Security . . . as well as a plethora of various social welfare programs. These payments have grown 1,067 percent during the past 22 years; from 21.4 billion in 1958 to about 249.7 billion dollars during 1980. As our chart indicates, the curve is getting steeper, with an increase of over 40 billion dollars for the year of 1980 alone.

State and local governments have had generous access to the Federal treasury over the past ten years, as have those receiving various government subsidies. These two categories . . . combined on our chart . . . accounted for almost 100 billion dollars in 1980. Interest paid by the government in 1980 . . . probably low; 1980 figures are estimated based on results through September . . . will undoubtedly grow as the Federal budget continues to run in the red.

As the Federal government has become more involved in the lives of its citizens, it has consistently failed to live within its income. This has caused great concern about the looming spectre called The National Debt. There was much viewing with alarm when this debt passed one trillion dollars in the Fall of 1981. This is a cause for concern, particularly when you compare gross Federal debt of 274 billion dollars in 1955 with the 914 billion 25 years later in 1980. But how much of a concern? To determine how threatening it really is, we have to stop comparing apples to oranges.

The "apple" dollar of 1955 would have bought $1.64 worth of merchandise in 1972; the "orange" dollar of 1980 would have paid for only 56 cents worth in the same year. The year 1972 is chosen for this example because it is the "base" year chosen by the U.S. Department of Commerce for its index used in comparative calculations involving the Gross National Product. As is the case with the Consumer Price Index, this index, with the frightening title of Implicit Price Deflator, uses an index figure of 100 for its base year. The dollar figures in the third chart for both the Gross National Product and the Gross Federal (National) Debt have been converted using the "Deflator."

As the chart indicates, the GNP, in terms of 1972 dollars, has risen much faster than the National Debt. The significant point is that the percentage of our Gross National Product that would be required to pay the entire National Debt has decreased over the 25-year period: in 1955, over two-thirds of GNP, 68.6%, would be needed; in 1980, just over one-third, 34.8%.

This is in no way intended as an endorsement of present government spending policies. Rather, it indicates that Federal debt, while it has some effect on inflation, is not the major cause. The major effect is upon interest rates.

Even though it is in inflated dollars, it should be reduced. The farther out you swim, the farther you have to swim back.

Our forefathers complained about taxation without representation. It has not been too good *with* representation.

CHAPTER 5

Energy Costs and Foreign Trade Deficits

"No man is an island," wrote John Dunne. Nor can the economy of a country be an "island." What happens in world markets profoundly affects inflation in the United States.

Since 1974, when the Organization of Petroleum Exporting Companies (O.P.E.C.) realized that the price of crude oil could be raised almost at will, energy costs and foreign trade deficits have been tied closely together. Crude oil on the open market went from $2.47 a barrel in 1972 to over $40 in 1980. The higher prices O.P.E.C. nations put on crude oil, the higher the foreign trade deficit.

As the foreign trade deficit climbs more U.S. dollars are sent abroad to pay for U.S. imports. As more U.S. dollars get into the hands of foreigners, the value of the U.S. dollar declines relative to other currencies. The lower the value of the U.S. dollar, the higher the prices of imports into the U.S.

With various inflationary forces forcing up the prices of what used to be the major U.S. industrial exports . . .

machinery, automobiles, airplanes, computers . . . the demand for U.S. goods has declined relative to total foreign trade. With U.S. imports of petroleum and automobiles soaring, U.S. dollars have been flooding Europe and Japan for several years, with U.S. dollars sinking lower and lower.

Until 1981 the U.S. dollar was weak. In 1981 the dollar recovered, for several reasons:

1. The amount and average price of foreign oil imported into the U.S. declined.
2. Foreign countries appeared to have more confidence in the Reagan administration than they had the previous one.
3. Business conditions in several major countries declined and trade surpluses turned into deficits, affecting the value of their currency.
4. U.S. exports of manufactured goods and agricultural products continued to be healthy, in spite of the increase in the value of the dollar.

For a few years after the initial 1973–1975 price increases the O.P.E.C. nations held the price line. Then the upward trend resumed. When the Shah of Iran was forced out of office, O.P.E.C. raised prices a tremendous amount. However, Saudi Arabia, the largest oil producer, did not go along with the highest price increases. The value of the U.S. dollar, in terms of Japanese currency, dropped as low as 180 yen from a par of 360. By 1980 the domestic buying power of the U.S. dollar had dropped 50% from 1972. Thus there was a vicious cycle. Many of the O.P.E.C. price increases were claimed to be justified by the decrease in the value of the dollar. However, these increases just forced the value of the dollar down further.

U.S. merchandise imports grew from $55.6 billion in

1972 to $240.7 billion in 1980. Exports grew from $49.8 billion in 1972 to $210.6 billion in 1980. The foreign trade deficit in 1980 was $30.1 billion.

In spite of the huge merchandise trade deficit (the U.S. imported $82 billion of oil in 1980), the net result of all transactions, including smaller adjustments, was a plus of $118 million. This is called the balance on current account. It would seem from these figures that the dollars owned by other countries did not increase in 1980, but U.S. investments in foreign countries, minus investments in the U.S. by foreign countries, resulted in a substantial outflow of U.S. dollars in 1980. This did not result in as big a decline in U.S. dollars in terms of German marks or Japanese yen, because both those nations also incurred foreign trade declines. During this period the British pound actually declined in terms of U.S. dollars.

So an examination of all the pluses and minuses in foreign transactions shows that other types of income from foreign countries offset the merchandise deficits. The big net outflow of American dollars in the past decade resulted from investments and loans, both private and government, military expenditures, and outright government gifts to foreign countries.

The value of the U.S. dollar dropped lower in 1977–79 than a free market setting of exchange rates would justify. Part of this drop was psychological, reflecting a lack of confidence in the U.S. The economies of Germany, Switzerland, and Japan appeared solid and impregnable, while the U.S. seemed to have lost strength and direction until 1981.

These trends are in the process of changing. The decrease in consumption of petroleum—with consequent decreases in price—will reduce the U.S. rate of inflation in two ways: by raising the value of the dollar and by lowering the cost of energy. A 10% drop in the price of

oil and its downstream derivatives might reduce the
C.P.I. and more likely the P.P.I. by almost 1%, but for
each additional 10% decrease the C.P.I. and P.P.I. would
decrease less.

A drop in the price of oil may result in an increase
in the demand for cars or other products and services
such as airline transportation. Foreign countries having
to import all their oil might buy more agricultural or
other products from the U.S. because they would be
spending less money for oil.

This is near-term. Over the long range prices of oil
and its derivatives will increase more rapidly than the
C.P.I. unless ways to decrease consumption or to develop
new economical sources of portable energy are found.

Petroleum production from oil-shale deposits is a possibility, but the logistics are staggering. At an estimated
½ barrel of oil from a ton of shale, the production of
enough to meet our needs would require processing (in
the words of one expert,) ". . . a mountain a day." Production of hydrocarbons from vegetable matter seems to
have the most promise.

How about the prospects for growth in U.S. exports?
Between 1969 and 1980 the dollar value of U.S. agricultural exports increased almost 600%. Prices of grain increased about 150%. Forecasts of food consumption
worldwide indicates that more U.S. agricultural products
will be needed. The big problem is how the Lesser-Devel-
oped-Countries (LDC's) are going to pay for them. To
get money to pay for food, the U.S. and other nations
will have to buy from them. But what will we buy?

The U.S.S.R., presently a major grain customer, is expe-
riencing a declining birth rate, an increase in infant mortality, and high abortion rates. Within a few years it
should be able to supply all its agricultural needs, except
in years of drought and unusual weather conditions.

Even in bad years, Russia produces about 90% of its grain requirements. We can expect more competition in international agricultural markets from countries like Argentina, Australia, and southern African countries.

Non-agricultural exports and imports, except for oil, have maintained about the same pattern as agricultural products. While foreign cars and steel imports have been getting great publicity, the total dollar value of exports and imports have matched fairly closely year after year. It is unlikely that there will be a big change in this pattern, even though Japan has cut into U.S. production and exports of high technological capital goods, in many instances under licensing agreements on U.S. patents.

If the U.S. can eliminate the major cause of inflation, its exports of manufactured goods will increase because its prices will be more attractive.

The Molded Fiber Glass Company recently helped an Israeli company get started in press molding of fiber glass reinforced plastic. We recommended what size presses to buy and obtained prices from several U.S. press builders, all of whom claimed to be very anxious for the order. The Israeli manager took our press specifications to a German builder, whose written quote was 40% below the U.S. quotes. Guess who got the order.

Floating foreign exchange rates tend to balance out exports and imports, except where the demand for a product (oil) or service is quite inelastic, or the supply quite inelastic. High tariffs and other restrictions on trade maintain inefficient producers, high costs, and national monopolies, such as unions. By so doing, these restrictions contribute to inflation.

To keep the value of the U.S. dollar from dropping lower when there is an oversupply of U.S. dollars in foreign hands (commonly called Eurodollars) the U.S. government and/or the Federal Reserve will keep U.S. interest rates high. This will attract foreign investors, who will use their Eurodollars to buy high-interest paying U.S. securities. But, this action is a two-edged sword, because high interest rates increase inflation and retard industrial growth, and imported dollars to meet internal government deficits add fuel to the fires of inflation.

In summary, the increase in petroleum prices and the possible eventual shortage of petroleum has caused about 1% a year increase in the C.P.I. since 1973. These increases may not continue if conservation efforts become increasingly successful and vegetable matter can be transformed into petroleum-type hydrocarbons. The decrease in the value of the dollar relative to the currency of the countries who export in large volume to the U.S. also increases inflation (possibly ½% for a 10% decline in the dollar) but only at the times the dollar goes down. When it goes up, inflation is reduced by about the same percentage.

The detailed analysis in Analysis 3 of the problems facing the steel industry in the United States gives an example of the forces that contribute to the balance of payments dilemma facing the nation in today's competitive world economy.

CHAPTER 6

Some Other Factors Contributing to Inflation

We have discussed four factors commonly blamed as the chief culprits in inflation: excess demand; money supply; government deficits; and foreign exchange deficits.

As we add these together, we see that, in total, they might cause a 2–3% annual increase in prices.

Well, then, what other factors might lead to our dreadful inflationary situation? Let's consider those which are cited most frequently.

1. DWINDLING NATURAL RESOURCES

Producers of minerals and chemicals are constantly forced to use lower grade ores, to dig deeper, to go to distant sources, and to substitute. This raises costs and prices. However, increased prices and the thinning out of competition may make it practical to work large-scale low-grade ore bodies, using efficient equipment that could not be justified previously at lower volume per mine.

There are millions of tons of steel, cast iron, copper,

lead, zinc, and aluminum gradually oxidizing in the form of junk cars, farm equipment, machinery, and even unused buildings. These could be reclaimed when scrap prices get high enough to justify the cost of collection.

The prices of important inorganic minerals can be expected to advance slowly over the coming decades in relation to other prices, but this will not be a major source of inflation.

The elimination in the early 1970's of the depletion allowance for mines and wells (27½% of production values could be exempt from income tax to allow for depletion of a consumed natural resource) reduced greatly the funds available for prospecting, development of new mines and wells, and modernization of old mines.

With less funds, mine and well owners did not gamble as much of their cash on prospecting for new sources, which resulted in lower U.S. production in relation to demand and more dependence on foreign oil.

Politicians and others are wont to rave about "loopholes" in federal income tax regulations. Every one of these so-called "loopholes," such as tax-exempt municipal bonds or depletion reserves, was put there for a sound economic reason, and elimination of the "loophole" just passes the cost along to someone else or restricts the U.S. economy in some way.

2. A DECLINING RATE OF INCREASE IN PRODUCTIVITY

This has several causes: people work less hours per year; many have lost the work ethic; the supply of skilled blue-collar workers is dwindling; new people are not being trained fast enough as replacements; production facilities are not being improved as rapidly as they should be because tax and depreciation policies of both federal and state governments have deferred such improvements; short-sighted featherbedding union policies have reduced output. One theory to justify increases in pay has been that productivity increases offset pay increases, but pay increases have greatly exceeded productivity increases, especially in the last few years.

The subject of productivity increases is discussed in more detail in Chapter 9.

3. INCREASING COSTS DUE TO GOVERNMENT REGULATIONS

Tremendous amounts of money have been spent on facilities which not only do not increase production one iota, but also frequently add to operating costs, particularly energy costs. Government agencies such as the Environmental Protection Agency (E.P.A.) and the Occupational Safety and Health Agency (O.S.H.A.) have forced private industry to make such investments without regard to the benefits obtained. In the long run, consumers and taxpayers pay these extra costs, whether or not the benefits were desirable or even necessary.

Consumer costs also have been increased by government regulations. Non-leaded, high octane gasoline is a prime example. It costs more everywhere, but its benefits are limited to a few concentrated areas where auto emissions are suspected of causing undesirable smog. The production of non-leaded high octane gasoline requires aromatic chemicals, which are by-products from gasoline refining and are indispensable ingredients of most plastics and coatings. Since the production of by-products cannot be increased without increasing the production of the main product, the prices of aromatic chemicals have shot up rapidly.

There is no question that government regulations add to inflation, though not in a major way.

4. THE GROWING COST OF PROTECTION AGAINST LAWSUITS

A little noticed cause of inflation has been the tremendous increase in product liability, malpractice, and similar type lawsuits and awards. Awards have become so astronomical, due to generous juries, that some attorneys concentrate entirely on taking such cases on a contingency fee basis. In no other major country are contingency fee cases permitted, either by law or by bar association ruling.

Court rulings made several years ago permit the plaintiff to sue everyone involved for damages, even though he was careless, and the machine on which he was hurt was old, obsolete, rebuilt, or in poor repair. Equipment manufacturers have been faced with unbelievable increases in insurance costs. In some cases their insurance companies have cancelled their policies. Some companies have gone out of business, while others have continued without insurance.

An example of how product liability insurance cost increases have resulted in higher prices: a marine motor manufacturer's insurance cost per motor produced used to be $3.00. In recent years the insurance cost increased to $57.00 per unit. This probably resulted in an increase of $120 to the consumer.

Doctors, particularly surgeons and anesthesiologists, have been faced with similar increases in malpractice insurance. Not only have doctors raised their rates to cover insurance increases, but the insurance increases have reduced the number of doctors, reducing service to the public, which is another form of inflation.

Attempts have been made, on both a national and state scale, to eliminate some of the excesses caused by the interpretation of product liability laws, but most of these attempts have been blocked so far by the Association of Trial Lawyers and by labor unions who do not realize how much this problem is costing their rank and file.

5. THE DEBT BURDEN

A condition that is both a cause and a result of inflation is the tremendous increase in debt owed by all sectors of our economy since World War II.

Consumer debt of all types, including home mortgages, increased 2,457% in 33 years. Business debt 2,350% total government debt 477% state and local debt 1,960% and Federal debt 370%.

The willingness of consumers, businesses, and state and local governments to go into debt certainly has kept business active. Where did the money come from? A large portion, possibly 90%, came from savings and loans, insurance companies, institutions, trust funds, pension funds, long-term bank loans, and corporate and individual investors. The purchasing power of such sources was reduced on a 1:1 ratio to the borrowings, so such expansion of credit did not result in much of a net increase in demand.

6. FEAR OF INFLATION ITSELF

"If we wait the cost will go up." Anticipation of greater inflation. This belief keeps the fires of inflation burning. Time and again when business activity has slowed down in the past decade, the tremendous consumer and business debt has been viewed with alarm, especially by those who were adults in the 1929–41 depression.

This points up the danger of seeking a system that would not only stop inflation but would also cause prices to decline. If people felt that prices were going to decrease

TABLE 5
TOTAL U.S. DEBT

Year-end	Net Public Debt (Bil.)				Net Private Debt (Bil.)			Grand Total (Bil.)
	Federal	Agencies	State & Local	Total	Business	Consumer & Other	Total	
1980	$742	$302	$330	$1,374	$1,617	$1,662	$3,279	$4,653
1979	663	255	305	1,223	1,475	1,545	3,020	4,243
1978	620	205	300	1,125	1,215	1,450	2,665	3,790
1977	564	167	271	1,002	1,065	1,240	2,305	3,307
1976	506	142	242	890	953	1,069	2,022	2,912
1975	437	123	223	783	898	940	1,838	2,621
1974	352	110	208	670	877	865	1,742	2,412
1973	339	88	191	618	787	788	1,575	2,193
1972	332	67	177	576	670	696	1,366	1,942
1971	317	58	162	537	592	621	1,213	1,750
1970	291	53	144	488	539	568	1,107	1,595
1965	258	20	100	378	323	407	730	1,108
1960	234	10	71	315	206	257	463	778
1955	228	5	46	279	137	166	303	582
1947	221	1	16	238	66	65	131	369
Avg. Ann. Inc. %								
1975–1980	14.0	29.2	9.6	15.0	16.0	15.4	15.6	15.60
1970–1975	10.0	26.4	11.0	12.0	13.3	13.0	13.2	12.80
1960–1970	2.4	43.0	10.2	5.5	13.7	21.0	13.9	10.50
1947–1960	0.46	0.77	26.5	2.5	16.3	22.7	19.5	8.54

rapidly they would cut their purchases down to the minimum needed to maintain their standard of living and not replace big ticket items until they were worn out.

A decline in the price of items whose purchases are normally financed by long-term monthly payments would result in much higher delinquency rates than now exist, especially if down payments have been small and interest rates high. The combination of a cut-back in purchases and increasing foreclosures on loans might result in a serious depression. No solution to inflation can be sought at the risk of serious deflation.

7. HIGH INCOME TAXES

Lawmakers do not seem to realize that increasing income tax rates, both personal and business, forces prices up. To cut down taxes, high earners look for tax shelters; for example, investments with low current income but high capital gains potential. Land around growing cities has this potential. Much such land has been bought up and held by large investors who can wait while holding individual lots at high prices. The potential home-buyer is forced to pay far more for his lot. This type of forced inflation is most common in real estate, but also permeates other types of property.

8. LOCAL TAX INCREASES

State and local governments, faced with tremendous demands for more pay by employees and rising energy and material costs, add "small" taxes to the cost of doing business in their area. The businessman adds these taxes to his costs of doing business. If he cannot do that because of competition, his business suffers, as do his employees, and eventually his customers. These state and local tax increases are inflationary and detrimental to long-range welfare of the area.

9. CAPITAL GAINS TAX

The capital gains tax adds to inflation in two ways. If A owns a piece of property that B has to have, and the property has increased in value since A acquired it, B must pay A what the property is worth plus the capital gains tax that A will have to pay on its sale. Otherwise, after the sale A would have less assets than before.

The second way the capital gains tax adds to inflation is caused by basing the capital gains cost on the original cost of a capital item less depreciation. A manufacturer may have bought a machine in 1961 for $25,000. It is completely written-off but has a current market value of $20,000. A new machine will cost $100,000. The new machinery maker will not take the old machine in trade-in, so the manufacturer has to sell his old machine. If he gets $20,000 for it, he pays the full corporate income tax rate on the difference between its current book value and the sale price.

The manufacturer should be allowed to apply all the proceeds he obtained from the sale of the old piece of equipment to the purchase price of the new equipment, which would reduce the book value of the new equipment accordingly.

10. INCREASING SOCIAL SECURITY TAXES

Social Security tax increases are inflationary. They increase the cost of living, but not directly the C.P.I., of everyone who has to pay the tax. Social Security payments started in 1937 with both the employee and the employer paying 1% of the first $3,000 earned by the individual into the fund, or $60 a year per employee. In 1981 the rate on each was 6.65% on the first $29,700 earned, an increase of 2,299%. Was the original 1% rate realistic? Yes—if there had been no inflation there would have been no reason to increase payouts to recipients and pay-ins by employee and employer. If Congressmen had not voted, every two years just before election, to increase benefits and coverage, the Social Security fund would now be adequate to meet the payments originally planned. Without inflation such payments would have provided real income as planned. Further, there would have needed to be no increase in the Social Security tax rate.

Since 1965 Congress and inflation combined have evis-cerated the Social Security Fund to a point where its neg-ative cash flow, even after a 2,299% increase in payments by employed people, is so great that it will be bankrupt shortly. The Social Security Security Fund should have now assets greatly in excess of one trillion dollars to be considered properly funded. Attempts by the administra-tion to reduce some of the excess coverages to help bal-ance its cash flow are met with hysterical outcries by people who have not examined the facts.

11. UNDER-FUNDED PENSION PLANS

Originally it was thought that private pension plans would consist of payments by the employer, and often by the employee, into a fund which was constantly being invested in income-producing securities. This fund was supposed to build up so that when the person retired he would get enough from it which, together with Social Security and some personal savings, would provide him an adequate retirement income.

What happened? As inflation continued, contributions

into the private funds became inadequate to meet their eventual liabilities. Pensions were increased with inflation, while reserves lagged. Since, most pension plans were written on a fixed benefit basis, actuaries were called in to estimate the amount by which these pension plans were "unfunded." No one knows the exact amount of the "unfunded" portion of all private pension funds, but it might run into a trillion dollars.

A government agency now guarantees private pension funds with fixed benefit provisions. It charges the employer an insurance fee of about $2.60 per employee per year. If a large company goes broke, the government can be stuck with a fabulous obligation, running into nine figures.

Employers are required by law to make up the unfunded amount over a period of 28 years and to contribute a sufficient amount per employee each year to meet the current funding requirements. Both the making-up of the unfunded and completely funding all future pensions are deducted as current expenses by employers and have to be covered in their pricing or taken from their profits. As long as inflation continues and pensions are increased, it will be impossible to catch up with the unfunded liability. This is not a major cause of inflation, but it raises prices somewhat.

12. GOVERNMENT PENSION COSTS

Extremely generous pensions and fringes to government employees have added to taxes of all sorts, which find their way back to the prices or taxes paid for products and services. Many government employees are not only "double-dipping" but even "triple-dipping." A military person has been able to retire at full pension after 20 years of service. The average age at date of retirement in the military is around 43 years. Such pensions escalate more rapidly than the C.P.I. (See Enterprise article in Analyses section).

The retiring government employee then gets another job, either in private industry or with a different government organization (federal to state to local) where full pensions are paid after a short period of service. By taking a third job covered by Social Security after retiring from the second government job, he can get three checks each month when he retires from the third job. The retiring general-level military man often gets a high-paying job with a military supplier.

13. INTERNATIONAL PRESSURES

Political and military upheavals in foreign countries have contributed to inflation in the U.S. over the past 45 years. These upheavals interfere with normal international trade, international sources of supply, and demand and supply patterns. The total impact on U.S. price levels is impossible to measure. Possibly 10% of the total inflation since 1936 and the Ethiopian and Chinese-Japanese wars has been caused by wars. We cannot legislate these conflicts away. Building up military strength to combat the threat of Russian action anywhere in the globe is inevitably inflationary.

14. EQUAL OPPORTUNITY REGULATIONS

A minor cause of inflation and low productivity is the forced use of less effective people in many occupations. While it may be socially and politically desirable to force employers to use these people, it is an economic burden paid for by consumers and taxpayers. Anything that reduces productivity per person-year, or reduces the quality of the product or service produced, adds to inflation.

15. UNEMPLOYMENT COMPENSATION

While the increase in percent rates paid on payrolls has not been tremendous, the ceiling has been increased 100% in the State of Ohio and similarly in other states. The increase in the rates and the ceiling add to inflation.

Originally unemployment compensation covered 13 weeks at a level of about 40% of average pay. Unemployed workers were supposed to hunt actively for any type of work. Now compensation is paid for 26 weeks or more, and the unemployed worker does not have to take a job much inferior in pay or different from the type of work he had been performing. The total output of the country is reduced by the lost output of workers who would be employed at some gainful, productive work but would rather stay home and loaf. This loss adds to inflation.

Many states have exhausted their unemployment compensation funds and are now borrowing from the federal government. This money must be paid back in two years. Regardless of the individual employer's merit rating, every employer in the state has to pay an extra $18 per employee per year until the federal government is paid back. The federal government shows this loan in its budget, but has practically no control over it.

INTEREST RATES

In the last few years interest rates have advanced far more rapidly than the rest of the C.P.I., with the result that interest costs alone have increased the C.P.I. as follows:

Some Other Factors Contributing to Inflation

		Additional Increase Due to:	
	CPI Increase %	*Mortgage Interest Increase Alone*	*Mortgage Interest Increase and Home Purchase Increase*
Dec., 1977—Dec., 1978	9.0%	0.9%	1.1%
Dec., 1978—Dec., 1979	13.3%	1.7%	2.2%
Dec., 1979—Dec., 1980	12.4%	1.5%	1.5%

Rents are affected by interest rates. While most rental units are financed on long-term mortgages with fixed interest rates, new units are often financed with variable interest rates. Regardless of fixed or variable, interest rates are considerably higher than they used to be, and rents have to be increased accordingly. Landlords owning existing rental units at old low fixed interest rates feel they should get more rent to cover the inflated value of their units, so up go all rents. Consumers have to pay much higher payments on installment purchases, which is also reflected in the C.P.I.

Producers of goods and services have to increase their overhead rates, which in turn increases their prices, to cover increased interest charges. Normally interest is a small cost factor in overall operations, but in recent years it has become a very large cost item. Both private industry and public operations have to increase their gross income to meet high interest costs. One of the biggest costs of any government unit is interest. Recent increases in interest have upset the administration's calculations on balancing the budget.

Inflation greatly reduces, and sometimes wipes out, real income from money loaned out. The lender, except in the cases of tax-exempt trusts or foundations, pays income tax on the full amount of interest received. If he receives 15% interest and is in the 50% tax bracket, he nets, after tax, 7½% before inflation. If the inflation rate is 10%, he loses 2½% a year on his loan.

Consequently the lender wants enough interest to cover taxes and inflation and leave him with a reasonable return on his investment. We cannot expect interest rates to go down permanently until inflation goes down.

Present interest rates are higher than they should be because the Federal Reserve is artificially tightening the market. We can expect high interest rates indefinitely in the future as long as compensation-cost-push inflation is allowed to exist, though short-term fluctuations could drop the market rates (not necessarily prime) into single digits.

The net effect of high interest rates on an individual or business will depend largely on their own situations, the amount of debt owed, owning or renting property, and the type of activity. Many people and businesses benefit from high interest rates, but more suffer from them.

All the factors discussed in this chapter plus those in Chapters 3, 4, and 5 contribute to inflation. None of them are dominant causes of inflation in America today. Some, particularly interest rates, speculation, and holding of real estate, will disappear when the major cause of inflation is corrected. I estimate that at the present time all of these minor factors together are responsible for 35% of our present rate of inflation; the major cause 65%.

CHAPTER 7

How the History of Industrial Employment Leads into Today's Inflation

As I stated at the outset of this book, the major cause of our present inflation is not one of the factors which are conventionally blamed for the situation. In the preceding chapters I have tried to show why these suspected causes—though they all have some effect—are not at the root of our critical economic sickness.

When we eliminate these factors as major causes, we are left with one dominant factor: *paying people more, year after year, for doing the same amout of work or less.*

That is why we are in the spot we are in today. Before we discuss what we can do about it, it's important to review the steps by which we got here.

We think of the world's present economic system as beginning with the Industrial Revolution, generally said to have started in England around 1750. Earlier, business was dominated by crafts, mercantilism, feudalism, and petty merchants. There was a vast gulf in income between the small upper class and the massive lower class. Members of the upper class did not work; they lived on the income from their land, their investments, and their ventures in exploration for profit.

The small middle class consisted of tradesmen, craftsmen and professionals. Factories were individually-owned small shops whose employees lived in—or close to—the shop. The owner was the full-time manager.

These conditions had existed for centuries, in slightly different forms in different countries. The nobles, whatever their titles, were generally descendants of warriors who controlled an area, protected the inhabitants, made and dispensed the laws, and extracted economic contributions from their subjects. Some nobles were appointed by the king and were given lands and income.

As kings gradually tried to consolidate their domains into larger homogenous countries they had to deal with these nobles, some of whom resisted domination and refused to contribute to the expenses of the central government. These fractious little countries within a country made expansion of trade and subsequent industrialization and specialization difficult. Even late in the nineteenth century Italy and Germany consisted of duchies and other independent small units, to be united into one country by Garibaldi and Bismarck.

Prior to the Industrial Revolution the average European worked on a farm. He lived on the farm or in a village. The farm was usually owned by a nobleman, whose area was totally or almost self-sufficient. Disease and famine kept the population from expanding too rapidly, and sometimes cut the population down to a point where production dropped and inflation occurred. As boys grew up, they were faced with few choices: stay on the farm; join the Army; go to sea; become an apprentice; join a monastery; or emigrate to the colonies. The latter choice required money unless one went as an indentured servant to a colonial landowner in the colony, who would pay the emigration expenses. The indentured servant was in effect a slave for a certain number of years, usually four. Girls had fewer choices.

Craftsmen protected their knowledge and skills very selfishly, fearing that too many craftsmen would drive rates down and split the available business. The number of apprentices was limited and the length of time the apprentice served, at no pay except subsistence, was unnecessarily long.

Economic philosophy before the Industrial Revolution was to restrict output and keep prices high. Once when a new textile plant was set up the craftsman weavers invaded it and smashed the machinery. They felt it would ruin their jobs.

We can illustrate the relevant historical developments most clearly by focusing on England.

All in all, the lot of the average Englishman before the Industrial Revolution was very tough, with many living only slightly better than the domestic animals they raised. There was little an individual could do about it. He earned a low-level subsistence income. While noblemen lived in large castles with many servants, their standard of living was still far below what we would consider satisfactory now. There was no big pie that could be split up more equitably to raise the average man's standard of living to any extent, and he had little power to force a redivision of wealth and income.

This limitation of any chance for advancement of the status of the individual British citizen bred a class-hatred that continues to plague England today. This animosity, stemming from the day of the feudal system, accounts for much of the strength of Britain's Labour Party, and of its labor unions.

England was eager to build up its exports. In the time of Queen Elizabeth I, 1558–1603, wool was an important export. A process called "Inclosures" for sheep pasture was adopted by the landed gentry to expand the wool supply. The inclosures displaced many tenant farmers from their lands and produced a class of wandering, unemployed "sturdy beggars." Poor laws, adopted in 1601, placed the responsibility for supporting the unemployed, the aged, the infirm, and orphans on local communities. The administration of these laws varied widely from community to community. People in need gravitated to the more generous towns.

The abolition of the Catholic Church by Henry VIII (1491–1547) resulted in large numbers of monks, nuns, and other church people being left with no means of support. Church lands were acquired by the wool growers, reducing the production of food and the need for agricultural workers. The increasing supply of wool helped establish the wool weaving industry in England, but created a problem of unemployment that has haunted England ever since. It also accentuated the lower classes' distrust and hatred of the upper classes, whose short-term greed and lack of concern for English workers has over the centuries made socialism and communism attractive to the masses.

To increase the amount of farm land available for larger commercial farms a second period of Inclosure (1750–1810) deprived many small tenant farmers of their land. However, the increasing demands for industrial workers absorbed most of them. In spite of migration of British people to North America, Australia, and other colonies won by Great Britain in the eighteenth century, the population of Great Britain (excluding Northern Ireland) grew from 7,500,000 in 1750 to 10,800,000 in 1801 (the first census) to 23,130,000 in 1861, primarily in urban areas. This growth created urban problems and squalor, much as in major Latin American cities now.

The British middle class increased rapidly during the Industrial Revolution, but had to struggle to gain its political power. A policy of free trade was adopted greatly expanding Britain's foreign trade. Britons began to eat better. Great reforms and improvements made in the nineteenth century improved the conditions and political power of British working people. Early in the twentieth century Britain adopted old age pensions, unemployment insurance, and health insurance.

Prior to the Industrial Revolution, lack of communication, education, trade between areas, and easily transferable capital had made progress very slow. With the discovery of the New World and the return to Europe of relatively huge stocks of gold the latter obstacle was largely overcome. However the capital did not immediately get into the hands of people who could put it to proper use. The New World offered expanding markets for manufactured goods, but it took hundreds of years before this helped spawn the Industrial Revolution.

The word "Revolution" implies rapid change. The Industrial Revolution could more properly be called an evolution. With the formation of the Bank of England in 1694, entrepreneurs had access to more funds than ever before. Some crude machines were in use, powered by wind, water, or wood. Markets slowly expanded. Manufacturing, primarily of textiles, grew rapidly, spurred by key inventions: A practical steam engine, James Watt, 1769; the flying shuttle, John Kay, 1733; the spinning jenny, James Hargreaves, 1770; the water frame, Richard Arkwright, 1769; the mule, Samuel Crompton, 1779; the power loom, Edmund Cartwright, 1783; the telegraph, several inventors, 1815–45.

The availability of both coal and iron ore in England facilitated the expansion of iron making. The Bessemer furnace was developed later to convert iron into steel.

Eli Whitney's cotton gin (1793) provided low-cost high volume short-staple cotton for England's mills. His subsequent inventions and production of interchangeable standard parts introduced mass production methods into American industry early in the nineteenth century.

With the springing up of new factories in England came a new opportunity for farm boys and girls. They could go to work in the factories. Much has been written, both by responsible historians and by various levels of hysterics, about this early period of the Industrial Revolution. Of course there were abuses, but the alternative for many of these young workers was semi-starvation on the farms. Employers hired children just big enough to perform the needed functions. They were sent orphans or children of large families whose parents were unwilling or unable to support them. These children became virtual slaves because they had no other place to go. According to a report written by a couple who studied the situation many years later, children were worked as much as 12 hours a day seven days a week, and shared their beds with other children who worked the opposite 12 hours. This report has been branded as grossly exaggerated, but it has been used by all shadings of social reformers as a Bible of what would happen if their particular philosophy were not adopted. It, with similar horror stories, was also used by early labor union organizers to elicit public sympathy for the "downtrodden workers."

It is certainly true that English employers took advantage of the abundant supply of workers. However, except for the orphans and abandoned children, workers were free to go back to the farms or villages, but most did not do so, probably because their living standards were lower on the farm or village.

England passed child labor laws in 1802 and subsequently individual States in the U.S. passed such laws, but not nearly as early. (Ohio 1908). The U.S. did not adopt a federal child labor law until 1938.

With slow but gradual improvements in living standards and sanitation the infant mortality rate went down and the farms and villages were left with more mouths to feed. The Corn Laws prohibited export of corn to keep the internal price of corn low, which in turn reduced the amount of corn produced and employment in agriculture. These laws were complex but in general mitigated against the working man.

In the 17th century after Cromwell the strength of Parliament increased while the strength of the rulers decreased. Representation in Parliament in those days was based on land, not on population. The members argued and legislated for their own self-interests. The landed gentry early dominated Parliament, but as industrial towns grew factory owners became an important factor in politics. By the twentieth century the working class became a political factor. The Labour Party has dominated Parliament much of the time after World War II.

There can be no doubt that the British working man was treated unfairly over the centuries until relatively recently. One of the arguments advanced by unions, in the U.S. as well as elsewhere, is that the workingman is entitled to extra compensation to make up for the centuries in which he was underpaid, or they consider he was underpaid. Both the people who may have benefited and the mistreated people are long since dead. The union proponents do not realize that competition generally kept the price of the products and services the workingman produced down, so low wages were mainly offset by low prices. Low productivity, not high owner profits, kept living standards low.

During the years that capital was scarce the share of

the wealth going to the owners of capital was greater than it is now. As capital became more plentiful, the relative share of the economic pie going to each dollar of capital decreased. It would have decreased with or without unions through competition. Without strikes and union-created restrictions on output, the total economic pie would have been, and would still be, greater. Everyone's share would have greatly increased.

Class hatred, which scarcely exists in the United States, has been very strong in Britain, causing destructive strikes, labor unrest and low productivity. The situation may be changing. Appalled by the extremism of the Labour Party, an influential group broke off in 1980 to form the new Social Democratic Party, with a more moderate orientation. The Social Democrats proceeded to win elections and become a major factor in British politics, primarily at the expense of the established Labour Party. In the fall of 1981 the *New Statesman,* an important weekly left-wing publication, attributed the decline of the Labour Party to a lessening of the class feeling which has festered so long in Great Britain.

After bearing the major brunt of two World Wars and suffering the loss of most of its colonies and its investments in O.P.E.C. nations as well as other unilateral nationalization of its properties, Britain cannot afford to have major strikes and lack of cooperation by labor groups. Britain has temporarily been rescued from financial insolvency by North Sea oil, but it must get a cooperative team effort from all Britons if it is to survive as a major Free World nation. Its almost confiscatory taxation makes it very difficult to establish new enterprises and expand existing ones.

The situation in the colonies and the United States prior to the end of the Civil War was considerably different than it was in England. Agriculture was the main source of income and foreign exchange. Prior to the Revolutionary War, British policies such as Mercantile Regulations, the Navigation Acts, and taxes, discouraged expansion of colonial industry. Britain wanted its colonies to supply food and raw materials, and to buy British manufactured products.

In the colonies large tracts of land were given out by English kings in the form of feudal grants, as rewards and to finance colonization. The proprietors generally continued to live in England, but supplied the money to develop their American properties. In the South small farmers were driven out as large plantations, worked by slaves, expanded. Southern crops prior to Eli Whitney's cotton gin were tobacco, rice, and indigo.

Workers were badly needed. It is estimated that 80% of the immigrants coming to the colonies before the Revolutionary War were brought in as indentured servants. After a person had served out his period of indenture, he was very likely to become a farmer, acquiring free a little tract of land from the government. He would live in abject poverty for several years. He preferred this to working for wages that would provide him a higher standard of living.

To attract and hold workers, colonial employers paid wages about twice as high as those in England. Colonial governments favored employers over employees in legislation, and particularly favored the government's need for labor. Workers could be impressed for a variety of public works projects, including road construction and repair, building bridges and fortifications, dams, etc. The wages were set by the local authorities. Workhouses were set up in major towns, where lawbreakers, even minor, worked out their sentences.

A debtor who could not, or did not, pay his debts was not put in prison as in England, but was bound over to work for his creditors until his debt was paid. This policy was continued until the 1830's.

The scarcity of workers greatly influenced the policies of the colonies, and subsequently the states, in regard to slavery.

Lifetime slavery started in the colonies in the 1640's. By 1775 half a million slaves lived in the colonies, primarily in the South. This resulted in the replacement of white workers on the plantations by slaves. These whites became southern poor whites if they did not migrate to the West. Many did not have the means or courage to move West, and some preferred the low-subsistence existence. These people were bypassed in the prosperous growth of the country.

The labor shortages in World War II brought hundreds of thousands of their descendants to the North. Gradually most of these people were assimilated into Northern communities.

Before the Revolutionary War the English government encouraged the emigration to America of unemployed poor, unskilled workers, and vagrants, as well as convicts who worked out their sentences. For a while England attempted to prevent the emigration of skilled workers and the exportation of machinery, plans, or models. These attempts were generally ineffective.

The feudal estates owned by loyalist residents or by loyalist absentee owners were broken up at the end of the Revolutionary War. Thousands of residents of the colonies who had remained loyal to England during the war fled to England, Canada, and other British possessions with what transportable assets they could carry, leaving all other possessions behind. They were treated very shabbily.

The French and Indian War (1754–60) was financed by England and won by a combination of English and colonial troops. Victory left the colonies with no worry or expense involved in defending themselves against aggression. After this war was over, however, Britain tried to collect some of its costs of financing the war from the colonies, the principal beneficiaries, by increasing taxes and control of the colonies. (The Stamp Act, The Townshend Act, other coercion). This resulted in gradually increasing friction. George III was an honest but stubborn man, involved in constant friction at home. He and his prime minister, Lord North, were unable to take the colonies' viewpoint on their problems and complaints, making the Revolutionary War inevitable.

Even before the colonies were united in the Revolutionary War, and to a greater extent after the war, the division between the viewpoints of the various factions within the colonies was almost as great and as bitter as it was between the colonies and England. The Democrats under Jefferson favored agriculture and exports and limited federal jurisdiction and activities. The Federalists led by Alexander Hamilton wanted a strong state, a strong currency, a protective tariff, and rapid expansion of American industry.

After the war industry, protected by tariffs, expanded rapidly in New England, New York, New Jersey, and eastern Pennsylvania. The southern states objected to such policies strenuously. With the cotton gin transforming the South into a great short-staple cotton producer, the friction between the high-tariff manufacturing north and the free-trade agricultural south kept increasing resulting in the Civil War (1861–65).

In the meantime, political parties changed rapidly. Hamilton's untimely death in a duel with Aaron Burr in 1804 weakened the Federal party. Jefferson adopted many of the Federalist ideas and substantially expanded the power of the Federal government. Suffrage was given to practically all men except slaves in the 1820's and 1830's. Jackson, 1829–1837, politicized the office with the spoils system and appealed to the common man for votes, a play that was quickly copied by the Whigs. Polk (1845–49) greatly expanded the size of the country, annexing Texas and taking the southwest away from Mexico, mostly California, Arizona, New Mexico, and Nevada. He lowered tariffs, he established an independent treasury, and he settled the Oregon territory dispute. After Polk until the Civil War, presidents Fillmore, Pierce, and Buchanan were mostly involved in pacifying the South.

While industry gradually grew more rapidly between the War of 1812, an inconclusive affair, and the Civil War, more exciting economic events were occurring. The invention of the John Deere hardened steel plow (1837) opened up the tough but fertile lands of Illinois, Iowa, and surrounding states to crop agriculture. The old cast iron plows wore out too fast. Cyrus McCormick's reaper greatly increased the acreage a man could cut. Agriculture expanded rapidly. The railroads followed to bring the crops to market. Peter Cooper invented the first successful steam locomotive, the Tom Thumb, in 1830, but until steel rails were developed a few decades later, high speeds and weights were not practical. The telegraph cut communication time down tremendously, making practical the management of far-flung enterprises.

The discovery of gold in California in 1848 started a westward movement that has been going on ever since.

The American Civil War created great pressure and opportunities to expand industrial production. Its foundation was steel. Railroads, the farm machinery industry, and construction grew rapidly after the war, also increasing the demand for workers. The effect of all these developments from the Deere plow onward is shown in the immigration figures:

TABLE 6
U.S. IMMIGRATION: 1820–1980

Period	No. of Immigrants (000's)	Period	No. of Immigrants (000's)
1820–30	152	1901–10	8,795
1831–40	509	1911–20	5,736
1841–50	1,713	1921–30	4,107
1851–60	2,598	1931–40	528
1861–70	2,315	1941–50	1,035
1871–80	2,812	1951–60	2,515
1881–90	5,247	1961–70	3,322
1891–1900	3,688	1971–80	5,064*

* Includes unpublished estimate of 808,000 for 1980; does not include any estimates of illegal immigrants.

The increasing need for workers generated by the young Industrial Revolution in the U.S. presented new opportunities to thousands who had formerly been farm-hands as well as those who had emigrated from Europe in search of a better life. The new concentrations of workers resulting from the switch from the former "cottage industry" format to larger industrial units provided new opportunities for labor union organization.

The latter half of the 19th century was thus characterized by extensive union organization and by bloody violence on both sides. Largely due to public indignation at this violence, the labor union movement made little progress until well into the present century.

The "Molly Maguires," a secret society of Irish miners, first came to public attention in 1862, and went out of existence in 1876 when 14 of its leaders were imprisoned and 10 executed for terrorist activities against the mine owners.

The Knights of Labor (1869–1917) grew to a memberships of 702,000 in the 1880's by soliciting all workers of a company as members. An unsuccessful Missouri Pacific strike (1886) and Chicago's Haymarket Square Riot, also in 1886, damaged the organization severely, and it gradually disappeared.

Public indignation ran high after the Haymarket riot and subsequent violence during the Homestead, PA, strike in 1892 which killed several Pinkerton guards as well as several workers. The public was becoming increasingly apprehensive at these continuing outbreaks of violence, which they saw as mini-revolutions inspired by Socialist labor leaders.

The labor leaders, however, applied even stronger pressure tactics in the Pullman Strike that started May 11, 1894. This was one of the most significant examples of this turbulent period in labor.

The city of Pullman, Illinois, had been founded by G. M. Pullman as a model community for the workers of the Pullman Palace Car Company. The company owned all the property, and attempted to create a "company family" atmosphere for its workers and their families.

In 1889, the residents voted to have the city annexed by Chicago, and the company was required by Illinois courts to sell all property not used for industrial purposes. This ended Mr. Pullman's hopes for a "family feeling."

Business activity had dropped sharply in the early 1890's, resulting in a bank panic in 1893. Wholesale prices had dropped sharply. The Pullman company—citing economic conditions—had reduced wages in early 1894. Pullman workers called a strike and appealed to their "mother" union, the American Railway Union, for support.

The American Railway Union, spearheaded by its fiery president, Eugene V. Debs, called for a boycott of all Pullman railway cars. Railway traffic out of Chicago ground to a halt as 50,000 railroad workers walked out. Produce and meat, then not mechanically refrigerated, spoiled and the public's normal food supply was interrupted.

The railroad owners asked the Federal government to intervene. On July 2, an injunction was obtained, prohibiting the strike. The injunction was not obeyed. On July 4, President Cleveland dispatched troops to Chicago to enforce it.

The immediate result was much rioting and bloodshed. Finally the strike was broken, ending one of the blackest chapters in American labor history.

In 1905, the Independent Workers of the World (IWW) started organizing unskilled workers in many trades. As its membership increased, the "Wobblies" became more and more militant. The group collapsed when its leaders were convicted under the Espionage Act during and after World War I.

In the 1890's the American Federation of Labor, under Samuel Gompers, brought a wide variety of craft unions under one leadership. The AFL made slow progress, because it remained primarily a collection of craft unions. As such, it was unable to put much pressure upon large employers since skilled craft workers made up only a small percentage of the employees of a large company.

Throughout this period in the latter 19th century and into the early years of the 20th, the posture of the Federal government and the courts was based upon the principle of protecting the rights and property of the owners. In 1913, the U.S. Department of Labor was established by law. It incorporated the functions of various bureaus already in existence and was headed by a Secretary of Labor whose duties included the responsibility to "act as mediator and to appoint commissioners of conciliation in labor disputes." It was perhaps prophetic that the first

Secretary of Labor was William B. Wilson, who, in addition to being a member of Congress, was also a trade unionist.

The first major test of arbitration by a Presidential commission was in December, 1919, when the commission awarded a 27% wage increase to bituminous coal workers. This increase gave John L. Lewis a great boost.

From this time through the onset of the Great Depression, Federal legislation drifted more to the side of labor.

The collapse of shipyards and the sharp business recession of 1920–21 reduced union membership. Through most of the '20's, unions made slow progress. Then came the Crash of '29 and the subsequent depression that lasted, in varying degrees of severity, until 1941. By 1933, union strength and membership had dropped by about 50% from the 1920 level, from some 4.5 million to about 2.25 million.

The new administration of Franklin D. Roosevelt felt that old business practices and economic theories had failed and could not be counted on to restore the nation's economic well-being. Great new experiments were tried. Roosevelt coined the term New Deal. Roosevelt had intended to work closely with business leaders. One of his major programs, the National Industrial Recovery Act, NIRA, seemed to have goodies in it for everyone. It floundered for many reasons, including the greed of those who took advantage of others who were trying to live within its guidelines. Roosevelt believed that business and industry had sabotaged the program. He gradually withdrew his cooperation and even-handedness from business and industry, and turned to courting the support of labor union officials and the "common people."

The N.I.R.A. was declared unconstitutional on May 27, 1935. Twenty-three days thereafter the Wagner Act was passed. It gave great new powers to labor unions to organize workers and rendered employers almost powerless to attempt to keep their employees from joining unions.

Thus the greatest inflationary force ever released on the face of the earth was spawned.

The purpose of reviewing briefly the economic and union history of England and the United States has been to get a better understanding of the beginnings of unions and the conditions under which most people worked during the last two hundred and fifty years.

Prior to the Industrial Revolution the standard of living of the average man, or of the feudal lord or plantation owner, had improved very slowly over the centuries. People did not expect improvements. What was good enough for their ancestors was good enough for them.

With the coming of the Industrial Revolution, countless inventions, massive increases in power, large investments in new and specialized machinery, the development of huge sources of mineral and agricultural wealth in the New World and Australasia, and the new mass markets provided by free trade among all the United States, the rate of increase in the standard of living for practically all people accelerated rapidly. It was a combination of productivity increases created by invention, investment, resources, markets, confidence, management, and restless pioneers.

The direct contribution of unions in this increase has been less than nil. Unions merely have argued over the division of the spoils, and during the arguments have often greatly reduced the spoils. A comparison of the C.P.I. over the last 181 years to wage rates paid shows that the average man's rate of increase in his standard of living was in most cases greater when unions had little power than when they had great power as in the late 1970's. The unions have increased the standard of living of some of the members (not all) more rapidly than that of all workers, but the net result of all their activities over the years has been to reduce the rate of increase in the average man's standard of living.

Much of the U.S. social legislation for which the New Deal, the Democratic party, and labor union leaders take all the credit, had been introduced and passed in other countries decades before, and had been introduced in the 1920's by Republican legislators in the U.S. Congress.

The major contribution unions have made to the increase in the standard of living has been to force employers to devise and invest in labor-saving machinery and procedures to cut down the labor content in the product or service produced. This can greatly increase the amount of capital investment needed per job, a problem that is particularly serious now with high interest rates and high corporate income taxes and a tax-created shortage of equity money.

Offsetting this is the untold number of companies who have been forced out of business by short-sighted union demands or have not been able to keep up with competitors because they do not make enough profits.

The progress of the last two hundred and fifty years should have provided our economy with an overabundance shared by a happy team of people all working together harmoniously to provide products and services for everyone at every-reducing costs. Instead, we have conflict everywhere, bankrupt people, companies, cities, states, and nations, and an ever-declining standard of value.

When mankind disappears from the face of the earth, and he will someday, God may comment, "What a mess man made of his golden opportunity."

CHAPTER 8

Compensation–Cost–Push: The Engine of Inflation

Or Which Came First—Wages or Prices?

When people are paid more and more for doing the same amount of work or less, the result is *compensation–cost–push* inflation (C.C.P.).

Labor unions argue that they need wage increases to keep up with price increases. But the key question is, which came first, the wage increase or the price increase? The answer—and here is the heart of the argument—is that in every case involving a major union, wage and fringe increases preceded the price increases. In addition, the percentage wage increase was greater than the price increase.

Compensation–cost–push (C.C.P.) inflation got its start in 1935 with passage of the Wagner Act. At the stroke of a pen, unions had vastly increased power, including compulsory union membership for employees and compulsory collective bargaining for employers, while the power of employers to combat unionization of their plants were greatly reduced.

The rationale presented by theorists was that the individual worker had no bargaining power, leaving the employer free to pay his employees only enough to keep them working for him. These theorists had not examined the history of wage rates and consumer prices. Over the years wage rates in an open labor market had gone up as productivity increases had reduced costs. Prices had gone down with increased productivity. For example, between 1800 and 1900 prices dropped 50% while general wage rates doubled. Thus the standard of living for the average American worker had quadrupled during that time.

The Wagner Act changed the ratio of bargaining power from 90% employer to 10% employee to close to 90% union and 10% employer. Even with 90% bargaining power the employer had to compete in the open market for good employees and his products had to be competitive in price. If his wage levels were low, his prices were low. If wage levels went up, his prices had to go up. In spite of popular belief to the contrary, American employers paying low wages to employees did not make, and generally never have made, excessive profits over the long haul. Competition will not let them do so.

Unions did not use restraint or common sense in the exercise of their new power. They demanded and obtained wage increases far in excess of productivity increases, and forced employers to accept programs which resulted in reduced productivity, excessive hiring, and retention of incompetent or lazy workers.

One of the reasons unions gave for making demands for large increases in pay was that they felt workers had been underpaid for centuries and the big increase would catch up to some extent the amount they had been underpaid in the past. This "catch-up" theory failed to recognize that new customers had to buy their products, people who had not benefited from any real or imagined under-payment in years past.

In the long run wage increases come from the employer's customers, not the employer. If customers will not pay the price the employer has to charge to stay in business, the employer will go out of business and union members will lose jobs. The unions failed to recognize this.

Employers had three methods to try to absorb their increased labor costs: 1. Increase productivity to offset part or all of the increased cost; 2. Increase prices; 3. Reduce their profit margins. In most companies all three methods had to be used.

Since 1936 the corporate income share of national income has trended downward, with employees' share of national income increasing. (See Analysis 7). The combination of a reduced share of national income, high corporate taxes, and inadequate depreciation charges, is largely responsible for the failure of American industry to keep pace in the last 36 years with foreign industries. Unions did not realize the importance of company profits to their members.

While most of the blame can be placed on unions and the legislators who gave them this excessive power in the first place and have not had courage enough to take it away from them, management has not been entirely blameless. In too many cases, executives gave in too readily to union demands, particularly in early negotiations. Most wage patterns were set by agreements involving large companies whose executives were employees themselves, rather than owners. As employees they were under pressure—from boards of directors and thousands of stockholders—to produce profits and pay dividends. In most cases their compensation, as well as their jobs, de-

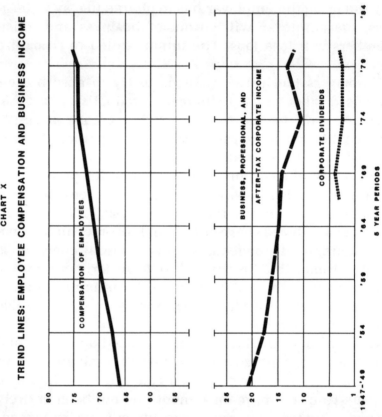

CHART X

TREND LINES: EMPLOYEE COMPENSATION AND BUSINESS INCOME

COMPENSATION OF EMPLOYEES

BUSINESS, PROFESSIONAL, AND
AFTER-TAX CORPORATE INCOME

CORPORATE DIVIDENDS

SOURCE: U.S. DEPARTMENT OF COMMERCE

5 YEAR PERIODS

80 75 70 65 60 55

25 20 15 10 5 1

1947–'49 '54 '59 '64 '69 '74 '79 '84

PERCENT OF NATIONAL INCOME
(AVERAGES OVER PERIODS INDICATED)

110

pended on producing profits in the near term. They could not do this with idle plants and workers on picket lines; it was often to their personal advantage to cave in to the demands.

True, they should have realized their responsibility for the long-range viability of their companies and resisted compensation–cost–push more effectively, but "the system" exerted pressure the other way. In many cases, also, they were afraid to take too hard-line a stance against the unions. Because of the failure of law enforcement officers to maintain labor peace, they had reason to fear physical violence.

THE THEORIES BACKFIRED

The original theory justifying labor unions was that unionization would enable the poorest paid workers in the country to bring their wages up to the average. It did not work that way. Union organizers went after the biggest groups of highest paid workers in the country. They organized industries like autos, steel, construction, and mining, because they were the easiest to organize and their employers, being generally profitable, would not want to be shut down by a strike for any length of time. As the rich workers got richer, the cost of living increased and the poor got poorer. Ever since the Wagner Act the disparity in wages has become wider and wider.

Prior to the build-up of union strength after the Wagner Act, great increases in productivity and real wages had been made. For example, in the auto industry the average wholesale price of an auto produced in 1929 was $621. In 1935 the average price was $522, a decrease of 16%—even though the 1935 auto was a considerable improvement over the 1929 model. Wage rates in the auto industry in 1929 and 1935 were almost exactly the same, while the C.P.I. (Consumer Price Index) had gone down from 122.5 to 98.1. Thus, the EMPLOYED auto worker's standard of living had increased 25%, as measured by the amount of goods and services he could buy for each hour he worked. Let's examine the 1930's in more detail.

When Roosevelt was inaugurated on March 4, 1933 there were close to 13,000,000 people unemployed. Business activity was very low and many corporations and individuals were bankrupt. The banks were closed. All previous business theories and policies were discredited. The public and government officials all were desperate to accept any new theories and programs that promised a change for the better.

Roosevelt assembled a "brain trust" composed of college professors, politicians, and liberal businessmen. During Roosevelt's first hundred days in office tremendous amounts of new legislation were passed merely on his request. One bill was entitled the National Industrial Recovery Act, (NIRA) which was administered by General Hugh Johnson and the National Recovery Administration (NRA).

The theory behind the N.I.R.A. was naive and simplistic. With 38 million people employed working 40 to 48 hours a week, and 12.8 million people (1933) unemployed, the idea was to cut the number of hours worked per week by the employed people by 10 hours. The "braintrusters" believed this would absorb practically all the unemployed. The hourly wages of those whose work-week was reduced by 10 hours would be increased so the take-home pay per week was the same.

The theorists ignored four things. First, raising wage rates raised costs and prices, while the decrease in hours worked reduced the production of wealth accordingly, so the average individual's real purchasing power was cut by this policy. Second, the unemployed workers did not have the skills to handle many of the job openings. Third, they were not always located where the jobs were. Fourth, many smaller employers could not increase their number of employees by roughly one-third more workers, nor could they raise their prices sufficiently to offset their cost increases.

The NIRA program did not result in reemploying 10 million people. Unemployment dropped about one and one-half million between 1933 and 1934, and about 700 thousand between 1934 and 1935, leaving 10.6 million unemployed, 20 per cent of the labor force.

Without these interferences in costs and distribution of purchasing power it can be concluded that the depression would have ended much sooner. Chart 12 shows the Business Week Index of Business Activity by quarters from July, 1929, its high point, through 1939. From the low point in March, 1933 (The Bank Holiday) it started up quickly before any New Deal experiments became effective. After mid-summer it started dropping again. NIRA pricing, hours worked, and wage policies were largely responsible.

The N.I.R.A. was declared unconstitutional in late May, 1935. Business activity started picking up shortly thereafter then continued upward on a steady pace until mid-summer 1937. Four million more people were employed by mid-1937. Business dropped precipitously from then till mid-summer 1938, recovering only partly and slowly until World War II started in September 1939. Three million people lost jobs by mid-1938.

What caused the business recovery of mid-1935 to mid-1937 to first start and then end so abruptly? Why did business not pick up strongly until the war? The 1935 demise of the N.I.R.A. allowed prices and wages to adjust themselves to the law of supply and demand. Demand and employment increased. Prices and wages were relatively

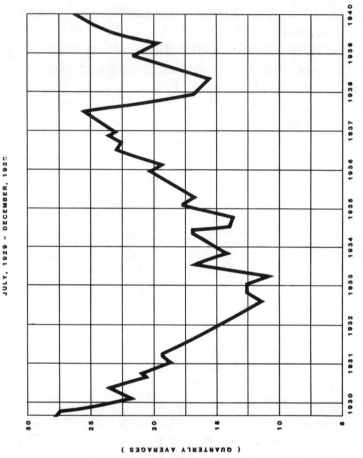

CHART XI

BUSINESS WEEK INDEX OF BUSINESS ACTIVITY

JULY, 1929 – DECEMBER, 1939

SOURCE : BUSINESS WEEK MAGAZINE

INDEX
(QUARTERLY AVERAGES)

CHART XII

U.S. UNEMPLOYMENT AS PERCENT
OF LABOR FORCE

(1929 - 1980)

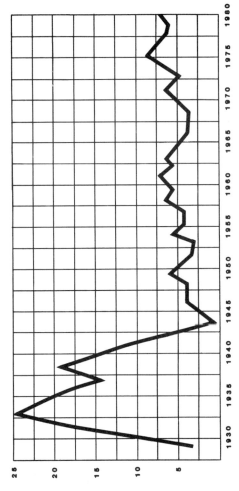

SOURCE : ECONOMIC REPORT OF THE PRESIDENT,

FEBRUARY, 1970 AND JANUARY, 1981

UNEMPLOYMENT

(% OF LABOR FORCE)

stable for two years. This was largely responsible for the mid-1935 to mid-1937 pickup. Sharp price increases in mid-1937 stopped it cold.

Roosevelt felt that business and industry had sabotaged the N.I.R.A. He had started out to work closely with businessmen, but switched his support to the fledgling labor unions. In 1934 he had vetoed the Wagner Act, but so strongly supported it after the demise of the N.I.R.A. that it was passed within a few weeks.

This act gave great new powers to union organizers. It took over a year for them to get their campaigns rolling.

In late 1936, the UAW Union staged a sit-down strike in a number of General Motors plants in Michigan. Local and State authorities were either unwilling or unable to dislodge the sit-down strikers. General Motors at first refused to negotiate until the strikers had left the plants. The strike was called off in February, 1937 upon the agreement of General Motors to negotiate with the union. By this illegal act of occupying the premises, the union forced GM to capitulate.

The union obtained a 10¢ an hour basic wage increase which covered about 300,000 workers. To forestall union activity at its plants, Ford Motor Company gave raises ranging from 5¢ to 15¢ per hour. Both GM and Ford increases averaged about 15%, on base rates around 50–60¢ an hour.

Subsequent to the increase in wages, the wholesale price of the average car jumped 12% from 1936 to 1938, while wages increased 19½%. This was the beginning of modern compensation-cost-push inflation.

In 1937 3,929,000 cars were produced. In 1938 output dropped to 2,020,000—a decline of 49%. People who had traded cars every year for $150 to $200, or every two years for $200 to $250, found that the difference they had to

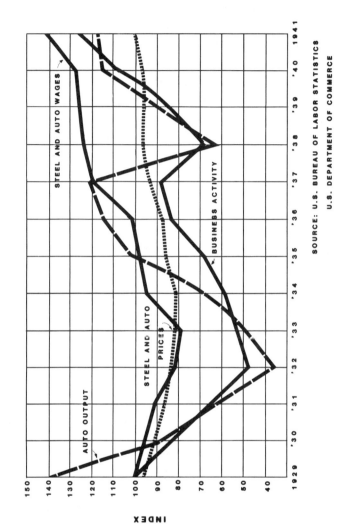

CHART XIII

STEEL AND AUTO WAGES AND PRICES, AUTO OUTPUT

AND BUSINESS ACTIVITY FROM 1929 TO 1941

STEEL AND AUTO WAGES

BUSINESS ACTIVITY

STEEL AND AUTO
PRICES

AUTO OUTPUT

INDEX

1929 '30 '31 '32 '33 '34 '35 '36 '37 '38 '39 '40 1941

150
140
130
120
110
100
90
80
70
60
50
40

SOURCE: U.S. BUREAU OF LABOR STATISTICS

U.S. DEPARTMENT OF COMMERCE

117

pay for a new car had increased substantially. So they postponed buying.

Instead of creating new jobs, these sharp pay raises actually wiped out many jobs. Business activity and employment dropped more sharply between late 1937 and mid-1938 than in any time in history.

The situation was similar in the steel industry. On February 28, 1937 the CIO and U.S. Steel agreed to negotiate. On March 16, they agreed to a 10¢ per hour increase to all hourly workers—a 19% increase. Subsequent to the wage increase, U.S. Steel and other companies raised the price of steel.

In most types of economic activity wage rates were much lower than in autos, steel, construction, and coal mining. People outside these highly unionized industries did not get the same percentage pay raises; in most cases they did not get any raise at all. Thus the higher prices for unionized products such as autos kept many of them from buying.

Some economists claim that the Federal Reserve brought on the 1938 recession within a depression by tightening the money supply. An examination of the facts shows this not to be true. Banks had billions of excess reserves. Interest rates on 3-month Treasury bills were below ½%, Fed discount rates were 1% to 1.5%. Banks had plenty of money to lend, but few borrowers. Others claim that Roosevelt stifled recovery by balancing the budget in 1937. Actually he did not. The difference in budget deficits in 1936, 1937, and 1938 was minimal.

What most economists appear to have missed was the mammoth stagflation of 1938. Chart XIV shows what happened to steel and auto wages and prices, auto output, and business activity from 1929 to 1941. It demonstrates that inflation got its start in steel and autos with 1938

CHART XIV

INDEXES OF MAN-HOUR EMPLOYEE COSTS
AND STEEL PRICES; U.S. STEEL INDUSTRY

(1967 : 100)

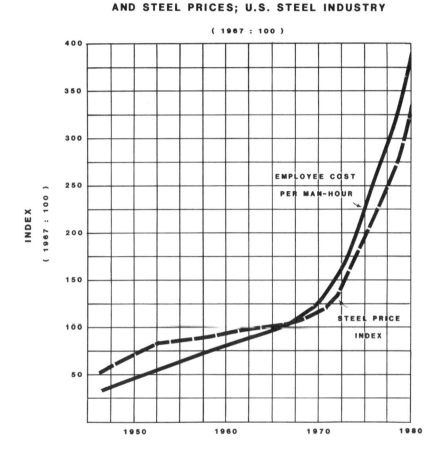

SOURCE : BUREAU OF LABOR STATISTICS

wage levels 25% higher than in 1929. The C.P.I. was 19% lower than in 1929.

Thus, the average EMPLOYED worker in these two industries had 54% more purchasing power than in 1929. A new set of economic royalists had been created by the

Wagner Act. The only fly in the ointment was that the high wage increases reduced demand and created widespread unemployment. If pre-Wagner Act wage setting procedures had been allowed to continue in force, millions more people would have been employed and everyone's standard of living would have increased, not that of just the favored few.

Most people felt, including some of the New Deal braintrusters, that once the unions won their 1937–38 big increases from their employers and the public they would be satisfied and not ask for more. Not so. When these first three-year labor contracts expired in 1941, they came back for more. Their new power made their demands irresistible.

In 1941 through strikes, threats of strikes, and some violence—the unions obtained substantial increases throughout the auto industry. Ford Motor Company was unionized. Average wages jumped from 94.9¢ per hour in 1940 to 111.6¢ per hour in the last half of 1941, an increase of 18%. Car prices went up 6.4% between 1940 and 1941, and 9.1% when the 1942 models were introduced. Then the war.

During World War II prices, wages, salaries, and fringes were fairly effectively frozen. The moment the war ended, the big unions made large demands for wage increases, even though the wage and price freeze was still in effect. President Harry Truman appointed a Fact Finding Board which granted a 19½¢ an hour increase to the steel workers with no increase in steel prices. The steel companies did not accept this ridiculous proposal. Finally, Truman backed off and allowed a $5.00 a ton increase in prices.

It should have been obvious to Truman and his Fact Finding Board that such policies guaranteed continued inflation. There was little gained by granting a wage increase which had to be followed by a price increase. General Motors workers went on strike on November 12, 1945 demanding a 19½¢ an hour increase and other fringes. This strike lasted 113 days. On January 10, 1946, Truman's Fact Finding Board recommended a wage increase for General Motors workers of 19½¢ an hour (18%). The agreement at the conclusion of the strike was 18½¢ an hour, a substantial increase in costs.

After World War II, the unions tackled, successfully, a large number of other major industries: oil, meat, electrical goods, farm equipment, and the metal mining industry. They already were well established in the coal mines and the railroads. The pattern of increase was about the same across the board; 18½¢ an hour, which in most cases was almost the same in percentage.

With big increases in wages and fringes, prices went up rapidly. Between 1945 and 1948 prices went up 34%, 11% a year. This price increase resulted both from demand-pull and compensation–cost–push.

These price increases did not result in a sharp drop in demand as they did in 1934 and 1937. There was a tremendous backlog of unfilled orders caused by the lack of production of consumer goods during the war. Most people had cash or war bonds because they could not buy much during the war. People were willing to pay any price to get cars and houses. All they had to do was scrape up the down-payment and meet the monthly payments.

The federal government made it very easy for veterans to buy houses through guaranteed loans, minimum down-payments, and longer term loans than had ever been considered safe by commercial lenders. The government became involved in guaranteeing loans to non-veterans as well. The law of supply and demand was not allowed to operate to hold in check the big increases in pay demanded by and obtained by the unions.

After every major war in past modern history prices had dropped sharply. The post World War II period was different. Even the recession of 1949 caused less than 1% drop in the C.P.I., with six of the nine C.P.I. components advancing. In 1955 the C.P.I. dropped .3%, but with those two exceptions, prices have increased steadily ever since 1945.

Gradually the unions expanded, moving into private service industries, and finally into public service industries. Public service unions create greater problems for consumers and taxpayers than private industry unions. Public services cannot be stockpiled; they are usually local monopolies; there is no substitute for such services; and without continuous service safety, health, and peace are difficult, if not impossible, to maintain.

While it may be argued that unions represent only 25% or less of all workers and should not be blamed for compensation–cost–push, their wage and fringe increases set the pattern for everyone else. Unionized employers with non-union salaried employees usually give their non-union employees about the same increases. Employers without unions generally unilaterally increase wages and fringes to keep their employees from joining unions.

The size of the non-union increase depends on the economics of the industry. Large highly-mechanized profitable companies will generally match, penny for penny, increases obtained by unions in the same industry, but medium and small companies, usually less mechanized and profitable, grant smaller increases in wages and fringes. Most of their employees understand their employers' problems and do not expect as big increases. At the same time, these smaller companies are unable to increase productivity as rapidly as the big, highly-mechanized companies, so the compensation increases they grant increase their costs the same percentage as the large companies. The net result is that the discrepancy between compensation paid to workers in large companies and smaller ones becomes greater and greater, yet the higher-paid worker may not have the skills nor work as hard. The person working for the smaller company may be more versatile.

All through this 45-year period of inflation the pattern has been the same; compensation increases first, followed by increases in prices or taxes, or reduction of public services. Great discrepancies in compensation have been created, because some unions have had far more power than others to extort unjustified raises. See Table 7.

Many people believe, because they have not investigated the facts, that this period of inflation started in 1965 with the escalation of the Vietnam War.

If compensation-cost-push existed from 1935 through the present time, why did prices move up more slowly from 1954 through 1965 than in later years? See Chart II. There are four main reasons.

First, there were three recessions during that time: 1954; 1957-8; and 1960-61. During periods of low business activity and high unemployment, unions cannot get as big increases from private employers as in boom times, but they still get increases.

Second, early unionization was concentrated primarily in the goods-producing industries, where productivity increases offset part of compensation-cost-push increases. In recent years unions have invaded the service industries, first private and then public, where there is little opportunity for productivity increases.

Third, the Vietnam War reduced the number of persons available for employment, particularly in the late

TABLE 7
AVERAGE HOURLY WAGES—HIGHLY UNIONIZED INDUSTRIES vs. RETAIL TRADE

Year	All Manufacturing Combination-Union and Non-Union	Basic Steel	Automobiles	Coal Mining (Bituminous)	Principally Non-Union Retail Trade	Consumer Price Index (1967 = 100)
1927	$0.54	$ 0.67	$	$ 0.73	$	51.3
1929	.56	.73	.76	.66		41.5
1936	.55	.82	.88	.77		43.0
1937	.62			.83	0.48	42.2
1938	.62	.85	.92	.85	.48	44.1
1941	.73	.95	1.04	.96	.52	48.8
1942	.85	1.03	1.17	1.03	.56	66.9
1947	1.22	1.45	1.47	1.58	.90	84.3
1957	2.05	2.70	2.46	2.92	1.47	100.0
1967	2.83	3.57	3.55	3.75	2.01	181.5
1977	5.87	8.36	6.92	8.28	3.85	195.4
1978	6.17	9.39	8.50	9.53	4.20	217.4
1979	6.69	10.42	9.08	10.28	4.53	247.0
1980	7.27	11.39	9.89	10.86	4.88	
Dollar Increase Per Hour 1937–1980	$6.73	$10.57	$9.01	$ 9.98	$4.40	

Note: Above figures *do not* include fringe benefits. With benefits added, for example, hourly labor cost for steelworkers reached $18.451 per hour in 1980.
Sources: U.S. Department of Labor, Bureau of Labor Statistics; American Iron and Steel Institute; United States Steel Corporation Annual Report, 1941.

1960's. This tightened the market for labor, giving the unions more power to force larger compensation settlements from employers.

Fourth, the 1965–80 period had a number of new factors and disasters that did not exist in the 1955–65 period. Each one by itself was not a major cause of inflation, but added on top of C.C.P. inflation, COLA, and the disastrous, poorly-conducted Vietnam War, they created sharp increases in prices. What were they?

By 1970–71 the demand for petrochemicals finally caught up with the inelastic supply. Speculators forced prices up as much as 1,000% in 1973–75. Other commodities jumped, but not to that extent.

The 1973-Israeli-Egyptian War resulted in quadrupling crude oil prices. Russian droughts shoved grain prices up. There was a tremendous increase in social programs involving transfer payments. There are more people now receiving transfer payments from the government than are employed in industry.

Fifth, more and more employers have come to believe that they not only can, but have to, pass along compensation-cost increases in their prices, so they do not put up as much resistance to such increases as formerly.

Sixth, *COST-OF-LIVING ESCALATION CLAUSES GUARANTEED INFLATION.*

In 1948 the U.A.W. and General Motors negotiated a cost-of-living adjustment (COLA) based on quarterly or longer changes in the C.P.I., in addition to a yearly annual improvement increase, which generally has been 3% of base pay. Starting in the 1960's COLA was widely adopted by all major unions. The government adopted it in not only wages and salaries but also in pensions and other transfer payments. Many private industry pensions are tied to the C.P.I., adding still more to compensation–cost–push (C.C.P.).

As soon as COLA became widespread, its spiral guaranteed constant inflation. Each major contract had an annual improvement factor or some other increase besides COLA. Seldom did productivity offset this increase, so costs went up even faster than the C.P.I. The total wage increase at General Motors from the COLA clause alone was $5.78 per hour from 1948 to April, 1981. A small annual improvement factor might not have been unsound in some industries where productivity increases were possible. However, in most industries productivity increases seldom occurred. That meant the entire wage increase plus COLA had to be added to the price or tax paid for the service, or the amount of service reduced accordingly. The increased costs of COLA and pension increases, particularly those paid to present retirees, are not only a big factor in C.C.P. inflation, but they are cost increases over which the employer has practically no control. COLA defeats the purpose for which it was devised.

Seventh, *PUBLIC EMPLOYEE UNIONS.*

Public-sector unions have been particularly destructive in recent years. While the combination of imports and the present business recession has resulted in a temporary let-up in the demand for more and more by most auto, steel, and rubber tire workers, practically all other unions, especially in service and transportation industries (both private and public) are still demanding and getting increases which are forcing and will continue to force price and tax increases in the range of 8–12% a year, with no let-up in sight. The rate of inflation will gradually but surely increase, as long as groups have the power to force their compensation demands onto the backs of consumers and taxpayers.

Recent compensation increase demands show how little power employers, consumers, and taxpayers have to resist such demands if the need for the product or service is inelastic and must be supplied on a continuing basis regardless of cost. People can put off buying new cars, or can buy cheaper cars, or can get along with their old house, or T-V, or stay home if personal travel costs get too high, but—they need most public services constantly, which gives such unions tremendous power, even if their strikes are illegal.

About the only major public service union that did not win a big increase in compensation and fringes to add to their already excessive pay was the Air Traffic Controllers. Their demands were so exorbitant and their attitude so cavalier that they had to be put in their place, even at considerable inconvenience and cost to the government, business, and the public.

While all other public unions should be given similar treatment if they choose to strike illegally to obtain their demands, it in most cases will be very difficult to provide their services by substitute personnel. Due to the widespread areas covered by most public services it is difficult to prevent violence and apprehend the law breakers.

While the Air Traffic Controllers failed, most other unions, both public and private, except in highly depressed industries, have still been able to obtain huge settlements in recent contract negotiations. For example:

Air Traffic Controllers:
Averaging $34,000 per year, demanded an increase of $10,000 and a 10% decrease in hours worked. They struck illegally after refusing an increase to $36,000 for 36 hours work.

Postal Workers:
Obtained an increase from the existing base of $21,146 of 26% over a 3-year period plus increased fringe benefits. If the C.P.I. increased more than 8% a year their wages would increase further.

Southern Bituminous Coal Workers:
Obtained an increase of $3.60 per hour in base pay over the 40-months contract, an ultimate raise of $7,488 per year. Fringe benefits were also increased.

Construction Workers on Federal Projects:
Under Davis-Bacon Act regulations would receive varying amounts, but always the highest in their area, such as about $31.00 per hour in wages and benefits for electricians in Los Angeles, or about $22.50 per hour for Operating Engineers in a Northern California local. Overall these construction workers increased their compensation from 30%–40% over a 3-year period.

Railroad Machinists:
25,000 railroad machinists in January, 1982, received a new contract resulting in an increase in total costs to the railroads of 39.5% by July 1, 1984.

In the case of some local, school, and state government workers the lack of funds has forced these unions to soften their demands, but only after compensation has been driven up to astronomical levels. The public is suffering severely from the lack of services as the number of government workers is cut back.

While a serious depression (which would do far more harm than good) might reduce the demands of these powerful groups, they still will have far more strength to obtain their compensation demands than the general public, so the inequity in compensation levels will get larger and larger.

TABLE 8
AVERAGE STRAIGHT-TIME PAY FOR PUBLIC SAFETY EMPLOYEES—SELECTED CITIES
October, 1977—September, 1978

	Firefighters		Police Officers		Police Sergeants		Refuse Collectors
	Monthly Pay	Hourly Pay*	Monthly Pay	Hourly Pay	Monthly Pay	Hourly Pay	Hourly Pay
Atlanta	$1,051	$4.33	$1,124	$6.49	$1,337	$ 7.71	$ 4.25
Boston	1,205	6.62	1,223	7.69	1,485	9.34	—
Chicago	1,645	8.08	1,615	9.32	1,994	11.50	7.63
Cleveland	1,379	6.63	1,374	7.93	1,586	9.15	5.79
Dallas	1,283	5.48	1,316	7.59	1,560	9.00	3.61
Denver	1,445	6.94	1,440	8.31	1,777	10.25	6.49
Detroit	1,487	6.79	1,493	8.61	1,947	11.23	6.95
Houston	1,526	6.52	1,562	9.01	1,853	10.69	5.82
Jacksonville	1,047	4.31	1,217	7.02	1,563	9.02	3.81
Kansas City	995	5.74	1,297	7.48	1,750	10.10	4.87
Los Angeles	1,727	7.12	1,695	9.79	2,081	12.00	6.27
Memphis	1,115	4.60	1,163	6.28	1,263	7.29	3.85
New Orleans	1,069	5.14	1,067	6.16	1,394	8.04	—
New York	1,545	8.91	1,575	9.09	2,011	11.60	8.15 (Drivers)
Phoenix	1,256	5.18	1,279	7.38	1,793	10.35	5.22
Pittsburgh	1,256	6.97	1,268	7.32	1,436	8.29	7.24
San Francisco	1,568	7.46	1,574	9.08	1,845	10.65	11.19 (Drivers)

* Calculated to take into account variations in hours worked in different cities.
Source: U.S. Department of Labor, Bureau of Labor Statistics.

Will the government do anything to curb union power? Not until government realizes the futility and destructiveness of trying to stop inflation by monetary and fiscal policies only, and until a large enough segment of the American public realizes the true cause of inflation. This is the first step. Another equally important step is for the individual to realize and be willing to accept that his compensation cannot be increased every year for doing the same work. Everyone has become accustomed to a yearly, or more often, increase in pay for doing a little less work than the year before; and since so many are deeply in debt they believe they need the next year's increase to pay for last year's purchases.

It is human nature to live up to one's income. No matter how much the average person earns, he spends it all and usually takes on more installment or mortgage debt. If he is an economic royalist with an income twice or three times the average, he not only spends it, feels he cannot get along without it, but sincerely believes he is entitled to every penny of it.

Another human nature problem that will make it difficult to eliminate compensation–cost–push inflation is that most people do not believe that prices of products and services will go down as productivity increases reduce costs. Over the last 45 years, the prices of many products and services have not gone up nearly as rapidly as inflation, because productivity increases have offset most of the compensation increase. Their prices, after adjusting for inflation, actually decreased. A prime example is major household appliances.

Stopping compensation–cost–push inflation will require a tremendous educational effort over a long period of time. Such programs require organization, dedication, and lots of money. The benefits of stopping inflation are immense; but they are not grasped by the average American. Union bosses would violently oppose any effort to reduce their powers and control over our economic system.

It is not a question of whether or not C.C.P. inflation can be stopped. It will eventually be stopped; *but can it be stopped under our present economic socio-political system—or will it require a new form of government?*

Four analyses follow this chapter. They are important in that they furnish concrete examples of the effect of major negotiated wage/benefit settlements upon today's escalating inflation.

ANALYSIS 3

The Steel Dilemma

For the first half of the twentieth century, the symbols of U.S. leadership in the world's economy were the production line and the steel industry. The awesome ability of these two entities to produce was basically the reason for the defeat of the Axis partners in World War II and the basis for the rebuilding of world industry thereafter.

In 1955, ten years after the war, U.S. steelmakers produced 39.3% of the world's steel and Japan, 3.5%. Twenty years later, in 1975, U.S. production represented 16.4%, while Japan had climbed to 15.8%; in 1980, Japan produced 15.4%, the U.S. 14.1%.

In 1955 the U.S. was a net exporter of steel; by 1975 we were importing 13.5% of our steel consumption. Present-day imports hover around 18% of our steel usage, with roughly half of the imported product coming from Japan.

In recent years, the news media have been full of stories of the virtual collapse of our domestic steel industry . . . abandonment of mills; indefinite postponement of construction; layoffs of thousands of steelworkers, etc.

What has caused this debacle in an industry that for generations has been regarded as one of the strengths of our industrial base? A number of reasons have been advanced; by those basically critical of U.S. business and industry in general; by professional economists; by productivity experts; and, by representatives of the steel industry itself. If we examine the theories advanced, we find that most of them have at least some validity, but that we can trace the root cause . . . the bottom line . . . to the cost of labor.

1. *From the critics of business:* the desire for high profits and dividends from the steel companies.

In 1977, a report to the President by The Council on Wage and Price Stability (*Prices and Costs in the United States Steel Industry*) stated that steelmakers need an after-tax profit of 5–6% on sales to generate a return equal to the all-industry average. From 1967 through the first half of 1977, the industry averaged an after-tax profit of 4.01%. For the past two years, results from the major producers have shown:

TABLE 2
STEEL INDUSTRY INCOME

	1979		1980	
	Net Income *$ Millions*	*% Return* *on Sales*	*Net Income* *$ Millions*	*% Return* *on Sales*
United States Steel	(293.0) Loss	(2.3)	504.5	4.0
Armco	221.0	4.4	265.3	4.7
LTV	173.5	2.2	127.9	1.6
Bethlehem	275.7	3.9	121.0	1.8
National	126.5	3.0	83.8	2.3
Republic	121.2	3.0	51.0	1.4
Inland	131.1	3.6	29.7	0.9
Wheeling-Pittsburgh	49.7	4.0	14.7	1.4

Excess profits are not even close to being a contributing cause.

2. *From professional economists and productivity experts:* our steel-making facilities are largely obsolescent while the competition, with more up-to-date facilities, operates more efficiently. The solution is new plants.

How feasible is this solution?

In 1964, construction of the Ogishima works was started in Japan. Construction of the first phase was completed in just two years; the second stage in 2½ more years. The mill was designed to produce 6.6 million net tons of raw steel, and construction costs were approximately $3.55 billion. This would result in a plant cost of $540 per net ton of capacity, with construction time of slightly more than 4 years.

The proposed U.S. Steel plant at Conneaut, Ohio (now dormant) was originally planned at a construction cost of $3.25 billion (an estimate which was subsequently raised to about $3.5 billion) to produce 4 million tons per year. This would result in a net cost of $812 per ton of capacity as contrasted with the Ogishima cost of $540 per ton. The biggest reason for the higher U.S. cost is the difference in construction labor rates, as well as construction labor practices. U.S. Steel also estimated a total of about 8 years to complete its mill's two phases, adding considerably to interest costs relative to those incurred by the Japanese. The longer construction time in the U.S. is caused principally by construction practices, government permit requirements (the Environmental Impact Statement alone required over a year in preparation, public hearings, etc.), and by union-negotiated work rules.

Using the comparative per-ton fixed asset costs of the Ogishima plant and the proposed Conneaut plant . . . $540 per ton vs. $812 . . . the Council's report also calculated the annual difference in cost for the use of the capital involved in the projects. Assuming a capital charge for both plants of 17% to cover interest costs (input at

8.5% . . . logical in 1977 . . . only a dream in 1981), return on equity, depreciation, and income taxes, these annual costs, based on a 77% yield from raw steel to finished product, would be $177 per net ton of finished steel at Conneaut vs. a cost of $119 for the Ogishima plant. If these estimates were still applicable today . . . and they are certainly optimistic vis-a-vis interest costs and depreciation . . . the Japanese would have a $58 per ton advantage in addition to the far lower wage rates they enjoy.

But, aside from the effect on our competitive position in world markets, how would such a plant affect the cost of steel to U.S. Steel's domestic customers? Peter Marcus, author of *World Steel Dynamics,* estimated an operating cost saving for the proposed plant of $54.00 per net ton in 1976 dollars over the average American plant in operation today . . . far less than the $177 in capital costs, even at an interest cost at about half of today's rate.

3. *From steel industry spokesmen, three principal complaints: The first:* environmental standards requirements are using up funds needed for capital improvements.

Over the past few years this has been true, but Japan is expending approximately 20% of construction budgets on such applications. U.S. producers *are* at a disadvantage, however, in having to deal with separate State environmental protection agencies as well as Federal. The amorphous nature of overlapping . . . and often contradictory . . . regulations result in delays and negotiations not encountered by Japanese producers.

Second: U.S. tax laws and depreciation schedules put our industry in a non-competitive position for plant construction and modernization.

This is certainly a factor, but the Reagan Administration has begun to alleviate the problem, and even Congress has been getting the message. More favorable depreciation schedules will help all U.S. industry, particularly capital-intensive operations such as steel production, but will not reduce the original investment cost.

Third: Foreign producers have been guilty of "dumping" steel into the U.S. market at below their domestic prices.

The Japanese claim that export prices of their steel have remained above domestic prices since 1974, but figures from the U.S. Bureau of the Census show that the weighted average of carbon steel prices sold by Japan to the U.S. fell from $286.32 per net ton in 1975 to $229.91 in 1976, then rose to $250.79 in the first half of 1977. It is rather hard to believe that the Japanese cost structure could vary so widely as to allow that much flexibility in pricing.

Since the Japanese industrial system guarantees its workers steady employment year after year, it is easy to understand why they would indulge in "loss leader" practices from time to time. This should be a spot occurrence rather than a trend.

While all the preceeding reasons for troubles in the U.S. steel industry make some contribution to its problems, we cannot help feeling that we are slapping gnats while the elephants walk by. Let's look at the real, or base, cause that puts the industry behind the competitive 8-ball.

First, raw materials. The basic materials that go into steel are iron ore, coal, limestone, and, in most U.S. processes, scrap iron and steel scrap. Two-thirds of the iron ore used in U.S. steelmaking originates in this country, where it is mined by union miners and shipped, largely through the Great Lakes, on American ships manned by union sailors. Before shipping, some 50% of the ore is pelletized at the mine site, also by union workers. Coal used to provide coke for reducing the ore to molten iron in the blast furnace is mined in the Eastern U.S. by union miners and shipped on trains manned by members of the various railroad brotherhoods. On arrival at the steel mills, the raw materials are processed by members of the United Steelworkers of America. The members of these unions are the highest paid of any similar workers in the world.

A look at the change in relative prices for basic raw materials in the U.S. and in Japan over the past 20 years shows one reason for the reversal of the competitive positions of the two countries. In 1956, iron ore cost $9.63 per ton in the U.S.; $16.70 in Japan. By 1975, the cost was $23.99, U.S., vs. $15.15 in Japan. Coking coal cost $9.85 in the U.S.; $22.14 in Japan. By 1975, Japan was paying $50.83, including a substantial percentage imported from the U.S. while our domestic producers were paying $40.04, reducing the U.S. competitive advantage from 125% to 27%. Scrap has always been cheaper in the U.S. than in Japan, so Japanese production is slanted more towards the Basic Oxygen furnace, more efficient than the older Open Hearth furnaces still widely used in the U.S. because of their higher tolerance for scrap. Overall, increasing relative raw material costs had reduced the U.S. percentage advantage in raw materials from 71.4% in 1956 to 9.1% in 1975.

So, in 1975, the U.S. still retained a slight competitive advantage in raw materials over Japan. The Japanese, however, had not been required to deal with the United Steelworkers of America. They had not granted workers 5 weeks of vacation after 17 years, nor a "sabbatical" vacation of 13 weeks once each five years for employees with 17 years service. The Japanese hourly employment costs had increased by 1975 to a total of $5.89 per hour, and their output to 9.35 metric tons per 100 man-hours, while in the U.S., 1975 employment costs were $11.10 per hour with an output of 8.13 metric tons per 100 man-hours. This translates into a labor cost per metric ton of $62.99 in Japan vs. $136.53 in the U.S.

The 1977 steel contract settlement was predicted to increase hourly compensation in the U.S. by 30% in three years, but that assumed a general inflation rate of 6%. As of the time of the 1979 published figures, the hourly wage costs had risen by 24% in only two years.

From the first year after World War II, 1946, through 1979, Bureau of Labor Statistics shows the average hourly earnings in the iron and steel industry, *not including* fringe benefits, increased 741%, while the C.P.I. increased 272%. Total employment costs, including fringe benefits, totaled $15.921 per hour in 1979, and have risen to $18.451 in 1980.

Some day, we are going to have to face the truth about the fate of our steel industry. It is getting late.

TABLE 3

BLS—MONTHLY CONSUMER AND PRODUCER PRICE INDEXES (1967 = 100)

SHOWING RECORD OF BLS INDEX OF STEEL PRICES

Period	Consumer Price Index*	Industrial Commodities	Total Iron & Steel**	Producer Price Indexes						
				Steel Mill Products			Other Iron and Steel Products			
				Total	Finished	Semi-Finished	Pig Iron & Ferro-Alloys	Iron Ore	Scrap I & S	Foundry & Forgings
1947	66.9	70.8	51.3	45.5	46.0	40.4	64.4	56.0	129.0	49.6
1948	72.1	76.9	59.6	52.0	52.4	48.7	76.8	61.0	162.9	57.3
1949	71.4	75.3	60.6	56.4	56.7	53.3	85.3	72.5	107.6	59.6
1950	72.1	78.0	64.6	59.4	59.5	57.8	87.3	77.8	139.3	60.6
1951	77.8	86.1	70.4	64.0	64.3	60.9	95.5	83.5	158.2	66.2
1952	79.5	84.1	71.3	65.4	65.8	62.3	98.8	86.9	152.0	66.5
1953	80.1	84.8	75.1	70.5	70.8	69.1	104.4	97.1	137.2	70.1
1954	80.5	85.0	76.0	73.8	73.8	74.2	103.9	99.6	106.2	71.7
1955	80.2	86.9	80.4	77.2	77.3	78.0	104.6	101.3	139.3	73.5
1956	81.4	90.8	88.5	83.8	83.8	83.5	114.3	109.2	176.3	81.0
1957	84.3	93.3	95.1	91.8	91.7	92.5	124.5	114.7	155.7	87.3
1958	86.6	93.6	96.5	95.0	94.9	95.9	125.1	111.8	124.8	89.9
1959	87.3	95.3	98.4	96.5	96.5	97.3	125.4	107.2	133.4	91.7
1960	88.7	95.3	97.2	96.4	96.3	97.1	120.4	108.0	110.2	92.4
1961	89.6	94.8	97.3	96.0	95.9	97.0	118.4	109.1	116.8	92.7
1962	90.6	94.8	95.9	95.8	95.7	97.0	113.9	104.4	95.2	92.8
1963	91.7	94.7	95.7	96.3	96.2	97.4	102.3	103.6	91.7	92.8
1964	92.9	95.2	97.1	97.1	97.0	98.6	97.1	100.8	109.4	93.8
1965	94.5	96.4	98.0	97.5	97.5	98.4	100.3	100.7	112.6	95.1
1966	97.2	98.5	98.8	98.9	98.8	98.8	100.3	100.7	106.6	96.8

1967	100	100	100	100	100	100	100	100	100	100
1968	104.2	102.5	101.9	102.5	102.5	102.3	100.9	98.1	93.0	103.0
1969	109.8	106.0	107.2	107.4	107.4	107.0	102.1	98.1	110.5	106.9
1970	116.3	110.0	115.2	114.3	114.3	112.2	114.6	100.1	138.9	112.6
1971	121.3	113.9	121.8	123.0	123.0	122.7	126.3	103.0	114.6	119.2
1972	125.3	117.9	128.4	130.4	130.4	130.9	125.4	103.0	121.8	124.3
1973	133.1	125.9	136.2	134.1	134.1	133.9	129.4	106.7	188.0	131.5
1974	147.7	153.8	178.6	170.0	170.0	169.0	188.1	123.3	353.2	161.4
1975	161.2	171.5	200.9	197.2	196.6	206.7	264.7	154.3	245.6	194.3
1976	170.5	182.4	215.9	209.8	209.0	223.1	261.6	171.0	259.0	218.6
1977	181.5	195.1	230.3	229.9	229.0	243.6	257.0	186.1	231.2	229.9
1978	195.3+	209.3	253.3	254.4	253.4	270.6	259.7	194.9	264.6	248.7
1979	217.7+	236.1	283.2	280.4	279.5	294.3	296.5	216.7	341.9	275.8
1980	247.0+	274.2	305.0	302.7	301.2	325.3	307.2	244.1	328.1	309.0

Current Months

	100	100	100	100	100	100	100	100	100	100
1979										
July	219.4+	237.2	286.2	284.2	283.1	301.2	305.8	219.1	346.1	274.6
August	221.5	240.3	285.9	284.6	283.5	300.0	305.7	223.2	332.0	276.0
September	223.7	243.8	285.3	284.8	283.8	300.0	304.5	222.7	316.7	277.7
October	225.6	248.5	289.0	288.4	287.6	300.0	305.0	226.3	311.5	285.5
November	227.6	250.2	291.6	288.7	287.9	301.0	307.6	226.3	328.2	291.5
December	230.0	252.8	292.7	289.3	288.5	301.1	307.6	227.6	333.3	293.1
1980										
January	233.3+	260.3	297.3	293.7	292.1	318.7	308.1	227.6	343.7	297.6
February	236.5	265.4	300.2	294.2	292.6	318.9	308.1	236.8	365.7	302.2
March	239.9	268.2	301.6	295.6	294.1	318.9	308.1	236.8	367.8	303.5
April	242.6	270.7	307.0	304.1	302.9	322.2	309.5	246.1	352.9	305.2

TABLE 3 (continued)

| | | | | Producer Price Index | | | | | | |
| | | | | Steel Mill Products | | | Other Iron and Steel Products | | | |
Period	Consumer Price Index*	Industrial Commodities	Total Iron & Steel**	Total	Finished	Semi-Finished	Pig Iron & Ferro-Alloys	Iron Ore	Scrap I & S	Foundry & Forgings
May	245.1	271.2	304.7	305.5	304.3	324.2	309.1	246.1	301.5	306.1
June	247.8	273.0	303.1	305.8	304.6	325.1	309.1	246.1	266.1	309.2
July	248.0	275.6	300.4	301.0	299.5	325.1	305.8	248.2	270.0	311.2
August	249.6	277.3	302.3	301.0	299.5	325.1	305.8	248.2	300.2	310.8
September	251.9	278.2	304.3	301.0	299.4	325.1	305.8	248.2	326.9	311.7
October	254.1	281.2	310.4	307.5	306.3	325.0	305.8	248.2	338.0	316.2
November	256.4	282.7	312.5	309.5	308.1	300.6	305.8	248.2	345.7	317.5
December	258.7	286.1	316.0	313.4	311.4	344.6	305.8	248.2	358.5	317.2

** Includes Purchased Ferrous Scrap
* Unrevised old series
+ Urban wage earners and clerical workers for 1978, 1979 and 1980.

Source: United States Department of Labor, Bureau of Labor Statistics (Released in January, 1981)

Sources: * Report to the President on Prices and Costs in the United States
Steel Industry by The Council on Wage and Price Stability, October, 1977.

* United States Steel Corporation and United Steelworkers (AFL-
CIO) March 1937–April 1974. Bulletin 1814, U.S. Department of
Labor, Bureau of Labor Statistics.

* Supplement to Bulletin 1814, 1974–80 (BLS)

* American Iron and Steel Institute: *Corporate Labor & Benefits
Analysis*, August 11, 1981

TABLE 4
TOTAL EMPLOYMENT COST PER HOUR
WAGE EMPLOYEES IN THE IRON AND STEEL INDUSTRY

| | Pay for Hours Worked | | | | | | Comparison | Other Payroll Costs | | | | | |
| | Straight Time | | | | | Subtotal | | | | | Total Payroll Cost per Hour | Employee Benefits Cost per Hour | Total Employment Cost per Hour |
Year	Regular	Shift Differential	Sunday Premium	Overtime Premium	Premium for Work on Holidays	Pay for Hours Worked	Avg. Hourly Earnings in Steel (BLS)	Pay for Holidays Not Worked	Vacation Pay	Adjustments			
1946	$1.228	$.022	—	$.029	—	$ 1.279	$ 1.281	—	$ .047	$.028	$ 1.354	$ .050	$ 1.404
1947	1.393	.022	—	.041	—	1.456	1.439	—	.051	.006	1.513	.050	1.563
1948	1.502	.022	—	.049	—	1.573	1.580	—	.054	.002	1.629	.050	1.679
1949	1.574	.022	—	.037	—	1.633	1.646	—	.068	.002	1.703	.050	1.753
1950	1.603	.023	—	.055	—	1.681	1.691	—	.064	.001	1.746	.162	1.908
1951	1.769	.023	—	.080	—	1.872	1.89	—	.070	.003	1.945	.169	2.114
1952	1.924	.029	—	.091	—	2.044	2.02	—	.099	.005	2.148	.167	2.315
1953	2.023	.036	—	.066	.020	2.145	2.19	.024	.095	.003	2.267	.173	2.440
1954	2.107	.034	—	.026	.023	2.190	2.23	.031	.109	.003	2.333	.179	2.512
1955	2.246	.036	—	.065	.029	2.376	2.41	.023	.105	.005	2.509	.213	2.722
1956	2.407	.036	.008	.066	.025	2.542	2.57	.028	.126	.004	2.700	.254	2.954
1957	2.582	.035	.029	.047	.036	2.729	2.73	.038	.147	.003	2.917	.299	3.216
1958	2.787	.038	.040	.031	.035	2.931	2.91	.056	.190	.004	3.181	.332	3.513
1959	2.896	.048	.060	.082	.058	3.144	3.10	.047	.220	.006	3.417	.381	3.798
1960	2.916	.046	.050	.045	.037	3.094	3.08	.054	.195	.006	3.349	.471	3.820
1961	3.054	.045	.050	.048	.044	3.241	3.20	.055	.200	.005	3.501	.488	3.989
1962	3.141	.046	.052	.052	.041	3.332	3.29	.058	.224	.008	3.622	.533	4.155
1963	3.166	.047	.055	.069	.053	3.390	3.36	.050	.240	.007	3.687	.560	4.247

TABLE 4 (continued)

| Year | Pay for Hours Worked | | | | | Subtotal | Comparison | Other Payroll Costs | | | Total Payroll Cost per Hour | Employee Benefits Cost per Hour | Total Employment Cost per Hour |
| | Straight Time | | | | | | | | | | | | |
	Regular	Shift Differential	Sunday Premium	Overtime Premium	Premium for Work on Holidays	Pay for Hours Worked	Avg. Hourly Earnings in Steel (BLS)	Pay for Holidays Not Worked	Vacation Pay	Adjustments			
1964	3.177	.049	.061	.090	.054	3.431	3.41	.048	.310	.007	3.796	.559	4.355
1965	3.261	.049	.064	.106	.056	3.536	3.46	.048	.343	.008	3.935	.540	4.475
1966	3.353	.049	.065	.110	.059	3.636	3.58	.049	.324	.008	4.017	.616	4.633
1967	3.398	.048	.063	.091	.056	3.656	3.62	.056	.349	.008	4.069	.689	4.758
1968	3.553	.049	.067	.126	.065	3.860	3.82	.049	.376	.018	4.303	.729	5.032
1969	3.776	.050	.072	.154	.068	4.120	4.09	.053	.370	.023	4.566	.809	5.375
1970	3.926	.054	.071	.118	.067	4.236	4.22	.077	.431	.023	4.767	.910	5.677
1971	4.242	.060	.075	.126	.071	4.574	4.57	.090	.519	.032	5.215	1.046	6.261
1972	4.813	.060	.087	.161	.100	5.221	5.15	.101	.528	.027	5.877	1.198	7.075
1973	5.159	.062	.135	.218	.114	5.688	5.56	.092	.507	.024	6.311	1.370	7.681
1974	5.921	.062	.212	.235	.120	6.550	6.38	.114	.653	.108	7.425	1.653	9.078
1975	6.634	.080	.218	.171	.124	7.227	7.11	.170	.874	.040	8.311	2.279	10.590
1976	7.247	.115	.249	.239	.148	7.998	7.86	.177	.912	.045	9.132	2.612	11.744
1977	8.029	.117	.280	.294	.193	8.913	8.67	.200	1.015	.123	10.251	2.785	13.036
1978	8.890	.120	.333	.391	.242	9.976	9.70	.194	1.051	.049	11.270	3.033	14.303
1979	9.822	.121	.368	.427	.281	11.019	10.77	.247	1.230	.055	12.551	3.370	15.921
1980	—	—	—	—	—	—	—	—	—	—	—	—	18.451

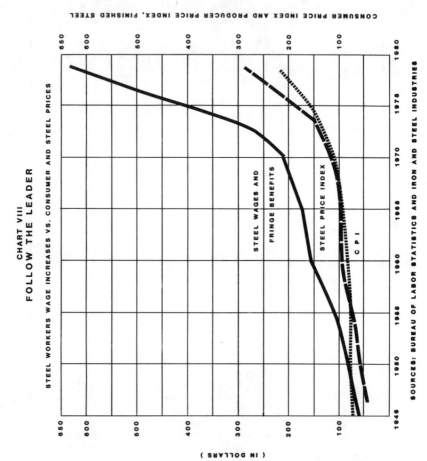

CHART VIII

FOLLOW THE LEADER

STEEL WORKERS WAGE INCREASES VS. CONSUMER AND STEEL PRICES

CONSUMER PRICE INDEX AND PRODUCER PRICE INDEX, FINISHED STEEL

(1967 : 100)

WAGES AND BENEFITS - 40 HOUR WEEK - IRON AND STEEL WORKERS

(IN DOLLARS)

STEEL WAGES AND FRINGE BENEFITS

STEEL PRICE INDEX

C P I

SOURCES: BUREAU OF LABOR STATISTICS AND IRON AND STEEL INDUSTRIES

144

CHART IX

EMPLOYMENT COSTS PER HOUR AND
PRODUCTIVITY IN THE STEEL INDUSTRY

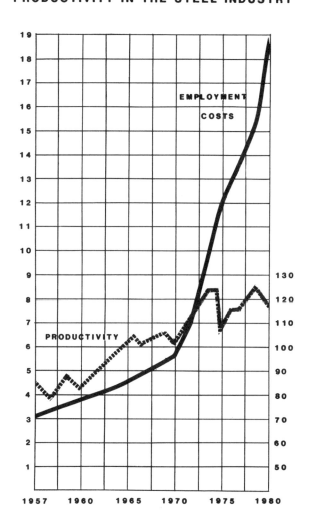

SOURCE: BUREAU OF LABOR STATISTICS

ANALYSIS 4

Steelworkers vs. Steelmakers

Or: How to Kill a 24-Carat Goose

In the old fable of the goose that laid golden eggs, the hero-turned-villain tired of waiting for one egg at a time, killed the goose to get all the eggs at once, and ended up . . . literally . . . with another kind of goose-egg.

From the preceding analysis of the steel dilemma, it appears that the United Steelworkers of America might do well to heed the lesson of the fable. For a substantial percentage of the United Automobile Workers, it may already be too late.

How did it happen . . . this battering of the steel industry? Why did it happen . . . did the workers not know that there are limits, or . . . did they just not care?

To find some answers, one must look at the history of the industry and of the union. We will start with the biggest of the companies, United States Steel Corp. It was formed through a combination of major steel producers and incorporated in New Jersey on February 25, 1901.

Prior to the passage of the Wagner Act in 1935, some of the steelworkers were represented by a craft union, the Amalgamated Association of Iron, Steel, and Tin

Workers of North America (AAISTW-AFL), on an open-shop basis, as well as some "inside" unions called Employee Representation Plans.

In 1936, the Committee for Industrial Organization (CIO) formed the forerunner of the present United Steelworkers of America, known as the Steelworkers Organizing Committee (SWOC). The first contract negotiated by SWOC was signed with a U.S. Steel subsidiary, Carnegie-Illinois Steel Corp., in March of 1937. SWOC later merged with AAISTW to become United Steelworkers of America, effective May 22, 1942.

The 1937 contract with Carnegie-Illinois provided a 10¢ per hour increase, bringing the average steelworkers hourly wage up to 86.4¢ per hour. The next contract settlement, in 1941, provided a similar increase. This increase, together with the effect of job gradiations, increased the average hourly rate to 99.4¢ per hour, according to U.S. Steel's 1941 Annual Report. Including these settlements, U.S. Steel's workers' earnings had increased at a rate of 3.75% a year from 1929 through 1941, with three-fourths of the total increase coming after 1937.

By 1938, steelworkers' average hourly earnings were 90.2¢, some 45% higher than the average for production workers in all U.S. industry. And in 1938, U.S. Steel posted a loss of $32,931,131.

So compensation-cost-push in the steel industry started with the escalation of hourly wages in the midst of the Great Depression. Although workers weekly hours were cut back in practically all industry during the "second trough" in the late '30's (from 37.6 hours in 1937 to 29.7 hours in 1938 for U.S. Steel) the higher wage-base remained in force.

Then came World War II. President Roosevelt had already declared the U.S. to be "the arsenal of democracy," and the steel industry had responded by setting new records in steel production. U.S. Steel alone increased tonnage output from 23 million net tons in 1940 to 30 million in 1942.

Wartime controls gave sweeping powers to various Federal boards. Early in 1942, the National War Labor Board began hearings in the landmark "Little Steel" case, involving various steel producers. None of the various U.S. Steel subsidiaries were involved in these hearings; their labor contracts contained a provision that either labor or management could reopen negotiations only after 20 days notice to the other party.

After the War Labor Board, in July, decreed that those involved in the Little Steel negotiations must pay wage increases retroactive to February, 1942, the United Steelworkers notified U.S. Steel that they wanted to reopen negotiations.

On August 18, 1942, the War Labor Board held a hearing. The U.S. Steel subsidiaries argued that any retroactive pay raises would directly violate the agreements between the companies and the workers. Eight days later, the Board, ignoring these arguments, directed the companies not only to pay a 5½¢ per hour more increase retroactive to February 14—more than five months before the application was made—but also to include a minimum daily wage guarantee as well as maintenance of membership and check-off provisions in the new contract. On September 1, 1942, Carnegie-Illinois wrote to the War Labor Board

"Carnegie Illinois Steel Corp. will comply with the Board's Directive Order. . . . The acceptance is predicted on one premise only; namely, that the country is at war and that your Board, created by the President of the United States of America, has ordered the Company to do certain things embodied in your directives. For the period of the contract now under negotiation, this Company bows to your decision and accepts that which it considers unneces-

148

sary, undesirable, and subversive of the workers' individual freedom. . . ."

During the war years there was a great deal of concern about "war profiteering." Governmental controls on steel prices, together with government-mandated wage increases, effectively took care of this for U.S. Steel. From the Annual Report of U.S. Steel for 1942:

> "The composite price of such representative steel products as bars, plates, rails, shapes, sheets, and strip in 1942 was two percent lower than in 1929. Increases in labor costs have not been offset by increases in steel prices."

Any profit increases engendered by high utilization of capacity were canceled out by various wartime surtaxes and excess profits taxes. During 1943, after paying the same dividends as in previous years, U.S. Steel had 3.4 million dollars left over for future needs . . . enough to cover operating costs for less than one day. From 1941 through 1943, the company's workers share increased by 45%, while corporate retention of money for future needs decreased 94%. In the 1943 Annual Report, the chairman of U.S. Steel warned:

> "A continuation of such a state of affairs may prove serious to U.S. Steel and ultimately to the Nation."

As is obvious from the figures quoted above, the United Steelworkers' position was strengthened during the war years, with more than "a little help from their friends" in the Federal government. As the record shows, this help did not decrease after the end of the war.

Shortly after World War II ended on August 14, 1945, the United Steelworkers demanded a 25¢ per hour wage increase. Based on reports of a fact-finding committee, President Truman recommended an increase of 19½¢ per hour, based upon an action by the Office of Price Administration that allowed an increase of $5.00 per ton in the still-controlled price of steel. For several years the steel industry had pleaded for an increase to cover previous government-imposed wage increases as well as increased raw material and freight costs, but had been ignored by the OPA. U.S. Steel offered its workers 15¢ per hour, claiming that the $5.00 per ton increase did not justify either the union figure of 25¢ or Truman's figure of 19½¢. After a four-week strike, the steelworkers and the company agreed upon a raise of 18½¢ per hour plus retroactive payment for any time worked from January 1 to February 15, 1946.

The iron-fisted long arm of government was not through with U.S. Steel. On November 25, 1944, the National War Labor Board directed U.S. Steel and the union to work out a plan designed for "correction of interplant inequities in wage rates." After years of study and negotiation between the company and the union, an agreement was reached on January 13, 1947, with changes effective in February, 1947. The plan grouped all jobs into 30 classifications; wage rates started with a "base common labor rate" and increased by 3½¢ per hour up through the 30 classes. There were a myriad of other details involved, but the end result was an across-the-board increase of 5.18¢ per hour *plus* an average *retroactive* payment of 3⅝¢ per hour for all time worked between January 4, 1944, and January 31, 1947.

During the 1940's and early 1950's, the union negotiated with each company separately. However the union contended that, because of the similarity between basic metal industries, negotiations with the steel, aluminum, metal container, and nonferrous metals industries should be coordinated. The steelworkers union established a Wage Policy Committee to outline the demands that the union would make during the coming year. Actual bargaining, starting in 1966, was done by "conferences" set up separately for each industry, using the Wage Policy Statement of the Wage Policy Committee as its guideline.

The Basic Steel Industry Conference is made up of a representative of each local steel union, generally the president, plus district directors and presiding officers designated by the chairman who is the president of the International. The Conference has the power to ratify contracts as well as to recommend strikes, which may be called by the Conference after a vote of the industry membership.

From the composition of the Conference, it is obvious that the negotiators are the "fat cats" of the union. Their positions in the union and their seniority in their jobs effectively insulates them from lay-off or disciplinary action by the companies. They can be the heroes . . . the rank and file union members are taking the risks. They are also politicians, and . . . like any other politicians . . . their continuance in office depends on their getting more and more for their "voters."

The larger steel companies, attempting to combat the pressure from industrywide bargaining, formed the Coordinating Committee Steel Companies in 1956 to negotiate on major issues at the national level. The original committee was composed of four members, two from U.S. Steel. The composition of the Committee (as well as the companies involved) has changed from time to time, but it continues as the negotiating team for the steel industry.

It would be unfair to say that the union was a better negotiator than the steel companies; the union had more powerful weapons, both economic and political. In any event, employment costs in the steel industry climbed steadily from 1956 until 1974, when hourly costs moved into the double-digit range for the first time.

Turbulence in company-union relations was nothing new in the steel industry. During the Korean War, President Truman briefly seized the basic steel industry, appointing the Secretary of Commerce as administrator. The U.S. District Court ruled on April 29, 1952 that this seizure was illegal, and the Supreme Court affirmed that ruling on June 2. The workers walked out, and did not return until July 24, when six large steel companies, including U.S. Steel, reached an agreement with the union for a sizeable wage increase and enriched benefits.

A review of wage and benefit settlements beginning with the War Labor Board's dictated settlement in 1942 reads like an invitation to inflation. The following list indicates the average increases in actual per-hour wage rates for the corporation.

February 15, 1946	18.5 cents per hour
February 1, 1947............................	5.18 cents per hour plus 3.5¢ per hour retroactive to January 1, 1944
April 1, 1947................................	15.0 cents per hour
July 16, 1948	13.0 cents per hour
December 1, 1950............................	16.0 cents per hour
March 1, 1952	16.0 cents per hour
June 12, 1953	8.5 cents per hour
July 1, 1954................................	5.0 cents per hour
July 1, 1955................................	15.2 cents per hour
August 3, 1956	10.5 cents per hour
January, 1957 (1st pay period)	3.0 cents per hour
July 1, 1957................................	9.1 cents per hour
July, 1957 (1st pay period)	4.0 cents per hour—First COLA increase
January, 1958 (1st pay period)	3.0 cents per hour—COLA-Semi-annual
July 1, 1958................................	9.5 cents per hour
July, 1958 (1st pay period)	4.0 cents per hour—COLA
January, 1959 (1st pay period)	1.0 cents per hour—COLA
December 1, 1960............................	9.7 cents per hour
October 1, 1961	1.5 cents per hour—COLA (Adjusted from 3¢ to offset insurance cost increase)
October 1, 1961	9.7 cents per hour
October 1, 1961	1.5 cents per hour—COLA (adjusted)

Steelworkers vs. Steelmakers

October 1, 1961	8.9 cents per hour
July 1, 1962	Existing COLA of 18.5 cents per hour continued; reaffirmed June 29, 1963.
September 1, 1965	12.2 cents per hour
January 1, 1966	Trade craft jobs increased by two full job classes plus other technical adjustments. Each trade or craft employee on incentive work was to receive 14.6 cents per hour added to all other earnings.
August 1, 1967	7.5 cents per hour
August 1, 1968	23.8 cents per hour
August 1, 1969	14.2 cents per hour
August 1, 1970	13.5 cents per hour
August 1, 1971[1]	64.8 cents per hour
August 1, 1972[2]	15.5 cents per hour
August 1, 1972	1.0 cents per hour—COLA (now quarterly)
November 1, 1972	2.0 cents per hour—COLA
February 1, 1973	3.0 cents per hour—COLA
May 1, 1973	7.0 cents per hour—COLA
August 1, 1973	7.0 cents per hour—COLA
August 1, 1973	15.5 cents per hour
August 1, 1973	8.0 cents per hour—COLA
November 1, 1973	9.0 cents per hour—COLA
February 1, 1974	9.0 cents per hour—COLA

[1] COLA paid 1¢ per hour for every .3% increase in the C.P.I.
[2] This included a 50¢ an hour general increase and 0.5¢ increase in increments between job classes resulting in additional increases up to 15.5¢ an hour for job class 33. 64.8¢ represents a combined incentive and non-incentive increase in base rates.

The above data are condensed from a special report by the Bureau of Labor Statistics covering wage and benefit information for U.S. Steel Corporation and the United Steelworkers of America from March, 1937, to April, 1974. The listing refers to wage information *only,* and does not reflect the increases in benefits. Total per-hour costs per employee from that time to the present are given by U.S. Steel as:

1974	$ 9.078 per hour
1975	10.590 per hour
1976	11.744 per hour
1977	13.036 per hour
1978	14.303 per hour
1979	15.921 per hour
1980	18.451 per hour

The per-worker cost of the fringe benefit package furnished by U.S. Steel to its average employee in 1980 was $4.274 per hour over 3 years, *not counting* the additional cost of paid vacations and holidays. This package of fringes alone is almost 2¾ times the *total* cost per employee at the beginning of the Bureau's study in 1947. Total employee costs per hour in 1980 were almost 12 times the costs during 1947.

Is there any way that an industry can pay its workers 12 times as much as before and still stay in business? Yes. There are two ways: increase production per worker; or raise prices. A look at the table relating productivity in the steel industry to employee costs reveals that the increase in labor costs far outstrips production increases. This leaves the other path as the remaining option; raise prices.

Sooner or later, however, any economy reaches a point where higher prices can no longer be absorbed by the market. We have reached that point.

At the beginning of this analysis, the rhetorical question was: ". . . did the workers not know . . . or did they not care?" The average worker might not know, but one can be sure that their union leaders *do* know. They are no longer "down-trodden workers" without knowledge or sophistication: they are hard-nosed businessmen with resources to hire top legal and accounting talent. Personally, they have nothing to lose but their tremendous power, and they will lose that only if they fail to keep their constituents satisfied.

Until this power is curbed, the inflation it engenders will continue to erode the U.S. standard of living, leaving only the choices of anarchy or bankruptcy.

Take your choice.

TABLE 9
HOW THE USW BEAT THE INCREASING COST OF LIVING
(Comparison of Increasing Employment Costs per Hour, Including Fringe Benefits, of Steelworkers to the Increases in the Consumer Price Index)

	Steelworkers			Consumer Price Index		
	From	To	Percent	From	To	Percent
1967 to 1968	$ 4.758	$ 5.032	+ 5.8	100.0	104.2	+ 4.2
1968 to 1969	5.032	5.375	6.8	104.2	109.8	5.3
1969 to 1970	5.375	5.677	5.6	109.8	116.3	5.9
1970 to 1971	5.677	6.261	10.3	116.3	121.3	4.2
1971 to 1972	6.261	7.075	13.0	121.3	125.3	3.3
1972 to 1973	7.075	7.681	8.6	125.3	133.1	6.2
1973 to 1974	7.681	9.078	18.2	133.1	147.7	10.9
1974 to 1975	9.078	10.590	16.6	147.7	161.2	9.1
1975 to 1976	10.590	11.744	10.9	161.2	170.5	5.8
1976 to 1977	11.744	13.036	11.0	170.5	181.5	6.5
1977 to 1978	13.036	14.303	9.7	181.5	195.4	7.7
1978 to 1979	14.303	15.921	11.3	195.4	217.4	11.3
1979 to 1980	15.921	18.451	9.0	217.4	246.8	13.5
	Total Increase: 287.8%			Total Increase: 146.8%		

Sources: U.S. Department of Labor, Bureau of Labor Statistics, American Iron and Steel Institute.

ANALYSIS 5

The Growing Adversary Relationship

It is difficult to define the relationship between union workers and their employers as anything but adversary when the record shows a total of 401,744,000 employee-days of production lost in the ten years from 1969 through 1978 from work stoppages. This is roughly equivalent to having all the workers in the heavily-industrialized state of Connecticut stay home for a full year.

The accompanying table shows a relatively slow growth in the total number of union members over the past few years, but a significant change in composition. This is particularly true in that sector to which the public is most vulnerable: governmental employees. From 1964 to 1978, union-member employees of the Federal government increased from 897,000 to 1,596,000 or 78%; State and local members from 556,000 to 2,030,000, or 265%.

Until recent years the idea of a strike by public employees was unthinkable. The majority were covered by Civil Service or, in the case of teachers, by tenure provisions in state laws. Job security was high, and retirement provisions, holidays granted, sick leave, and other benefits bet-

TABLE 10
NATIONAL & INTERNATIONAL UNIONS AND MEMBERSHIP—1956–1978
(Membership (000's) and Classification)

Year	Number of Unions	Manufacturing	Non-manufacturing	Federal	State	Local	All Government	Total Membership
1956	187	8,839	8,350				915	18,104
1958	186	8,359	8,574				1,035	17,968
1960	184	8,591	8,375				1,070	18,037
1962	181	8,050	8,289				1,225	17,564
1964	189	8,342	8,125	897	556*		1,453	17,919
1968	189	9,218	8,837	1,351	804*		2,155	20,210
1970	185	9,173	9,198	1,370	948*		2,318	20,690
1972	177	8,920	9,458	1,369	270	821	2,460	20,838
1974	175	9,144	9,520	1,392	444	1,085	2,920	21,584
1976	75	8,568	9,549	1,301	389	1,322	3,012	21,129
1978	74	8,119	9,998	1,596	473	1,557	3,626	21,742

Source: Handbook of Labor Statistics–Bureau of Labor Statistics
*Totals which included both State and Local

ter than in most jobs in the private sector. True, wages were generally somewhat below those of industrial workers, but compared favorably to those of, for example, store clerks. And the work pace was usually slower than for employees in the private sector.

As the numbers of public employees increased, they looked at the wage increases in highly unionized industry. Then they began to think, "Why not me, too?" After all, they had better weapons: if the Ford plants were closed by a strike, people could buy Chevrolets, but if your house is on fire where can you find a competitive fireman? Of course, strikes by public employees against the Federal government were illegal, and many states had similar laws. Consequently, most of the earlier public employee strikes were thinly disguised: "sickouts" by teachers, "blue flu" by policemen, etc.

Since nobody was enforcing the laws against public employee strikes, their unions became more and more militant, and their effect on debt-plagued municipalities more disastrous. New York City, already unable to pay its debts, was forced into an inflationary settlement by a crippling garbage collectors' strike. Although the city had to be bailed out by the State of New York, which issued its own obligations by underwriting the Municipal Assistance Commission (Big Mac) to get the money, union pressure has not lessened. The New York City Transit Authority (Subway and Surface) granted an increase of 9% effective in April, 1980, a further 8% due October 1, 1981, plus a COLA increment as of August 1, 1981 *and* a 95¢ per hour "catch up" raise for some 3,400 employees hired since the 1978 settlement. Employees of the commuter-essential bankrupt Long Island Railroad also received an increase in 24% over 3 years, with the settlement retroactive to January 1, 1979.

In Philadelphia, the city's transit workers, after tying

up the populace with a 19-day strike, received a package containing, along with other benefits, raises of 2% beginning March 15, 1981; 4% starting June 15, 1981; COLA increases of up to 12¢ per hour effective in December of 1981 and 1982; plus, a further 6.5% on March 14, 1982. Their ancillary benefits included a prescription drug and dental plan as well as an increase in life insurance benefits.

Strike-induced or strike-threatened settlements against the general public involving essential services are by no means confined to the populous Eastern Seaboard. The huge Illinois State, County and Municipal Employees union recently received a two-year contract with 8 percent increases effective June 1, 1981 and 1982; the State, County, and Municipal employees of Hennepin County, Minnesota did a little better, with 9% each year, improved benefits and additional pay adjustments of from 2.5% to 20% for workers in some categories.

In many settlements involving public service workers, increases have exceeded municipal budgets, inviting financial disaster for the municipalities. Although this does not make sense, what choice do the public officials have? No city can operate without its safety forces . . . its public transportation . . . or its power and water supply. The fact that the money is not there has had little effect on most militant public service unions. In effect, they say to the public officials, "That's your problem."

In a few cases, officials have taken a "hard line" approach. After a bitter five month strike by school teachers in Ravenna, Ohio, the school board did grant an increase, but only upon the condition that the voters approve an additional levy to provide the money. The voters turned down the additional levy. The strikers returned to work without an increase. A vote on an additional levy will be held in the Spring of 1982 and further negotiations will be conducted. For one of the few times in its history, Ohio's Ferguson Act, which makes strikes against public entities illegal, was invoked. When a number of the striking teachers spent a short time in jail, the television newscasters, union members themselves, pictured them as martyrs; the fact that they were defying the law seemed unimportant.

The proliferation of union activity against government is frightening to students of labor relations . . . where will it stop? Certainly, it shows no sign of abating.

The U.S. economy, already buffeted by years of cost-push-induced inflation, held its breath in anticipation of a strike by U.S. Postal Service workers in the Spring of 1981. The strike was averted by a last-minute settlement padding the $21,146 wage base by some 26% over a three year period . . . *if* the C.P.I. did not increase over 8% per year . . . more if it were higher, plus increased fringe benefits. The illegality of the threatened strike did not seem to be a concern to the workers or their union leaders.

President Reagan's decisive action in face of threats by the air traffic controllers might have finally given the "enough!" signal to public employees unions. At least, it was a firm step in the right direction. Obviously, it has shaken union bosses all over the world. Boycott-type threats from air traffic controllers in Canada and Western Europe indicate the concern of other union members over what they see as the erosion of their ever-growing power base.

As concerned citizens look at the growing power of public service unions to hold them hostage, they increasingly ask, "How did all this start?" If we look at the record, perhaps we can come up with some answers.

Since the days of the Roosevelt Administration politicians have promoted the idea that government can solve anything, and that governmental treasuries are bottomless. One cynical observation expresses the opinion that, "The American system of government will survive until the politicians learn that they can bribe the people with their own money."

This "bribery" started with emergency measures during the near-panic depression of the 1930's. Since that time, and principally during the "Great Society" days of Lyndon Johnson's administration, things began to get out of control. "Federal money" became the watchword for more and more municipalities as well as states. Participation of the Federal government in local projects became a way of life. Government grants became so much a part of the cost of the massive volume of building . . . and rebuilding . . . that a new profession was born: the "grantsman." Urban Renewal became a horrible example . . . thousands of properties were condemned and purchased with 75% Federal funding. Buildings were torn down, often leaving weed-covered vacant lots when developers could not be found to purchase the properties, even at a giveaway price, for redevelopment.

Billions of dollars were spent on government projects ranging from sewers to low-income and senior citizens' housing. Wage rates were dictated, under the watchful eyes of Federal inspectors, by the Davis-Bacon Act. These "regionally prevailing" wage rates were usually the highest union rate in the area . . . even if the government watchdogs had to travel 75 miles from the project being built to find a suitable "prevailing wage."

In the midst of this building boom local governments found that they were hard-pressed to meet the expenses generated by the increasing wage and benefit demands of employees and the push of inflation. Local taxpayers were beginning to vote down tax hikes proposed by their

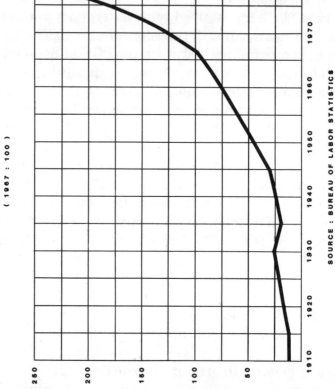

CHART XV

INDEX OF MINIUM HOURLY UNION WAGE RATES

BUILDING TRADES FROM 1910 TO 1978

(1967 : 100)

SOURCE : BUREAU OF LABOR STATISTICS

HANDBOOK OF LABOR STATISTICS – DECEMBER, 1980

WAGE INDEX

officials. Since the Federal government had been generous with construction money, why not operating money? This resulted in the birth of "Revenue Sharing" . . . probably the most dangerous step of all.

Indicative of what George Orwell called (in his book *1984*) "newthink" is a recent concession announced by Northern California Local 3 of Operating Engineers to spur flagging construction. Of their hourly rate of $22.50, (including $6.98 in benefits), they have agreed to accept a decrease of $4.00 per hour in their benefit package for *privately financed* projects *only*.

By the way, how much longer is it until 1984?

ANALYSIS 6

Bituminous Coal Mining

Or: Whatever Happened to the 16-Ton Syndrome?

Its thumping rhythms reverberated from the Nation's juke-boxes for months, reminiscent of the depression-dampened '30's. The name of the song: *Sixteen Tons*. Beetle-browed, irascible John L. Lewis probably loved it; it underscored his campaign to elicit public sympathy for his coal miners.

> "You load sixteen tons and what do you get?
> Another day older and deeper in debt.
> Saint Peter, don't call me 'cause I can't go,
> I owe my soul to the company sto'(re)"*

Today's coal miner no longer owes his soul to the company store, though he may have contracted some debts in keeping up his present lifestyle. In fact, one 29-year-old miner, interviewed during a protracted bituminous coal miners' strike, expressed concern about his payments on his automobile, his motorcycle, his house, and his motorboat.

The miners have come a long way since the days of

---

* *Sixteen Tons*, by Merle Travis. Copyright 1947 by American Music, Inc.

"sixteen tons." Output per man-hour has increased too; but the following analysis of the discrepancy between output and wages illustrates the inflationary effect of the "success" of the miners in their negotiations.

Output per man-hour in bituminous coal mining rose from a Bureau of Labor Statistics index figure of 27.9 in 1939 to a high of 103.6 in 1968, an increase of 271%. Most of this increase was due to the introduction of more sophisticated machinery in mining operations, particularly in rapidly expanding open-pit mines with the development of huge shovels, drag lines, and cranes. During the same period, average hourly wages rose from $0.853 to $3.86, an increase of 353%.

Since the high-productivity year of 1968, man-hour output had dropped from the index figure of 103.6 to an average of 74.1 for the last five years of the period, 1974–1978, a decrease of 28%. Much of this decrease was due to more stringent regulations imposed by governmental agencies and by union contracts, but, during the 1968 to 1978 period, an increase in average wage rates of 147% exacerbated the soaring price of the product.

From 1978 to 1980, average wages rose another $1.36 per hour. Terms of the new contract negotiated between the United Mine Workers and the Bituminous Coal Operators Association during the prolonged strike in 1981 increase base pay, across the board, by $3.60 per hour to $14.49 over the 40-month term of the contract, an ultimate raise of $7,488 per year. Using the average hourly earnings figure for 1980, $10.89, as given by the Bureau of Labor Statistics, this calculates to an annual cash income for a coal miner of over $30,000 per year, an increase of 33% for the five-year period from 1980 to 1984.

But, this is not the whole story. When we add the effects of shift differentials, hours paid but not worked, such as holidays and vacations; various items such as clothing allowances and a one-time bonus for returning to work, the cost to the mine operators per worker-hour actually worked climbs to almost $18 per hour. When one adds the cost of fringe benefits such as pensions, a medical plan, a dental plan, and life insurance, total cost per worker-hour reach just over $25.50 per hour actually worked. (NOTE: The accompanying chart uses basic hourly rate only to avoid complications of various one-time special fringe benefits, such as bonuses for returning to work after strikes, etc.)

If we look at the BLS base-year, 1967, we find that hourly labor costs (not including fringe benefits) were $3.75 for 100 units of the productivity index, or 3.75 cents per index unit. The historical high point for the index was reached in 1968, at 103.6 units of output per manhour. At a labor rate of $3.86 per hour, this gave a unit cost of 3.73 cents per unit, a slight improvement . . . but . . . the *last* improvement.

The figures for the subsequent 10 years were:

TABLE 11
LABOR COSTS, IN CENTS, TO PRODUCE EACH UNIT OF THE
BITUMINOUS COAL PRODUCTIVITY INDEX
(1967 = 100)

Year	Productivity Index	Hourly Wages	Cents per Index Unit
1969	103.1	4.24	4.11
1970	98.3	4.58	4.66
1971	92.0	4.83	5.25
1972	83.9	5.32	6.34
1973	85.9	5.75	6.69
1974	83.9	6.26	7.46
1975	72.1	7.25	10.06
1976	70.8	7.78	10.99
1977	69.0	8.26	11.97
1978	74.7	9.53	12.76

Productivity—Bureau of Labor Statistics, *Handbook of Labor Statistics,* Dec., 1980 Table 105.

Earnings—Bureau of Labor Statistics–Basic Economic Statistics & Wage Chronology.

As these figures indicate, the hourly wage cost of producing one unit of coal has more than tripled in the ten years between 1968 and 1978. If we assume that the productivity index will not drop from the 74.7 figure for 1978, the unit basic wage cost will reach 19 cents by 1984, a further increase since 1978 of 6.24 cents, or 48.9%.

These figures show that, *not* including fringe benefits, the labor cost per index unit will have almost quintupled in the 15 year period.

OUTPUT PER MAN-HOUR VS. WAGES
BITUMINOUS COAL MINING

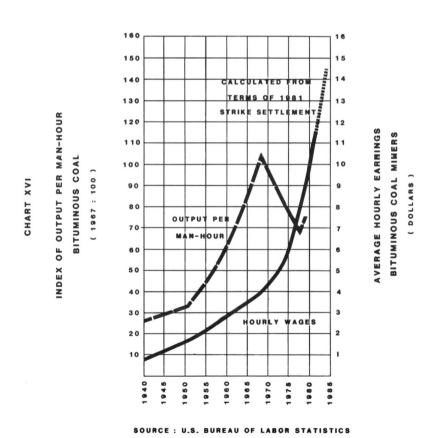

SOURCE : U.S. BUREAU OF LABOR STATISTICS

167

CHAPTER 9

Can Productivity Increases Stop Inflation?

Producing more, at less cost, would certainly reduce inflation. Theoretically, if the increase were great enough, it could offset the increase in costs caused by compensation increases.

Can it be done?

Well, in many situations it has been done. The development of the assembly line lets us drive to work in the time it would take to hitch a horse to a buggy. If our automobiles were still handmade in somebody's bicycle shop, only those who did not need to work could afford the drive.

Increased productivity, and better products for less, have resulted primarily from better tools; seldom from paying higher wages. The pay increases came from increases in output made possible by better tools.

USING THE TOOLS

The term, "Tools," as used here is a generic term. Tools that can improve productivity are not limited to mechanical or electronic devices; they can include anything from ideas to silicon chips; from marketing to hybrid seeds. For example, the analysis, "Farming-Bright Spot in Productivity," highlights the tremendous strides in agricultural productivity stemming from research since World War II and new equipment.

If productivity increased at the same rate for every type of economic endeavor (work) and this increase could be accurately measured, everyone would be paid the same rate of increase and compensation–cost–push would not exist. Unfortunately, not only do productivity rates of increase vary widely between various types of economic endeavors, and in many situations productivity does not increase at all and may actually decrease, but also it is very difficult to measure productivity in many types of work.

MEASURABLE AND UNMEASURABLE PRODUCTIVITY

Automobile productivity is a *measurable* quantity. The same is true for output data from other factories, in units; from farms, in bushels, pounds or bales; from mines, in tons; in transportation, ton miles or car loadings. A look at services, or service industries, presents a different problem: how do you measure the productivity of a policeman, a fireman, or a teacher? In retail or wholesale trade, or in restaurants, no meaningful measure of employee productivity has been developed.

Electric utilities can increase the productivity of their plant workers by installing larger generators. But this does not increase the productivity of most of their workers, who are field installers and repairmen, meter readers, and clerical help. Gas utilities are primarily distribution systems, requiring the same number of employees winter or summer; yet their sales peak in winter. Telephone companies might compare the number of customers to the number of their employees, or their billings per employee, but neither figure would measure the output of the telephone system.

Banks, insurance companies and brokers employ millions of people, but have no good way of measuring output. Counting numbers of transactions does not give an accurate measure; they vary widely in complexity and time required.

In local, state, and federal government employment, measurement of production is generally impossible. Presumably the work performed by government employees has economic, social, or political value, but there is no accurate way to measure it, and no way to prove its value.

Measuring productivity in our complex economy, then, becomes as ephemeral as Francis Bacon's attempt to answer Pilate's question, "What is Truth?"

The Federal Government tries, though. For years the U.S. Department of Commerce has calculated a figure usually called the Gross National Product (GNP). The full title is Gross National Product and Expenditures, but the full title is rarely used, which is unfortunate because the "expenditures" part of the title is significant. Actually, the GNP does not measure output at all. It measures input, in dollars, by assuming that everyone who gets paid or otherwise earns income is producing a product or service equal in value to the income he receives, or that the amount he invests is equal in value to the assets created by the investment.

These are broad assumptions. For example, Federal expenditures for goods and services are a significant part of GNP, and government is primarily a *user,* rather than a producer.

The GNP figures for the fourth quarter of 1980, annualized, are as follows:

	Billions
Personal Consumption Expenditures	$1,751.0
Gross Private Domestic Investment	397.7
Net Exports (+) or Imports (−) of Goods & Services	+23.3
Federal Defense Purchases of Goods & Services	141.6
Federal Non-Defense Purchases of Goods & Services	70.4
State & Local Purchases of Goods & Services	346.6
TOTAL Gross National Product & Expenditure	$2,730.6

The Department of Commerce constantly refines and updates these figures. The totals are suspect but are better than nothing. They can be used as a rough approximation of which way the economy is going, but not of exactly where it was in the period for which the statistics were taken. For example, in the June 1, 1981 Business Week magazine section entitled, "Business Outlook" the following statement appears:

"The slump in housing in the first quarter was not reflected in the first quarter G.N.P. That will hit in the second-quarter figures."

In an attempt to measure productivity in our overall economy, the Bureau of Labor Statistics divides the GNP by their estimate of total hours worked during the period to arrive at a figure called "Output per Man-hour." It would be more accurate to call it "Input per Man-hour." Since there is no accurate measure of hours worked, this measure of productivity per man-hour is at best a forced figure, but, like the GNP figures, it does reflect trends.

Though it is difficult to quantify changes in productivity, no one can deny that increasing it has a significant role in holding down inflation, *IF* increases in productivity are allowed to hold prices down. Over the past few years, increases in productivity have been more than absorbed by escalating wages, which have made no contribution to the increases.

Table 12 shows the number of people working in various types of economic activity in 1930 and 1979, the per-

TABLE 12
CHANGES IN DISTRIBUTION OF U.S. WORK FORCE, 1930–1979
(Thousands of Workers)

Goods Producing Industries

Year	Total Workers	Mining		Construction		Manufacturing		Farming*		Total Goods Producing	
		Number	%	Number	%	Number	%	Number	%	Number	%
1930	41,906	1,009	2.4	1,387	3.3	9,562	22.8	12,497	29.8	24,455	58.3
1979	93,256	957	1.0	4,644	5.0	20,972	22.5	3,774	4.0	30,347	32.5
Change in % of Total Workers		(−58.3%)		+51.5%		(−1.3%)		(−86.6%)		(−44.3%)	

Service Industries

Year	Transportation & Public Utilities		Wholesale & Retail Trade		Finance, R. Estate & Insurance		Other Services**		Government Federal		State & Local		Total Services Producing	
	Number	%	Number	%	Number	%	Number	%	Number	%	Number	%	Number	%
1930	3,685	8.8	5,797	13.8	1,460	3.5	3,361	8.0	526	1.2	2,622	6.3	17,451	41.6
1979	5,154	5.5	20,137	21.6	4,963	5.3	17,043	18.3	2,773	3.0	12,839	13.8	62,909	67.5
Change in % of Total Workers	(−37.5%)		+56.5%		+51.4%		+128.7%		+150.0%		+119%		+61.9%	

* Farming includes Forestry and Fisheries.
** Other Services includes workers in such fields as laundry and dry cleaning, appliance and auto repair, social workers, medical and legal services, etc.

Source: Bureau of Labor Statistics, *Handbook of Labor Statistics*, December, 1980, Tables #72 and #99.

centage of each type to the total workers in each year, and the change in this percentage from 1930 to 1979. The percentage of service industry workers increased 61.9%, goods producing workers decreased 44.3%. This illustrates the difficulties encountered in determining productivity increases for the nation as a whole.

While increases in productivity for the "unmeasurables" in the service industries are hard to determine, we can assign some plus value to their efforts in light of our changing work patterns. With over 50% of married women now in the work force, the use of more prepared foods and laundry services has replaced some jobs formerly done at home.

THE TOOLMAKERS

Economic history shows that better tools yield productivity increases. Besides such obvious tools as the production line, the speed wrench, and the grain drill, technology has produced other tools that have not only boosted productivity, but have also created entirely new industries.

Computers have opened up new worlds. Operating at speeds once measured in microseconds, then in nanoseconds, they record trillions of transactions for banks, guide astronauts into space and back, and teach children to read.

Robots, under various names, bore engine cylinders to ten-thousandths of an inch, spot-weld entire automobile frames in one operation, and cut intricate patterns from blocks of steel by using instructions from paper tape.

TOOLS AND TAXES

Obviously, these and other productivity-generating tools are not free. They represent enormous investments in research and development before they can go into service to produce better goods at lower prices. The money to develop these tools comes from the savings and investments of people . . . not just today's people, but those of past generations . . . for the capital base of our economy has been built over hundreds of years. Without this capital base growing from savings and investment, we would still be living in caves. Yet many people feel that payments to investors in the form of interest, dividends, rents, or profits are somehow anti-social and immoral. This feeling has made it politically popular to load investors with an ever-larger share of taxes. This has resulted, in many cases, in the destruction of viable economic enterprises, with a loss to society as well as to employees and communities. It is ironic that the "soak the rich" attitude usually hurts the non-rich; the savings eroded might be a workingman's share of his pension fund or a mutual life insurance company.

Taxes will always be with us, but taxation that diverts money from the productive to the non-productive does much to defeat the goal of stopping inflation.

Increases in manufacturing productivity are created by a wide variety of factors, most of which require substantial investment by the employer:

1. Improved machinery.
2. Improved tooling.
3. Better material handling.
4. New plants—better plant layouts.
5. Improved products.
6. Improved raw materials.
7. Improved quality control.
8. Improved scheduling.
9. Improved methods.
10. Simplification-standardization-specialization.

11. More efficient marketing.
12. Greater use of power.
13. Automation.
14. More efficient use of all assets.
15. Better planning.
16. Better management.

This list is not complete, but it illustrates the point that practically all productivity increases result from the expenditure of money, time, and brainpower. The individual worker has little to do with it.

The person attempting the productivity increase must believe he is going to benefit if his attempt is successful. The benefit may be in terms of a lower cost or a higher quality product at the same cost. If a higher quality product at the same cost results, the businessman is likely to sell it at the same price to get more volume. If the demand for his product is elastic, either a higher quality product at the same price or a lower-priced product at the same quality will result in higher unit sales.

The main reason for increasing productivity is the bottom line . . . to increase profits. Often, increased profits have to wait until the businessman has "played catch-up" in offsetting compensation increases.

Surprisingly, he gets little help from his workers in these efforts. In many cases workers resist and often prevent moves that could increase productivity. Such short-sighted attitudes have resulted in tremendous economic losses. "Featherbedding" in the railroad industry certainly contributed to the demise of Penn-Central, while many manufacturers have failed because worker resistance prevented their keeping plants modern and efficient and their balance sheets strong.

Workers, management, and owners should realize they are on the same team with the same aim: to produce a product or service which customers will continue to buy year after year, to improve both the product or service and the facilities used; and to split the proceeds of their endeavors equitably so conflicts over the disposition of the proceeds will not result in disruptive interruptions of production.

Many attempts at productivity improvements require increased unit production. The capital investment in machinery, tooling, and other specialized assets can be justified and recaptured only if increased volume is obtained. Normally the way to obtain increased volume is through lower prices on quality products, or greater marketing effort, or both.

Savings from productivity increases should not be passed along to workers in that specific company or industry. They should be, and will be, under free competitive conditions, be passed along to customers in lower prices, better products, often both. This usually gets the increased unit volume needed to obtain the productivity increase.

Most people unfamiliar with competitive conditions in private industry believe that the income created by productivity increases, if not passed along to employees in that company in the form of higher compensation, would be kept by the company. They have not studied the history of prices in industries where major increases in productivity have occurred. For example, the prices of major household appliances actually declined for decades after World War II, in spite of the cost increase of most major raw materials. At the same time, quality improved. In recent years prices of major appliances have increased, but not as rapidly as the C.P.I.

Many other examples of price decreases, or price advances much slower than either the C.P.I. or the P.P.I., could be recounted. These have all resulted from productivity increases. Computers are the outstanding example of management, technology, capital, and competition combining to provide the computer user with astronomical increases in output per dollar of cost. The output of commercial airplanes in passenger-miles produced per hour of operation, per gallon of fuel burned, or per airline company employee has increased tremendously. At the same time safety and reliability have also increased.

TODAY'S TRENDS

Using the technical advances over the past few years, we should be setting records for productivity. We are not. Table 13 shows the record over the past five years for the private business sector.

TABLE 13
**PERCENT CHANGES IN PRODUCTIVITY AND WAGE RATES
IN THE PRIVATE BUSINESS SECTOR, 1976–1980**

Year	Total Output	Output per Worker Hour	Compensation per Worker Hour
1976	+6.3	+3.3	+8.6
1977	+6.3	+2.1	+7.7
1978	+4.7	−0.2	+8.4
1979	+2.8	−0.3	+10.1
1980	−0.8	−0.3	+10.1

Source: U.S. Bureau of Labor Statistics

Bluntly, this record is dismal. The only category showing a consistent increase is compensation of workers, and this during the first period in our history that output per worker-hour has declined. For years, unions have been getting compensation increases which they have justified in part by claimed productivity increases. This has been particularly evident in the auto industry.

There is nothing wrong with workers getting incentive pay, profit-sharing bonuses, or other compensation for extra effort and output, but only if the extra effort and output reduces the unit cost of production, but:

There is no economic or ethical justification for passing the benefits of productivity increases along to workers doing the same work at the same speed.

Such a policy negates any inflation-lowering effect of increased efficiency in production. But it has been done, as the figures in the table show. If there are no productivity increases in an industry, unions still demand . . . and usually get . . . about the same percentage increases as in the industry having substantial productivity gains. The unions argue that they work as hard. They may even work harder, because their plants may not be as modern, efficient, and automated.

Many people believe that the company developing the productivity increase will keep all the savings for its stockholders. Actually, the stockholders are usually the last to benefit. After recovering the cost of whatever innovation yielded the increase, management either plows the savings back into the company or goes out after new business by quoting lower prices. By getting new business, it spreads its overhead across a larger unit volume and makes more profit at a lower price. This happens constantly: productivity increases benefit not only the company with higher profits, but also the customer with lower prices. Since the workers are also customers, they will also enjoy the benefits of these lower prices.

Thus, under free market conditions over a period of time, a person working at the same job at the same rate of pay will enjoy an increase in his standard of living as prices and taxes he pays for products and services gradually trend down. This did happen during the earlier development periods in the United States. Prices declined after the War of 1812 until the Civil War, and after the Civil War until 1901, when the combination of labor unions, industrial consolidations that "rigged" markets, and other interferences in free market conditions started to offset the benefits of productivity increases.

PRODUCTIVITY INCREASE—A LIMITED PLUS

For increased productivity to completely stop inflation, it would have to come in all areas of the economy . . . manufacturing, farming, retail stores, distributors, financial, etc. . . . and even in government. There is no way this could happen. We have seen how difficult even measuring productivity can be; to attempt an across-the-board increase would be futile. With better equipment, the fry-cook at McDonald's might turn out twenty more Big Macs per hour, but this does not mean that the chef at "21" would produce more steaks from a larger broiler.

Productivity increases are not industry-wide; they come as individual companies improve their efficiency. Chart XVII shows the wide divergence in productivity gains (or losses) in a number of typical industries, but these are net effects; undoubtedly some companies within these industries were more efficient than others. It also shows that, even in industries that still showed gains, the gains were inconsistent.

Today's productivity figures are discouraging, especially compared with recent U.S. history. From the early 1800's until the beginning of the present century the standard of living increased steadily, productivity soared, but prices, except in wartime, gradually decreased. (See Chart II, Chapter 1).

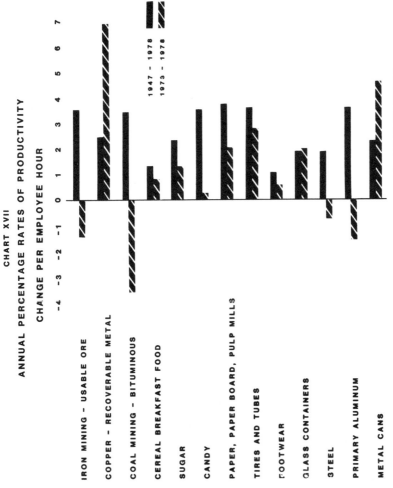

CHART XVII

ANNUAL PERCENTAGE RATES OF PRODUCTIVITY

CHANGE PER EMPLOYEE HOUR

1947 - 1978

1973 - 1978

IRON MINING - USABLE ORE

COPPER - RECOVERABLE METAL

COAL MINING - BITUMINOUS

CEREAL BREAKFAST FOOD

SUGAR

CANDY

PAPER, PAPER BOARD, PULP MILLS

TIRES AND TUBES

FOOTWEAR

GLASS CONTAINERS

STEEL

PRIMARY ALUMINUM

METAL CANS

SOURCE : U.S. DEPARTMENT OF LABOR, BUREAU OF LABOR STATISTICS

181

If prices decreased why aren't they doing it now?

There are a number of reasons, some of them minor, others of real importance. We will examine the two most significant.

1. Capital Investment . . . Risk vs. Rewards

In the 19th Century, investors could count on high returns on their investment in a new or expanding enterprise, if the venture was successful. Today the shareholders' return must come *after* taxes paid by the company (about 50+%), and *after* personal taxes on the dividends (formerly up to 70+% but still up to 50% Federal, plus State, local, etc.). And this assumes that the venture itself can earn a profit *after* complying with OSHA, ERISA, EPA, SEC and other regulations; *after* paying product liability insurance premiums to protect against lawsuits with no statute of limitations; and particularly *after* meeting competition at home and from overseas.

2. Escalating Costs of Labor

During the growth years in the 1800's, people wanted "more," but did not really expect it. They expected to work hard to "put food on the table and keep a roof over their heads," but had not come to expect more pay each year for doing the same amount of work or less. This is not to say that greed did not exist . . . it just was not organized. The reward for good work was keeping a job, and being able to buy ever-better products as productivity improved. Extra effort was applauded and often rewarded. It was not, in union parlance, "killing the job."

Although we cannot hope for an overall increase in productivity for every dollar paid to every worker, we can improve our present record. It will require not only a change in attitudes, but also a change in our present system.

THE ROAD BACK

Obviously, we are going in the wrong direction today. This is evident, as Table 13 and Chart XVII both show. Why? And . . . what can we do to turn it around?

First, let's look at the fundamentals.

The ability to make productivity increases depends on the company having the money to spend on . . . and often to gamble on . . . the new facility; the time and mental attention to devote to its development; and the assurance that production will not be interrupted by costly destructive strikes. To accomplish an "about face," all three of these factors must be addressed.

Available money can be less of a problem. Current liberalization of restrictive depreciation rules will help. When the Federal Reserve Board stops its up-pressure on interest rates, even more help will result.

Workers, and certainly union bosses, must come to realize that their most valuable asset is sound company management . . . that a company manger who is wrapped up in labor troubles has neither the time nor the energy to tackle new projects.

The real income and standard of living of the workers will improve through productivity increases, but getting people to believe this will be hard. People want more for themselves than others get, and if the present system gives them the power to gouge their neighbors, they will not willingly give it up. Only when conditions get bad enough and the gougees rise up enmasse will the system be changed.

Look at the record of the recent past. And, look at the prospects for the future. Do we dare wait longer?

CHAPTER 10

Can We Be Saved by a Return to the Gold Standard?

People who are being drowned by inflation grasp at straws. One of the straws which is grasped at is a return to the gold standard. The glitter of this solution has been a lure throughout the years. Once again we are hearing that our problems can be solved by the magic of gold.

The appeal of gold is often felt most strongly by people who have only a cloudy idea of what a return to the gold standard would really mean. So it's useful to examine the concept.

If a country is truly on the Gold Standard, anyone can take his paper money to the bank and exchange it for a piece of gold worth the face value of the currency turned in for it. When the United States was on a full gold standard (1900 until 1933), gold was valued at $20.67 an ounce. Twenty dollar gold pieces were the most common form of monetary gold.

Early in 1933 President Roosevelt increased the value of gold to $35.00 an ounce, which theoretically decreased the value of paper money and bank deposits by 41%. Surprisingly, prices were little affected by this change, Irving Fisher not withstanding.

Other factors, including NIRA experiments, increased prices about 3% between 1933 and 1934, but they leveled out. As a whole prices increased less than .8% per year until the start of World War II. Obviously, devaluing U.S. currency in terms of gold did not devalue the currency in terms of general purchases of goods and services.

France's return to the gold standard in the 1920's is quoted as an example of what would happen here if the U.S. returned to the gold standard. This ignores the fact that France made important changes, improvements, and austere corrections necessary to make returning to the gold standard possible. Its situation had been a classical case of old-style inflation, caused by an unbalanced federal budget, unfavorable balance of trade, transition from a wartime to a peacetime economy, a post-war business boom with excessive private speculation, and expanding debt, both public and private. The French government corrected most of the above causes and excesses, which stopped internal inflation. There was not worldwide inflation, so import prices were not advancing as they are now. With the franc lower in regard to other currencies, French exports grew. Confidence in French financial solidarity returned.

Moreover, the price of gold, $20.67 an ounce, was controlled by the U.S. Returning to the gold standard was simple. With the franc stabilized, the French central bank could buy gold at $20.67 and people could go to the bank and get gold for their paper francs. Since there was no frantic turning in of paper francs, the central bank did not have to buy much gold.

Stopping the *causes* of inflation made it possible for France to return to the gold standard. Returning to the gold standard by itself not only did not stop inflation; it would have been impossible without stopping the causes of inflation.

The mechanics of a return to the gold standard in the U.S. today would be so complicated and difficult as to make the move practically impossible, economically and politically.

For example, gold would have to be pegged at a set price. But what price?

If the U.S. returned to the gold standard at the current market price for gold, without eliminating the major cause of inflation, the price of gold would keep going up, owners of paper dollars would change them into gold at the banks, U.S. gold reserves would be rapidly drawn down, and the U.S. would again be forced off the gold standard.

But above all, the gold standard would do nothing to stop the major cause of inflation—*compensation–cost–push*. It would not even affect the minor causes.

A look at history yields some interesting facts. The worth of gold in relation to silver, called "bimetallism," was the foundation of the monetary system of most countries during the 19th century. The classical ratio was 16-to-1, or a pound of silver to an ounce of gold. This relative value was arbitrarily set with little relationship to market demand. During the 19th century, bimettalism ceased to be an acceptable monetary standard for increasingly sophisticated societies.

The moves by the U.S. back to a bimetallic gold standard after the Civil War—and then to a full gold standard in 1900—were intended to stabilize the dollar and increase the public's confidence in it. It was also supposed to work wonders in evening out the peaks and valleys of our economy. It did neither.

After the Civil War came a succession of business cycles. See Table 15 on the following page. The mild depres-

TABLE 15
CONSPECTUS OF BUSINESS FLUCTUATIONS—UNITED STATES, 1790–1925

1790	Revival; prosperity	1832	Moderate prosperity
1791	Prosperity	1833	Prosperity; panic; recession
1792	Prosperity; financial distress		
1793	Prosperity	1834	Mild depression
1794	Uneven prosperity	1835	Revival; prosperity
1795	Prosperity	1836	Prosperity
1796	Recession; depression	1837	Prosperity; panic; recession; depression
1797	Depression; panic		
1798	Depression		
1799	Revival	1838	Depression; slight revival
1800	Prosperity		
1801	Mild prosperity	1839	Revival; panic; recession
1802	Recession		
1803	Mild depression	1840	Depression
1804	Revival	1841	Depression
1805	Prosperity	1842	Depression
1806	Prosperity	1843	Depression; revival
1807	Prosperity; recession	1844	Revival; prosperity
1808	Depression	1845	Prosperity; brief recession
1809	Depression		
1810	Revival	1846	Recession; mild depression
1811	Moderate prosperity		
1812	Brief recession; uneven prosperity	1847	Revival; prosperity; panic; recession
1813	Prosperity	1848	Mild depression; revival
1814	Prosperity; financial distress		
1815	Prosperity; panic; recession	1849	Prosperity
		1850	Prosperity
1816	Depression	1851	Prosperity
1817	Mild depression	1852	Prosperity
1818	Mild depression	1853	Prosperity; recession
1819	Severe depression; financial panic	1854	Recession; depression
		1855	Depression; revival
1820	Depression	1856	Prosperity
1821	Depression; revival	1857	Prosperity; panic; recession; depression
1822	Mild recession		
1823	Revival		
1824	Prosperity	1858	Depression
1825	Prosperity; panic; recession	1859	Revival
		1860	Prosperity; recession
1826	Depression; revival	1861	Mild depression; revival
1827	Moderate prosperity		
1828	Prosperity; recession	1862	War activity
1829	Depression; revival	1863	War activity
1830	Moderate; prosperity	1864	War activity
1831	Prosperity	1865	Boom; recession

TABLE 15 (*continued*)

1866	Mild depression	1897	Depression; revival
1867	Depression	1898	Revival; prosperity
1868	Revival	1899	Prosperity
1869	Prosperity; monetary difficulties	1900	Prosperity, brief recession
1870	Recession; mild depression	1901	Prosperity
		1902	Prosperity
1871	Revival; prosperity	1903	Prosperity; recession
1872	Prosperity	1904	Mild depression; revival
1873	Prosperity; panic; recession	1905	Prosperity
1874	Depression	1906	Prosperity
1875	Depression	1907	Prosperity; panic; recession; depression
1876	Depression		
1877	Depression	1908	Depression
1878	Depression; revival	1909	Revival; mild prosperity
1879	Revival; prosperity		
1880	Prosperity	1910	Recession
1881	Prosperity	1911	Mild depression
1882	Prosperity; slight recession	1912	Revival; prosperity
		1913	Prosperity; recession
1883	Recession	1914	Depression
1884	Depression	1915	Revival; prosperity
1885	Depression; revival	1916	Prosperity
1886	Revival	1917	Prosperity; war activity
1887	Prosperity	1918	War activity; recession
1888	Brief recession	1919	Revival; prosperity
1889	Prosperity	1920	Prosperity; recession; depression
1890	Prosperity; recession		
1891	Depression; revival	1921	Depression
1892	Prosperity	1922	Revival; prosperity
1893	Recession; panic; depression	1923	Prosperity; recession
		1924	Mild depression; revival
1894	Deep depression		
1895	Depression; revival	1925	Prosperity (preliminary)
1896	Recession; depression		

Source: National Bureau of Economic Research 1926.
For later data see Business Week Index, Analysis 10, pg. 323.

sion of 1866–1867 was followed by a short-term revival during 1868, then a brief period of prosperity until the Black Friday Panic in September, 1869. However, good times or bad, prices declined steadily, even though the price of gold was supposed to be steady. Neither tight nor easy money supply appeared to have any noticeable effect on consumer prices nor any lasting effect on wholesale prices. See Chart II, in Chapter 1.

From 1870 until September of 1873 the economy enjoyed recovery and prosperity. Consumer prices changed little, even though money supply became increasingly tight and gold premiums rose steadily. The panic in the Fall of 1873 brought many business failures and a suspension of payment of currency by banks. As a result, the country endured some five years of depression. During the lean years, both wholesale and consumer prices declined: the former by 46%; the latter by 23%. Money supply was easy, but business demand for it was light.

This gloomy period was followed by a boom starting in 1879 and lasting until late 1881, when signs of recession began to emerge. During the boom years wholesale prices rose sharply. The stock and commodity markets, lacking the controls built into today's markets, were rife with speculation. Both markets performed erratically, particularly during periods of prosperity. In 1880, for example, those markets collapsed in May, then boomed in October. During this period consumer prices rose only moderately.

The decline that started in late 1881 reflected a bad crop year that pushed up commodity prices. Labor problems, including an ironworker's strike and the Chicago riots in 1882, deepened the recession; the slump continuing through the tight-money panic of 1884 until the slow recovery that started in late 1885.

One would assume that consumer prices would show a rollercoaster effect during these spells of boom and bust. Interestingly, after dropping sharply from the peak after the Civil War, the consumer price index changed little until the early 1890's; this in spite of four swings in business activity between 1885 and 1893, and variations in agricultural yields from excellent to poor.

The depression which began in 1894 continued with varying degrees of severity until 1898. Consumer prices dropped about 8%, then remained on a plateau until two years after the country went on a full gold standard in 1900. Prices then started to rise except for a brief dip after the money panic of 1907. By 1912, they reached a level not seen since the high point of the 1881-'82 boom, and continued their upward trend. During World War I the pressures of wartime wages and shortages plus help from the government, pushed prices to double the 1912 level by 1920.

During the twenty years before the gold standard was adopted, the Consumer Price Index varied some 20%. During the gold standard years, 1900–1933, the C.P.I. varied as much as 140%. True, it can be argued that part of this 140% difference was a result of a wartime economy, but if we drop the war years from our calculations, we still find a variation of 100% during the years of the gold standard. Historically, the gold standard apparently had no stabilizing effect on consumer prices. Indeed, it created problems of its own.

Before the establishment of the Federal Reserve System in 1913, the U.S. suffered frequent financial crises, caused primarily by the inflexibility of bimetallism and then the gold standard. With the Fed available as a stabilizing influence in the money markets as well as a "lender of last resort" for banks, these crises were virtually eliminated until 1933. Then the prolonged deflation caused by the depression reduced asset values backing up bank loans, both tangible and intangible, bank liquidity, and depositor confidence. Huge withdrawals of paper money by frightened depositors necessitated the closing of all banks for a couple of weeks, after which solvent banks were permitted to reopen. People had not lost confidence in paper money; only in banks.

Recent innovations have added flexibility to our monetary system, enabling banks and other institutions to borrow money to accommodate short-term peak needs. This is known as "managing their liabilities." Banks and other deposit institutions no longer have to rely on regular checking and savings deposits for their "inventory." They can borrow from the public or from business with Certificates of Deposit, which are actually IOU's; they can sell portions of their portfolios of various government securities with an agreement to buy them back at a certain time at a price calculated to give the purchaser an interest return on his money; they can borrow from each other in what is known as the Federal Funds Market, usually on a one-day basis. The use of these—and even more esoteric methods of money management such as trading in Eurodollars and foreign currencies—enable the banking system to have money and credit available where, and when, it is needed.

This new look in banking has indeed eliminated major crises in the money markets, except those caused by the Federal Reserve's futile efforts to stop inflation by tightening the money supply and raising interest rates.

Returning to the gold standard might have some psychological effect; but it would create great problems both nationally and internationally, without getting at the real causes of inflation. The inflexibility of the gold standard on the international market would force countries with unfavorable trade balances and government deficits off the gold standard, including the United States. Floating international exchange rates automatically adjust a country's money value to correct for unbalanced trade and budgets. This maintains the free market concept.

When the value of a country's money goes down, its

goods are cheaper in the international market, helping to increase exports. At the same time imports become more expensive, and are reduced, both by consumers and business. This is the way it should be. The important thing is to let the value of currency respond to the inflow and outflow of funds. Trying to maintain the value of money against a negative cash flow accomplishes little and makes the eventual drop in its value even greater.

CHAPTER 11

Compensation–Cost– Push Inflation, the Contax Plan to Stop It

"There is nothing more difficult to take in hand, more perilous to conduct, or more uncertain in its success, than to take the lead in the introduction of a new order of things."

Niccolo Machiavelli, 15th Century

I feel sure that many of the economists, bankers, and others who claim inflation can be stopped by tightening the money supply and/or reducing government expenditures know in their hearts that compensation–cost–push is the major cause of inflation. But they wishfully think that inflation can be stopped by monetary and fiscal policies. They realize that trying to stop compensation–cost–push inflation means fighting entrenched and powerful groups. In addition, general economic ignorance, indifference, and short-sighted greed make it seem very difficult—in fact, virtually impossible—to root out the basic cause of inflation. Many are afraid to speak out against c.c.p. inflation because they will incur the wrath and pressure tactics of union bosses.

The signers of the Declaration of Independence and other patriots of the American Revolution knew they might be hanged if the Revolution had failed. They were not cowards. Are we?

Someone must speak out!

People have been known to take aspirin for appendicitis, refusing an operation until the appendix has burst and peritonitis has set in. Stopping inflation requires a major operation. Over the years people have often said to me, "Your program will stop inflation, but you will never be able to get it adopted. Come up with a simpler solution."

There is no simpler solution to inflation. Economic aspirin will not cure it. Tinkering with the money supply has done little except put a lot of employers out of business. As long as compensation–cost–push inflation continues, government deficits will continue, since government pay-outs—most tied to the C.P.I.—increase more rapidly than income.

Let's face it. To stop inflation we must stop compensation–cost–push. It will take both courage and continued dedication on the part of the Contax Plan leaders just to get the effort under way. We can be sure that neither major political party—as presently constructed—will adopt this plan. Only when thousands of each Congressman's constituents start demanding that compensation-cost–push inflation be stopped will legislators even dare to talk about the plan.

Regardless of whether or not it can be adopted, let's get on with the solution to inflation.

Here are the truths on which my program is based:

1. Continuing inflation will eventually destroy our financial institutions, the value of our money, our economy, our society, and our international strength.
2. The major cause of inflation is compensation–cost–

push: the continuing escalation of prices resulting from people being paid more and more for doing the same work or less.

3. If business were free of compensation–cost–push, productivity could be increased, better products marketed, and prices gradually and continuously lowered.

4. Some wages are kept artificially high and constantly escalating because labor unions have been given legal monopoly status.

5. While the intent of the original legislation conferring this monopoly status . . . the Wagner Act . . . was to correct abuses by employers, the abuses committed by organized labor swung the balance much too far in the other direction.

6. Artificially high compensation levels are obtained by threats, boycotts, violence and strikes.

7. The power to maintain compensation at destructively ever higher levels must be eliminated.

8. The plan to eliminate these abuses must assure that employers do not take advantage of the situation to carry out their own abuses.

A theoretical economist could argue, with considerable justification, that the law of supply and demand alone should determine compensation. If there were an over-supply of labor in one area the price of labor (compensation rates) would go down so low as to be very attractive for employers to move operations into the area and employ the surplus workers. With this lower-priced labor, so the theory goes, he could undersell competitors and build up his sales volume and his employment. Gradually compensation rates would rise as the demand for labor started matching the supply. The economist would argue that there should be no minimum wage to keep the labor surplus area from underpricing other areas and thus build up the demand for its labor.

Letting supply and demand alone determine compensation would take decades, or even generations, before areas of surplus unskilled labor would be eliminated. Present government payments such as Aid to Dependent Children with welfare payments increasing with every additional child, born in or out of wedlock, practically guarantee continued surpluses of unskilled workers who have little desire to work and who could not produce enough to cover present minimum wage costs.

If the supply of labor could be turned on and off like a faucet; if people could be trained in new skills promptly; and if they could be quickly and economically transferred from a surplus to a shortage area—then the law of supply and demand could determine the price of labor. But there are practical problems.

Moving from one section of the country to another is a harrowing experience for most people. People cannot be switched around to the best markets like cattle, pigs, or chickens. Neither can employers. A large percentage of capital investments in facilities is lost even if machinery can be moved. The knowledge and skills of the working force would likely be lost to a great degree if a plant were moved to take advantage of a surplus labor supply in another area. The plant might be out of operation for months, incurring devastating expenses and loss of income.

Many smaller employers cater to a local or regional market, and have local or regional suppliers. Both markets and suppliers would have to be developed in a move to a new area. Thus employees and employers are relatively immobile.

If there were a shortage of people with a needed skill in an area, supply and demand would result in the compensation rate being bid up as employers compete with each other for the short supply. The unusually high wage for this particular skill would encourage more people with that skill to move into the area, or people already in the area to learn that skill. Gradually the compensation rate for that skill would come down toward the national average rate for that skill as supply began to match demand.

While the present minimum wage may be too high to justify private industry employment of the young, the unskilled, and the chronically-unemployed, this is not the major problem to be faced. Possibly 80% to 90% of all employed adult workers make more than the present minimum wage. If group power to set compensation rates were eliminated, they would worry about what would happen to their incomes. A precipitous drop would bring disastrous economic results to their families and their creditors, along with riots and political upheavals. A satisfactory method of determining equitable compensation is needed to replace the present system.

If group power to negotiate and strike for wages were eliminated, people would fear that unscrupulous employers would take advantage of local surplus labor conditions and pay much lower wages than they are presently paying. The people whose wages would be cut would not be willing to go through the long period of time necessary to increase demand so that their wages would go back up and their unemployed neighbor would have a job.

This illustrates a very important point in attempting to find an acceptable and equitable method of determining compensation to take the place of the present method. Practically everyone views change of any sort in the light of how it will affect him personally *now*. What might be better in the long run is of little interest.

So, if the public and legislators will not accept letting

the law of supply and demand determine compensation rates, what alternatives are there?

As we have seen, a price and wage freeze does not work for many reasons:

1. It would perpetuate the great inequities in compensation that now exist.
2. It would be very difficult and expensive to enforce. Black markets would appear when a product with an inelastic demand became scarce.
3. Many currently low-profit items would become scarce, as producers concentrated on more profitable products.
4. Strong unions would, as they have done in the past, ignore the freeze and force employers, and through them, consumers and taxpayers, to pay them more.
5. The law of supply and demand would not be allowed to operate to increase the supply, through price increases, of items for which demand was increasing rapidly.
6. A wage and price freeze has been acceptable over a short period of time with a definite end, such as a war, and where unusual conditions (very limited production of civilian goods) occur. Freezing prices and wages in peacetime solves nothing; it does not get at the real cause of inflation. When the freeze collapses, as it inevitably has done in the past, inflation will get worse.
7. Monitoring wage and price changes over some forty centuries since Egypt's Pharaohs first tried to control them has always resulted in a bureaucratic nightmare.

If freezing prices and wages is not the solution? what else?

Many people, particularly in unstable foreign countries, think Communism or Socialism is the answer. It is true that in many of these countries which have subsequently gone Communistic or Socialistic, the apparent difference in income and wealth between most people and the wealthy few was greater than it appears to be here. Compensation levels and standards of living for unskilled and semi-skilled working people have been much lower than in the United States, a situation blamed on the wealthy and ruling classes. Compensation levels have been low primarily because productivity has been low. Smaller countries have had smaller markets, which is why the European Economic Community united Belgium, France, Italy, Luxembourg, The Netherlands, and West Germany in 1957, then further expanded to include Great Britain and other countries. With limited markets, factories could not justify the machinery, facilities, engineering, and tooling necessary to obtain high productivity. In Britain restrictive practices by labor unions, nationalization of key industries, and extremely high taxes combined to make Britain's post-World II economy extremely inefficient. The dole made recipients feel that the government owed them a living and should take over everything, greatly reducing individual initiative. Doles practically equal wages, after taxes.

It will be interesting to watch France, now under a socialist government for the first time in 25 years. It had made much progress during that time, its currency was sound; inflation was no worse and no better than in most developed countries. Will Socialism reduce the destructive strikes for which France has been noted? What will happen to its productivity and progress?

If a Communistic or Socialistic country were completely self-contained and self-sustaining, neither importing nor exporting products or services, and had a reasonably sufficient supply of natural resources, it could keep prices level. It is unlikely to accomplish much to raise the standard of living; but, this would result from its economic system, not its lack of inflation.

However, when a Communist country must import large quantities of commodities, products, and/or services, inflation will occur as the prices of imports go up. If exports do not match imports, the value of the currency will gradually decline, further adding to the cost of imports and inflation.

The United States is relatively self-sufficient, with foreign trade making up a small proportion of its economy. It is more self-sufficient than any other non-Communist country. It could adopt a practical system to stop inflation and the system would work. With costs and prices of U.S. products and services not rising, but either steady or gradually declining, the value of the U.S. dollar would be steady or stronger, so that the price of imports, in terms of U.S. currency, would not increase.

What other methods of stopping inflation are there? Profit-sharing bonuses tend to get workers and management to realize they are both on the same team and to reduce, to some extent, workers' demands for more pay. However, unless a profit-sharing bonus system were nationwide and benefitted everyone, it would not be effective in stopping inflation. I do not see how a profit-sharing bonus system could apply to civil employees such as school teachers, firemen, policemen, or people in many service industries. Profit-sharing bonuses can increase productivity in industries where profits and bonuses can be calculated and are attributable to the combined efforts of all members of the company.

Tinkering with the money supply won't stop inflation. Freezing wages and prices won't do it. Bonus plans won't do it.

We must eliminate group power to force compensation levels ever higher.

For years I puzzled over how to permanently and equitably stop compensation–cost–push inflation and what to establish in its place. Every idea I dreamed up had its faults. When I challenged the Federal Reserve economist on April 22, 1970 by telling him that this period of inflation would not be stopped by monetary and fiscal policies he asked me what would stop inflation. I told him I would write up my ideas and bring them to him.

Telling him the cause of inflation was simple. Devising a solution was far more complex. About 4 o'clock the next morning the idea of using job evaluation on a nationwide basis occurred to me. The more I thought about it, the better I liked it. There appears to be no other practical, equitable solution.

My answer is the *Contax Plan* (Contax stands for Consumer-Taxpayer).

In its essentials this plan is simple. It consists basically of three sweeping steps.

1. Remove from workers the power to strike over economic issues.
2. Establish minimum pay levels for all jobs so that employers cannot exploit the elimination of the power to win higher wages by striking.
3. Eliminate the power of professional groups and others to set their own compensation unilaterally.

These three steps will require legislative action.

How to accomplish Steps 1 and 2 will be discussed in the next several pages.

First, how do we set up the "safety net"; the way of protecting employees from abuses by employers?

To accomplish Step 2 I propose a program of National Job Evaluation.

What is Job Evaluation? Job Evaluation has been used for decades to determine within an organization what the differential in pay rates should be between different jobs. It is a relatively exact science as social sciences go, and it is fair. Practically all large and medium-sized organizations employing a few hundred people or more use job analysis and evaluation. It is very helpful in collective bargaining discussions to determine wage rate differentials between jobs. It is a continuing operation, not a one-shot study, since job requirements may change. It is the fairest way to determine what a person's compensation should be.

At first I envisioned a nationwide program which would apply to all wages, a comprehensive study which set *ceiling* rates on each of the 7,000 or more jobs. While this plan would stop c.c.p. inflation, it could never be accepted.

So now I favor National Job Evaluation as a *protective* device, by which *minimum* rates would be set on all jobs. In this manifestation, NJE is not the cure for inflation but rather the protective system which enables the cure to be applied without disastrous side effects.

What is Job Evaluation?

Job Evaluation consists of analyzing a job for its various requirements. In brief, a typical job analysis would consider the following items:

1. Amount of physical effort required.
2. Peak physical effort required.
3. Continuity of effort requirements throughout shift.
4. Minimum physical requirements. Size, weight, age.
5. General education level required.
6. Prior special training and/or education required.

7. Amount of on-the-job training required.
8. Care and skill required.
9. Attention required.
10. Mental requirements. Judgment, decisions.
11. Amount of cooperation and type of personality required.
12. Environmental conditions—heat, cold, fumes, irritants, standing, sitting, indoors, outdoors, safety problems.
13. Importance of job.
14. Value of production added by job.
15. Responsibility for equipment, product, safety, and welfare of others.
16. Degree of loyalty and dependability required.
17. Appearance requirements.
18. Importance of years of service.
19. Steadiness of employment.
20. Availability of personnel with needed requirements.
21. Amount of time away from home.
22. Outside activities expected.
23. Social obligation requirements.

These are just some of the items considered. On a local basis some other factors would be considered in comparing rates between localities. Some of these might be:

24. Proximity of job site to labor supply.
25. Differences in cost of living.
26. Competitive labor conditions.
27. Amount of suitable labor available.
28. Availability of housing, schools, and other social requirements.
29. Long-range conditions, both internal and external.

Both of these lists could be expanded considerably. A typical Job Analysis discussion write-up for a manufacturing company covers 42 typewritten pages. Job Evaluation can be applied to all types of work, whether industrial, utility, transportation, wholesale and retail trade, service work, or government work. Jobs with the fewest requirements would rate low on the J.E. scale. Those with the greatest total requirements, such as that of a neurosurgeon, would rate very high on the Job Evaluation scale.

Under the Contax Plan, National Job Evaluation would apply to all group-determined or negotiated wages. For the purpose of this discussion, wages have been defined as all compensation for personal services of all types. Any group, whether industrial workers, service workers, public employees, or construction workers, etc., which sets its rates by negotiation with its employers, shall be covered by National Job Evaluation.

There are two major employee groups who would be primarily affected by Job Evaluation. First are employees whose compensation has been in the past determined by group negotiation with employers, strikes, threats of strikes, violence, economic pressure, political pressure, boycotts, etc. Second are other groups whose compensation has been influenced by the first group. Most employers keep the second group's compensation in line with the first group to discourage unionization. Strong unions set the pattern so their influence on compensation and costs is greater than their numbers.

In most cases elimination of group power to set compensation would not, and should not, result in substantial decreases in compensation. Over the years most employers have built up an experienced work force and would not take a chance on losing them by pay reductions. Their best people would find jobs elsewhere easily, and they would be left with poorer workers. Be that as it may, I believe the general public would not accept the elimination of group power to determine compensation without any assurance that the compensation rates to which they have become accustomed would be protected. National Job Evaluation rates as floors below which compensation rates could not go would be this protection.

SETTING UP NATIONAL JOB EVALUATION

There are about 7,000 different classes of work listed by the Department of Labor. This list actually has about 25,000 jobs, but many are different names for the same job. I have discussed N.J.E. with many private and some government experts on job evaluation. None of them view National Job Evaluation as a particularly difficult task. Much of the work has already been done by employers of all types and sizes, either formally or informally. Industry associations have collected compensation data showing compensation rates throughout the industry from the lowest paid worker to the head of the company. Most large companies have formalized written job evaluation studies covering almost all employees. Medium-sized employers may not have a formal written study, but the actual wages paid to the various employees are in effect determined by job evaluation.

For example, take three press operators. "A" is a beginner, able to produce 80% of standard with 5% scrap on one or a few different parts, with normal absenteeism. "B" has worked several months, can produce 95% of standard on most parts, 3% scrap, and has better than average attendance. "C" has worked more than a year, can produce 100%+ of standard on all different parts at 2% or less scrap rate, and has an excellent attendance record. N.J.E. rates would provide different compensation rates for different performance levels at the same basic job. People would not only move up within a job classification, but also would be able to move up from one classification to another as jobs opened up and they could qualify. Provision should be made for a short period of training as a worker attempted to qualify for a higher-rated job.

At the start of developing N.J.E. dollar rates for various jobs need not be determined. The data needed are the relationships between the various jobs. The simplest, easiest, lowest-paid job would be given a rating of 100. All the other jobs would be rated above it. It would probably be impractical to try to rate top management jobs. Compensation for top and middle-management and similar jobs are usually negotiated on a face-to-face basis.

Since practically all employers must submit payroll reports, etc., to the federal government, it would be relatively easy to have each employer turn in a one-time report showing the number of people employed at each pay level, with the lowest pay being given an index number of 100. No dollar figures need to be submitted. The employer should write a job description telling what type of work is being performed. There might be several different kinds of work being performed by different people, all of whom receive the same rate of pay. Job descriptions for each type of work should be submitted.

Each industry should take the initiative and responsibility for evaluating all the jobs created by it. This would cover a large proportion of workers. Data would be collected by mail from other employers. It is not essential that the data be obtained from all employers. It *is* essential that the dat obtained be representative of the industry or economic activity.

Reports would be received from public employers, federal, state, local, schools, as well as institutions, both public and private.

At what general level should N.J.E. rates be pegged? I suggest about 20% below average rates paid for such work at the time N.J.E. and the Contax Plan are adopted.

Compensation data should be reported in index numbers, or if reported in dollars and cents, should be converted to index numbers.

Why should this data be obtained in the form of index numbers rather than dollars? One industry may be highly unionized, steel, autos, construction, with compensation rates for both unionized and non-unionized employees very much higher than rates paid in another industry for work that under National Job Evaluation would be rated equal. For example, a beginning telephone operator or receptionist at a nearby U.S. Steel division receives higher pay than an experienced, trained secretary to the general manager in a medium-sized company, where an inexperienced telephone operator or receptionist is paid about 60% of what the secretary receives. No wonder the steel industry is hurting.

These index numbers obtained by industries and other forms of economic activity and employment do not have to relate to each other from one industry to another. They should adequately cover the one industry. After these data have been obtained, the next step is to relate one industry to another. This requires people experienced in job evaluation covering many different types of activity. They must be able to relate compensation for example for a beginning school teacher with a B.A. degree in education to an over-the-road truck driver, a bricklayer, an auto assembly line worker, or a stockboy at a supermarket. All the factors listed earlier in this chapter must be evaluated and an index figure for each job determined. This index figure will then relate to the index figure for every other job listed regardless of type of work.

After indexes for all jobs have been determined they then should be translated into average dollar compensation rates. Due to local factors, such as items 24 to 29 listed earlier in this chapter, N.J.E. rates for that particular locality (it should be a fairly large area) might be adjusted upward or downward (i.e. surplus labor) possibly 10 to 15%. Gradually most of these local differences should disappear.

Care should be taken to prevent N.J.E. rates from being higher than average actual rates paid for the job or service rendered for the industry or activity as a whole. If an employer's rates were below N.J.E. rates, he might be required to increase his rates 5% a year until he reached N.J.E. rates, or faster, if he were taking unfair advantage of a surplus labor situation. Many people no doubt are underpaid in comparison to rates determined by N.J.E., but an abrupt escalation to N.J.E. rates might put some employers out of business. Adopting the Contax Plan should be done as smoothly as possible.

The thousands of N.J.E. rates cannot be all added up and divided by the number of rates to get an average rate because there will be many high rates with only a few people entitled to such rates. There will be many times as many low-rated people. For the purpose of calculating the average rate, the N.J.E. rates must be weighted by the number of people in each index classification. A figure for the average compensation earned will then be obtained, as well as the average index number.

For example, this calculation may arrive at an average N.J.E. minimum compensation rate across the board of $6.00 per hour, at an average N.J.E. index figure of 185. With 100 as the lowest index figure, the lowest rate would be $3.243 per hour. These figures are examples, not recommendations.

As pointed out in Chapter 12, the problem in arriving at present average rates and N.J.E. rates is complicated by the fact that as time goes on inflation will continue, even while N.J.E. rates are being determined. Further, any earnings reported by the B.L.S. will be past history, not exactly applicable to the date the Contax Plan becomes effective. The Contax Plan should result in neither an increase nor a decrease in prices or average wages at the time it is adopted.

With *Step 2,* the "safety net" in place, we are ready for the step that will abolish the monopoly situation which has brought upon us the disaster of compensation–cost–push inflation.

Workers will be forbidden to obtain higher compensation by means of strikes, threats to strike, boycotts, or other concerted action, including negotiations for higher pay.

Within those few words lies a sweeping change in our system. Within them also lies—I am convinced—the salvation of our system.

The positive step will be the law which spells out the limits to which concerted employee action may go. Workers may have a collective voice in such matters as safety, working conditions, etc.—although within limits. *They will not be permitted to strike for higher wages or economic fringes.*

Any employer who is paying N.J.E. rates or above would have no restrictions on him or regulations to follow. He could pay whatever wages he felt necessary to get the quantity and quality of help he needed. He could not negotiate with his people in a group about compensation or other fringes which would increase unit cost, but he could negotiate with them on non-economic factors. They could not force him to negotiate with them as a group on economic issues.

What about union contracts in effect on the date when the Contax Plan becomes adopted? Let's assume that the rates set in a typical contract are considerably above the N.J.E. rates. This contract still calls for future increases in basic pay rates, COLA, and other fringe increases. All increases, including COLA, after the adoption date would be cancelled. This will obviously cause much wailing and gnashing of teeth. The rates being paid at the adoption time will continue to be paid to the specific individuals receiving them as long as they worked for the company in the same job classification. The employer could not unilaterally terminate them. Contract rules governing termination, seniority, and retirement will remain in effect.

What about new people hired by the company after the adoption date? They could be hired at the N.J.E. rate or above. Fringes called for in the contract would not automatically be granted to new employees, but most reasonable ones would likely be continued.

There would be two situations that would need special treatment. Company "A" has been in business for years, but is not growing. It has a union contract. Its total direct labor cost is $16.00 per hour. It has practically no labor turnover. Skills needed can be quickly learned.

Company "B," established after the Contax Plan adoption date, hires a new work force at a total direct labor cost of $10.00. Company "B" goes out after Company "A's" customers, offering a 12% decrease in prices.

What does Company "A" do under these circumstances? The employer can not force his present employees to take a cut, but they can agree to take a cut, if they think it is necessary to preserve their jobs.

Under such conditions Company "A," and its workers, should make great efforts to increase productivity and to decrease the percent of direct labor cost in its products. Maybe high-priced new equipment will do this. The company might get the employees to help finance such purchases. In the final analysis, real unit production costs at Company "A" would have to come down to match Company "B's" costs if Company "A" is to stay in business. The employees have been highly paid for years and should be able to live comfortably on competitive rates which can not be below N.J.E. minimums for the jobs filled.

Here is another situation. Company C has a high-cost labor contract and competes with other companies, both domestic and foreign, who have lower-cost labor contracts. Company C's owner feels he must have lower labor costs to compete. Under the Contax Plan it is conceivable that the owner could set up another company (Company D) and start off paying lower wages, at or above the N.J.E. level.

Company C cannot get out of its labor contract unless it goes bankrupt or shuts down. This is a sticky problem, because the owner of Company D knows all Company C's processes, products, secrets, costs, and customers. I suggest the following restrictions to make setting up Company D less attractive:

1. No money or other assets could be withdrawn by owner or with owner's approval from Company C in excess of amounts normally withdrawn in salaries, bonuses, expenses, dividends, etc., and no earlier than usual in fiscal year.
2. Company D could not solicit and/or accept business from Company C's customers for a period of five years after Company D is set up.
3. Company D could not hire key people away from Company C.
4. Without sound economic justification Company C could not shut down its operation.

These restrictions would apply to Company C only if the owner or owners set up a competing company in which he, or they as a group, owned 30% or more of the controlling equity.

Step 3. Eliminating the power of organized groups to negotiate, threaten to strike, strike, use violence, etc., to obtain compensation demands is one major element of the Contax Plan. It does not, however, address the inflationary effects of individuals, groups, businesses, and institutions with little or no competition who now unilaterally determine their own compensation without open-market bid-and-asked pricing; for example, doctors, hospitals, and lawyers. In this discussion they will be called U-Groups. There is no effective way the average buyer can bargain about the price of the product or service supplied. How to eliminate inflation in their charges is Step 3 in the Contax Plan.

Let's examine the problems caused by these U-Groups and the conditions faced by the consumer when needing the service of a U-group member.

Members of the U-group generally have no formal written agreement concerning prices, and probably would get into trouble with the anti-trust authorities if they did. They might not even discuss their rates and fees in a group meeting, such as medical or bar association, but there exists a tacit understanding about charges and non-competitiveness.

A prime example of U-group charges were the fees charged by the lawyers for closing a real estate deal in Virginia. The fee was 1% of the sale price, regardless of the paperwork involved. On a $50,000 house, the fee was $500 for very simple work, probably one to two hours, primarily clerical. Title searches, mortgage deeds, etc., were extra. Some government agency finally dug into the situation and ordered the practice stopped but did not order rebates of the hundreds of thousands, possibly millions, of overcharges.

Apparently this type of practice is still going on. Supreme Court Chief Justice Warren Burger was quoted as follows in the January 10, 1982 issue of the Cleveland Plain Dealer:

> BURGER BALKS AT BAR'S ETHICS
>
> "Supreme Court Chief Justice Warren Burger says the nation's law schools and bar associations are neglecting professional ethics and lawyers are overcharging their clients. 'Surely the failures of the law schools in teaching legal ethics and professional responsibility are responsible in some measure for the ethical problems in our profession,' Burger says in the Cleveland State University Law Review. He adds, 'In all too many cases—the purchase of a home being a good example—clients are 'ripped off' by fees that are greatly out of proportion to the complexity of the transaction or the time spent by the lawyer."

In Ohio the bar associations generally have established exorbitant fees for all sorts of work. For example, the legal work in handling an estate is charged at 3% of the value of the estate in Ashtabula County, regardless of the simplicity of the estate. A person might have only cash, life insurance, and marketable securities in his estate, to the total value of $1,000,000, with only current expenses, etc. as total liabilities, and yet his estate would be charged a $30,000 legal fee for work that on an hourly rate of $50 an hour would total only a few hundred dollars.

This 3% fee has been set by the probate court judge, who is also an attorney. The excuse I received from an attorney for this 3% fee was that it limited the charge an attorney could make against an estate. Without the 3% ceiling some attorneys had charged more. 3% on a $10,000 estate might be right, but 3% on a $10,000,000 estate is ridiculous.

Doctor's fees are an even more painful (to the public, that is) example of the unilateral increases in charges that have occurred in recent years. Now many doctors have incomes of hundreds of thousands or even millions a year. Medicare and Medicaid have been so loosely and carelessly administered that doctors have been able to raise fees with impunity. During an investigation by a Senate subcommitte into charges billed under Medicaid, the committee learned that, prior to Medicaid's adoption in 1965, Missouri doctors were charging $100.00 for cataract surgery. Beginning in 1965, billings under Medicaid for the same operation were $495.00.

People without insurance, either private or governmental, have been bankrupted by a prolonged illness. Hospital rates have escalated far faster than the C.P.I. Exact historical data on doctors' fees are difficult to obtain, but the percentage increases in most rates have greatly exceeded the C.P.I.

A number of years ago (1951–52) the local doctors raised their charge for a simple quick pre-employment physical exam from $3.00 to $5.00. (Our cost for a physical exam is now $20.00, up 567%. The C.P.I. is up 145.4% from 1952). My company was struggling along barely breaking even, and because of the Korean War available labor quality was poor and turnover very high. Physical exams were a big expense.

I phoned our doctor and told him that a 67% increase in this fee was too much. You would have thought that I was criticizing Jesus. The doctor took great offense. What right had I, a lowly businessman, to try to tell doctors what they should charge. He said, "We don't tell you what you should charge your customers." I replied, "We have to price our products against competition. If we are two cents higher, we do not get the business." I accomplished nothing with my phone call.

Sometime later a young fellow working in the plant got into a motorcycle accident and had to have his leg cut off. He had not been working long enough to be covered by our insurance. His father also worked for us. He brought in the doctor's bill. It was another doctor. He had charged this boy $5.00 for every time he stuck his nose into his hospital room, every day for about 20 days, in addition to the surgical bill. I suggested the bill be lowered because the charge was too high and the father would have a hard time paying the bill, and the boy could not. Again I was told it was none of my business what the doctor charged. Our exchange got rather heated, but it was a useless effort.

While doctors and lawyers are the prime examples of unilateral setting of charges and no effective competition, the same situation exists with many other groups, from barbers to real estate agents. The latter group operates on a percentage commission basis, and in spite of the fact that real estate prices had been increasing at an accelerating rate, which automatically increased their commission, they have increased their percentage as well. On a local basis this increase was voted in a meeting.

I am not sure that the Contax Plan should attempt to correct obvious present excessive charges made by various groups or how it should be done. It should be able to prevent such charges escalating. National Job Evaluation should cover the functions performed by these groups and set dollar values on them, but as long as there is no effective competition between members of the group, N.J.E. minimum rates would have little effect on them. Attempting to use N.J.E. rates for maximums for these services, without using N.J.E. rates as maximums for employees, would create tremendous friction and no doubt myriads of lawsuits by affected people.

National Job Evaluation rates for medical services might be used by administrators of Medicare and Medicaid, and by group insurors, to set the amounts they would cover. It is likely that Job Evaluation would arrive at charges substantially different from those being levied at present, particularly in metropolitan areas. Under the present system, the "Medicare B" portion of the program that covers charges by doctors, physical therapists, etc., is administered by some 66 different "carriers," mostly health insurance companies. These "carriers" set the amounts Medicare will pay for specific services by formulae based on prevailing costs in various areas. Medicare pays, after an annual deductible amount of $60 (for the year of 1981), 80% of what the formulae determine to be a "reasonable charge." This "reasonable" figure is often below what the doctor might consider an appropriate amount for his services, even though, in the 16 years since Medicare was introduced, medical and hospital charges have far outstripped the increase in the C.P.I. There has been little complaint from the public as these charges have mounted . . . after all, Medicare or other insurance covered most of them. Publicizing the rates under National Job Evaluation should get the publics' attention, and be a strong deterrant to further increases. Under the Contax Plan there will be no increases.

It can be argued that over a period of years the supply of lawyers, doctors, or personnel in other U-groups will grow more rapidly than demand for them, because of the attractiveness of the excessively high income earned by the established people. This increase in supply would, it is argued, create competition and force established practitioners to reduce their fees. Over the years doctors and medical colleges have effectively kept the domestic supply of doctors down, to a point where 50% or more of the medical men in small towns are foreign-born and educated. This so far has not resulted in any price competition since the supply has not yet caught up with the demand.

Even if N.J.E. maximum fees were set for people in non-competitive fields who now set their own fees and charges I doubt if this would be practical. A specialist usually charges more for an operation than a general surgeon. The specialist is supposed to be more skilled and knowledgeable than the general physician and is justified in charging more. When I had a prostate operation some time back I went to a specialist even though some preliminary work had been done by a general physician.

At the moment the only solution I can figure out to the ever-increasing charges and fees for the U-groups would be for every member of a U-group to prepare and make public a list of the fees charged for all the various products and services each supplies. To attempt to prevent the prices on such a list being increased above prices previously charged before it became obvious that the Contax Plan would be adopted, comparable lists of charges made one year and five years previously should be supplied. Some products or services might not have been supplied five years ago, but that would not invalidate the list.

As soon as the Contax Plan were adopted, the C.P.I. would stop increasing, unless a serious drought or a war occurred. With no increase in prices or the general cost of living, there would be no justification for any increase in the charges made by the U-groups. Consequently the listed fees charged would be the maximum the U-group could charge. The charge could be less than the maximum but not more.

It is likely that many of the charges listed would be higher than would be justified under a National Job Evaluation study. It is also likely that one member's list would show charges that exceeded the charges on another list within the same community by 100- to 300% or even more. Even within a member-group, such as a firm of lawyers, the services of one professional man might cost far more than the services of another equally educated but not equally experienced professional man. This group's list should show the individuals whose services cost different rates, whether per hour or per function. There is nothing unethical in that.

What is unethical is not telling the client or patient in advance what the product or service will cost, and then submitting a whopping big bill later. The Contax Plan should require a discussion and agreement on charges prior to starting to supply the product or service. I do not recommend that the Contax Plan be empowered to reduce charges submitted on a list except when it can be proved that the charges on the list are higher than the person or group or institution actually charged recently, or that such charges had increased in the last five years at a rate considerably higher than the increase in the C.P.I. One factor that has tended to increase rates faster than the C.P.I., especially for surgeons and anaesthesiologists, is the increase in malpractice insurance rates. See Chapter 6.

Another group which at times in the past has been able to increase their charges unilaterally has been landlords of residential property. Some have been subjected to rent freezing, which aggravates the supply shortage rather than increasing the supply of rental units. Under the Contax Plan interest rates will settle down into one-digit levels, people will not be hoarding real estate as a hedge against inflation, and the cost of building will not increase. Except in rapidly growing areas competition will keep rent costs from increasing.

Where rentals controls exist, their elimination will result in rents increasing to, and temporarily possibly beyond, the level justified by costs and a reasonable return on investment. This could cause hardship on those living on fixed incomes. Controls are currently causing hardships on the landlords, who generally are not pitied, and on tenants because maintenance is neglected and gradually the number of rental units declines. Under the Contax Plan rent controls would be gradually abandoned. The reason for gradual, rather than immediate, is that a few years would be required for enough new rental units to be built to bring the supply up to the demand. Rents on new buildings should not be controlled.

The tremendous increase in the number of new condominiums has resulted from the deductibility of interest and real estate taxes in owner's income tax returns. At the same time landlords and specialized firms who buy property from landlords have been converting old apartments into condominiums and forcing long-term tenants to buy the condominium or move out. The converter marks the property up tremendously and makes a huge profit without contributing anything to the national income or the quality of the rental units. Older people living on pensions and social security do not have the money for the down payment on the condominium or do not want to tie up all or a major share of their assets in one.

Converting existing apartments into condominiums should be either prohibited or regulated so that present long-term tenants can remain as renters. Further, prices charged for condo units should be based on the price paid for the apartment building, plus actual repairs and improvements, or if the landlord is converting, on a valuation based on rents received. There should be no controls on new condo units. Maintenance charges and agreements should be fairly determined and not unilaterally increased.

There seems to be no universally equitable way to handle housing costs and rents. I favor letting the free market determine rents. Over a long period of time after the Contax Plan is adopted equity will be approached, but local conditions will often result in rents being either too high or too low. The supply of housing units is to inelastic in the short-term.

What about unilateral changes in charges by large manufacturers? For example, when I first became a Ford dealer in Ashtabula in late 1937 the charge for delivering a full-sized Ford passenger car from Detroit to Ashtabula was $22. This charge was fairly constant until the war. After the war it increased, but still was in the $30 range when I sold out in early 1948. Now the so-called delivery charge is around $500 on cars, at least double the increase in delivery costs since 1937. The car manufacturers now charge the same amount for delivery whether the car is delivered in Detroit, Miami, San Diego, or Seattle. They also claim that some of the delivery cost covers delivery of components to the assembly plants, which was not the case in the past. Most manufacturers buying parts and components from distant plants have in the past included the delivery cost as part of the unit cost of the part or component. By changing their method of pricing delivered components, the list price of the car does not increase as fast, but the total price paid by the buyer increases just as fast. The dealer gets no discount on the delivery charge. The delivery cost on a Japanese car in the U.S. is $165.

It seems part of the increase in delivery charges on U.S. cars was just to cover up price increases. This subterfuge must have been detected over the years by dealers and government wage and price agencies, but it was not publicized until recently. Possibly one reason was to show list prices on U.S. cars lower than the Japanese cars delivered in the U.S., while actual prices to the consumers were not that low. Another subterfuge involving car prices is the treatment of extras. A car will be announced with a list price, but when a customer goes to buy it, he will find it has from several hundred to more than $1,000 of extras on it. The car is not available at all with the minimum equipment called for in the announced list price, even if the customer is willing to wait months for it.

In 1975 I ordered a six-cylinder stick-shift Ford 4-wheel drive half-ton pick-up truck. I waited months for it, and many more months for a snow-plow blade for it. When I ordered the truck I was assured I could get it with a six-cylinder engine and a stick-shift. It came through much later than promised with a big 8-cylinder engine and automatic transmission at a price several hundred dollars higher than the six was supposed to be. By that time it was early winter. In desperation I took it, thinking getting the snow plow blade installed was a matter of days, which it was not. It was late February, 1976 before the plow was in operation. The truck performs well, but it is a hog on gas. Fortunately it is driven only a few miles a year.

The Contax Plan would require that any price quoted a consumer is the complete delivered price and further that equipment specified by the customer would be available at that price. If cars, or other consumer equipment, are not available without the "unwanted extras" which add to the price, the list price should be increased to include the extras.

The same principles should apply to prices and other charges the consumer pays. Too many so-called businessmen are shysters and feel they should get everything they can from their customer, client, patient, or borrower each time they do business with him. They rationalize, with some truth, that their customer will not realize the rip-off he is getting, or they may never get another crack at him.

One way consumers and others get ripped off is in the price charged for repair parts and service on mechanical, electrical, and other equipment, cars, airplanes, etc., after they are purchased and run out of the guarantee period. Certainly there are extra costs in handling and storing parts but not anywhere near enough to justify the prices charged, which may run from 500% to 1,000% of the price the manufacturer paid for the part, or its internal cost, when it was installed on his machine. Some companies break even on the sale of new equipment and make all their profit on the sale of service parts.

I am not recommending that some government agency dictate the prices charged for service parts, because they might disappear from the market if priced too low. What I suggest is that the manufacturer supply, with the original sale of the equipment, a complete list of all the service parts needed to repair the unit and the total price of all the parts, as well as individual parts prices. A list of service charges for repairing the equipment or installing new parts on it should also be supplied. The buyer could then compare the costs to the price he pays for the equipment. He may change his mind about buying the equipment. The manufacturer may decide to reduce his profit margins on parts to keep from losing sales of new equipment. He might also train his field repairmen to be more efficient. The user could decide in advance whether he wanted to repair his equipment or not.

This problem may not seem to be earth-shaking enough to be included in a tally of factors contributing to inflation, but as homes, offices, factories, and transportation systems get more mechanized and automated, costs of repairs and service take a greater slice out of budgets.

The proposals discussed above as Step 3 of the Contax Plan certainly do not cover all the unilateral charges made by U-groups, but they cover the main ones. The theory of Step 3 is to control charges and other costs imposed by people, institutions and businesses (U-Groups) which are not controlled, or strongly influenced by competitive forces.

Unfortunately the proposals made in *Step 3* will not correct most of the great excess charges currently being made by many members of U-groups, but it should keep them from getting greater. Putting the spotlight on these situations should give the people who have to buy their services a somewhat better bargaining position. Competition from within over a period of years should help bring down some of these excesses.

OTHER BENEFITS PROVIDED BY THE CONTAX PLAN

Besides eliminating inflation, the Contax Plan provides additional benefits.

1. With the constant threat of prolonged strikes eliminated, a company can invest more confidently in plant facilities and improvements.
2. Crippling losses from prolonged strikes will be practically eliminated. (Under this plan strikes for noneconomic issues will still be permitted.)
3. Employees can plan their futures with more confidence and will not have to undergo the occasional poverty and semi-starvation periods caused by strikes.
4. Production and productivity per man-year will increase as facilities are used more fully and human

brainpower is concentrated on how to make more and better products for less money.

5. The value of the U.S. dollar will go up on international markets while the price of U.S. products will go down.

6. If the U.S. adopts the proper program to stop inflation, other nations will gradually adopt such programs too.

7. Animosity between management and labor should be substantially reduced as both begin to realize they are on the same team, with the same ultimate employers: their customers.

8. Individuals who are angry with their supervisors over wage issues would have less cause to be. Employers and supervisors would follow N.J.E. guidelines, even though actual wage scales may be considerably above the N.J.E. minimums.

9. People training for a specific job classification would know beforehand the compensation level they could expect. This will tend to channel people into work requiring skill, training, and education. Present exorbitant rates for jobs requiring little skill, etc. make people believe all they need to do is join the right union, get a job, and do only the minimum amount of work to keep from getting fired.

10. Government revenues, local, state, and federal, would increase. Business losses caused by strikes are tax-deductible. Loss of personal income during strikes reduces not only taxes collected from the strikers, but also the incomes and taxes paid by others in the community where the strike occurs.

11. With the increase in government revenues, tax rates will go down, or government services will be improved at the same tax rates. Tens of thousands

of government personnel are now engaged permanently in activities made necessary by the present system of determining group compensation. The N.L.R.B. is an example. Peace officers are now forced to devote much attention to strikes and related violence and crime. Adopting Job Evaluation on a national basis will require a large temporary work force, but once the N.J.E. rates are determined, this force can be reduced 90%.

12. With no further increases in government salaries, wages, pensions, and prices of government purchases, all governmental units should be able to balance their budgets.

13. Without inflation, interest rates will drop into the middle single-digit range, further helping governmental units to balance their budgets and eventually reduce taxes.

14. With a return of interest rates to normal levels, purchases by consumers, businesses, institutions, and governments will be greatly stimulated, resulting in improved business activity.

A much longer list of the advantages and benefits to be gained by everyone from the adoption of this program could be written, but the above should suffice. This whole program is not entirely peaches and cream. There are some problem areas, but nothing that cannot be overcome.

Admittedly the Contax Plan to stop, not just hold back, inflation can be criticized, even ridiculed, by people who have other beliefs about the cause and cure for inflation or who do not want to see inflation stopped. Those who criticize do not have a practical plan to stop inflation and those who do not want to try to stop inflation have not studied enough economic history to realize that eventually they will suffer severely from inflation. The choice is not the Contax Plan or some other way to stop inflation. The choice is either the Contax Plan or nothing.

HOW WILL THE CONTAX PLAN AFFECT TAXES?

By relieving the upward pressure on Federal, State, and local government expenditures, the plan would result in lower taxes.

Most of government expenditures are for employees' salaries and fringes, pensions, and other transfer payments and interest. (A large portion of defense costs are salaries, fringes, and pensions.) Most of these payments are increased as the C.P.I. increases. Under the Contax Plan, compensation and pension payments should not go up at all, because the Consumer Price Index will not go up. The strain on the Social Security system would be eased because payouts to over 31 million recipients would no longer increase; nor would the payments to some 2½ million retired government and military retirees and survivors. Reduction in interest rates will ultimately lower government expenses at all levels.

Present compensation levels for most government employees, local, state, and federal, have been increased by strikes, threats of strikes, political favoritism, and comparison with equally inflated private compensation rates. While it is unlikely that existing public employees would have their compensation cut under the Contax Plan, new employees could be hired at N.J.E. rates or above, resulting in the long run in cutting government costs for the services performed.

The Contax Plan will also eliminate tens of thousands of government employees who are now involved in all the various tasks and projects that are required, particularly in the area of labor disputes and price regulations, etc. The Contax Plan will require some additional personnel initially, but over the long run the net total of government employees will be substantially reduced.

The theory beind the Contax Plan, and the origin of its name, is that the country and the economy should operate for the benefit of all consumers and taxpayers, and not for organized minorities, pressure groups, or privileged U-groups. Legislation of any sort that benefits a few at the expense and detriment of the many should be carefully scrutinized before passage to see if there is some other way the problem could be solved, if there is a problem. Much proposed legislation benefiting small groups is entirely unfair, unethical, anti-social, and uneconomic. Costs versus benefits analyses should be conducted before practically any legislation is passed.

The transition to adopting the Contax Plan will not be simple. There will be lots of problems and some inequities, but they will be temporary and small compared to the present permanent and devastating inflation.

It is easy to find fault with the Contax Plan, but it will stop inflation, whereas no other program already tried or presently suggested will.

CHAPTER 12

What Should the Price Level Target Be?

Prices and compensation levels will continue to increase over the coming years. Let's assume the Contax Plan can be adopted before runaway inflation wipes out the value of the dollar.

Let's say it will take five years to adopt the Contax Plan and that during that five years the C.P.I. and other price indexes will have increased 50% over the 1981 average.

Should those then administering the Contax Plan aim to reduce average prices, compensation, and charges from the then 1986 level, or to hold them as much as possible at that level?

I believe they should try to maintain the 1986 level and should not try to restore prices, etc. to a lower previous level. There are several reasons for this:

1. If people felt that prices were going to go down soon, they would hold off buying, creating a serious depression which would feed on itself. Such a depression might result in political changes and the adop-

tion of programs and policies that would completely negate the Contax Plan.

2. The value of collateral used to back loans, such as real estate mortgages, inventories, equipment, cars, household goods, etc. would drop, increasing foreclosures and further depressing business.

3. As the probability of adopting the Contax Plan became greater, and if it were thought that prices would drop precipitously after it were adopted, speculators could and would seriously upset the market prices of many commodities, securities, and other easily-traded items.

4. Consumers will have made long-term commitments, for houses, cars, etc., based on their income and its future prospects at the time of the commitment. A decrease in income would create hardship and losses to them and their creditors both.

5. Exports and imports and international money markets, etc. would be greatly upset by a sharp decline in U.S. prices. Even now foreign nations are quite concerned about the suggestion that the U.S. return to the gold standard.

While it might appear to be desirable to go back to the price and income level of 1940, or some other relatively stable time, this would be impossible without great disruptions to our economy. If and when the Contax Plan were adopted, it should be administered so as to disrupt the economy and price levels as little as possible at that time. Its purpose is to stabilize prices, to prevent their continued increase, to avoid sharp deflation and depression, and to see that consumers and taxpayers get a fair deal.

Prices of many items, particulary land, are artificially high because many people want them as a hedge against future inflation. With the control of inflation, land values will decline, possibly in some places as much as 60–70%. While some people will get hurt, the majority will benefit through lower rents, lower prices for housing units, and lower prices at the supermarkets.

The Contax Plan is not set up to go into a market to support the price of a commodity; it should neither have the funds nor have any responsibility for price supports.

Price supports are a form of minimum compensation for the farmer, as would national job evaluation rates be for employed people. However, price supports have been used as political footballs, and often have been higher than a protective minimum price should be. Unfortunately costs of production vary widely even from farm to adjoining farm, and from farmer to farmer. One farmer can make a handsome income selling to the government at price support levels; another cannot break even.

Right now there are too many inefficient, underequipped, undercapitalized farmers on marginal land, for which they may have paid an excessive price, or a confiscating inheritance tax. They expect the government to rescue them from this hopeless situation. The government has generally done so, at the taxpayers expense. This adds to inflation.

The Contax Plan is aimed at stopping inflation without the destruction created by present ineffective programs being tried. If it stops inflation without causing deflation, which it can do, many of the other inequities and problems will be solved.

CHAPTER 13

Is the Contax Plan
Anti-Worker?

The Contax Plan's major aim is to develop a permanent and equitable anti-inflationary system of determining compensation for all working and investing Americans. The unions are not to blame for compensation–cost–push inflation any more than a fox in a henhouse is to blame for killing hens. If there is blame it should be placed on the legislators who set up and perpetuated the system giving unions and letting others have the power to set their own compensation.

The Contax Plan seeks to eliminate the present system of determining compensation, in which compensation bears no relation to the value of the services rendered. The person doing the paying, consumer or taxpayer, has no choice but to pay or go without. Today most unions are able, within limits, to increase the compensation of their members without regard to the value of the service rendered. Other groups have acquired similar power.

This power is the major cause of our prolonged period of inflation. It is grossly unfair to those who do not have the power. It is a power that can result in complete deval-

uation of the dollar. What will happen to this nation—
its political, social, and economic structure—when that
cataclysm occurs is hard to predict. In the past when
the currency of a small or medium-sized country reached
such a point, other nations came to its rescue. When the
value of U.S. currency dwindles to practically nothing,
the currencies of most other nations will be seriously
affected. In most democratic countries with popularly-
elected governments, compensation–cost–push inflation
will have gone as far as in the United States. When this
point is reached in the U.S., there will be no other democratic nation large enough to come to our rescue. Russia
may set the terms.

The Contax Plan seeks to protect everyone, including
union members, from this disaster. We cannot expect
unions of their own volition to give up this power.

By taking away the power of groups to determine their
own compensation, the Contax Plan is protecting the so-
cio-economic-political system under which most Americans, including union members, have prospered during
the last 200 years. Under any other system, union power
and real union compensation would be much lower, and
freedom would be greatly limited. Even though the Contax Plan will be difficult medicine to take, it will cure
present ills. With between five and ten million people
out of work or working only a few days a week, union
members are suffering. The percentage of union members out of work is higher than non-union workers. Unions have priced themselves out of work.

This does not mean there is no place for unions. Protection of workers against favoritism by supervisors, job security, promotion patterns, safety, health, seniority,
working conditions, working hours, hiring and discharge
procedures, discipline procedures, retirement; all are ar-

eas in which workers as a group can function better, with better results for both employer and employee.

The best thing a union could do for its members is to get them to understand that both employer and employees are members of the same team, all trying to make a product or service that customers or taxpayers will buy in sufficient quantities to keep everyone fully employed at his maximum ability. Employees' prosperity depends on the prosperity of the employer company. It might be hard for public employees to see the necessity of satisfying taxpayers with the service they render—until they see that unhappy taxpayers vote down tax levies, public employees lose jobs, and public services deteriorate.

Unions must also realize that protecting the lazy, incompetent, malingering, uncooperative, frequently absent, member is in the long run damaging to every member of the union. It threatens the very existence of both the employer and the union.

It may be difficult for union officials to see far enough ahead to realize the Contax Plan is the solution to their long-range existence. (See 1980–81 correspondence with Douglas Fraser, Analyses 18). However, I believe there are many concerned union members who are appalled at the present situation and realize that union excesses have created great problems. Union officials' primary job has been to get more and more for their members. The Contax Plan will greatly reduce their power and their perks, but they still will have a role under the Contax Plan. Union members will be permanently better off.

CHAPTER 14

What If Some Groups Do Not Go Along?

It is unlikely that legislation could be passed to make the Contax Plan effective until a clear majority of Americans strongly supported it, but even this support would not guarantee that everyone would go along with it. Some groups—for example the already grossly-overpaid construction electricians and plumbers on the West Coast—might refuse to work unless they got another increase. They would picket and otherwise obstruct work in process.

There is no way a free person can be forced to go to work. Every worker on a project or in a factory would be free to quit. If they all quit at the same time it would be the economic equivalent of a strike. However, under the Contax Plan such workers would be considered as quitting. They would give up all fringes normally sacrificed when a person quits, such as seniority, some pension funds, insurances, vacations, etc. If it could be proven that the wholesale refusal to work was perpetuated by a concerted group action, penalties could be assessed against the individuals involved, and/or the union.

"Peaceful" picketing would be illegal, since this would constitute a strike. Under the Contax Plan strikes for economic benefits are illegal. Penalties against picketing and violence or threats of violence, etc., would be established by federal law. People who have quit (non-workers) would receive no public-funded financial support of any type, including unemployment compensation, welfare, food stamps, aid to dependent children, etc. Union strike benefits would also be prohibited.

Employers would be prohibited from rehiring those who had quit except as probationary workers (or whatever classification they use for starting employees) and at starting rates for the skill involved. The employee would receive no credit for previous time worked. If more than 50% of a work force quits, the employer may not grant benefits or change employee classifications so as to increase the average rate of compensation, including fringes, within his operation.

It is conceivable that a group might have such a strangle-hold over the supply of an essential product or service (local services or transportation) that there would be a great temptation to raise the classifications of the workers involved or to otherwise bend the regulations.

If those who quit in no way interfered with other workers who were hired to take their place, no action could be taken against them. Those affected by the shortage of the product or service would just have to sweat it out until the new work force was increased and trained to supply the same level of products or services as before the quit.

Those who quit might picket violently, attack workers, and in effect create a virtual civil war. Using hit-and-run tactics, the individual law breakers could be very difficult to identify. Some in the group of quits might want to continue working, but would be intimidated by others in the group. Every member of the quit group would have to be treated equally. Since they are in effect preventing consumers and taxpayers from receiving a desired product or service, all services to these people might be cut off. The cut-off of services might include utilities, police, fire, and similar local services, schools, etc.

The most effective weapon is economic pressure. With no money coming in from any source, with positive government policies assuring that quitters will gain nothing and lose much; and with proof that such policies can be made to stick, (Air Traffic Controllers) people would be reluctant to try to use group power to satisfy their greed. They must be convinced that they will get increases in real income as productivity increases.

In the next several months after these words are being written some highly-paid unions may be forced to take substantial cuts in compensation, including costly fringes, pensions, etc. just to keep their employers from going bankrupt. Whether the unions will move fast enough to prevent bankruptcy in some large companies is questionable, but if they do and their employers become profitable again, the unions will want a quid-pro-quo catch-up increase in compensation again, and the yearly increase in costs will start all over again.

Other unions whose product or service is still in fair demand at this time will not feel much pressure to reduce their demands for an increase in compensation, let alone take a cut in pay. With inflation continuing they will expect an increase.

If and when the Contax Plan is adopted, militant unions will likely institute strikes and accompanying violence to try to destroy the Contax Plan before it becomes effective, and also to test the strength and resolve of those administering it. If the unions run up against a stone wall, they will adapt themselves to it. Everyone will benefit.

Under the Contax Plan an employer is free to increase the compensation of any and all his employees, as long as group coercion was not used in obtaining that increase, and the increase does not result in an increase in the price of the product or service produced. In general, the producer can increase his prices at any time as long as effective competition exists in his industry. He may reduce prices at any time.

CHAPTER **15**

Will Businessmen Support the Contax Plan?

In 1970 I became acquainted with Heath Larry, who at the time was Vice Chairman of U.S. Steel and chief negotiator for the steel industry with the United Steel Workers union. He, at that time, approved of the Contax Plan.

In 1973 I started giving talks, radio and T-V interviews, etc., to try to get people to realize the seriousness and inevitability of inflation and to do something about it. I wanted to talk to a group of Pittsburgh industrialists. I called Larry to see if he could set up such a meeting.

He turned me down cold. Why? In 1972 the steel industry and the United Steel Workers had signed a no-strike agreement. Before the end of every contract they would get together and agree, or submit the disagreement to binding arbitration. This resulted in some of the most extravagant give-aways in the history of labor negotiations, (see Analysis 4, Chapter 8) but it bought labor peace. It also resulted in cost and price increases which opened the U.S. market wide to foreign competition and prevented the relatively backward U.S. steel industry from earning enough money to modernize plants.

There are three main reasons why most large and medium employers are not likely to openly support the Contax Plan.

1. Employers with unions are afraid to take a public stand that appears to be anti-union.
2. Employers who do not have a union do not want to antagonize union officials, who might mount an organizing campaign against their companies.
3. Businessmen who sell to consumers do not want to antagonize any customers, pro-union, anti-union, black, white, Democrat, Republican, Protestant, Catholic, or Jew. So they take no stand at all on controversial subjects.

The Contax Plan does not propose any restrictions on business as long as there is concrete evidence of fair pricing and competition. Powers to investigate business pricing already exist, so the Contax Plan should need to go no further. U-groups, professionals and others, will be subject to some controls.

At first many companies will withhold support, for the reasons stated above. Individuals working for those firms will be able to support it, but more likely by money rather than by their time. At this stage, time and advocacy are more important than money.

Putting the Contax Plan over requires that millions of individuals take an active part in such an effort. How this might be accomplished is discussed in the next chapter.

CHAPTER **16**

What Can You Do to Stop Inflation?

The first thing you must do is to decide that inflation must be stopped. The second is to resolve that you will do what you can to help stop it. Continuing inflation will destroy your assets and your standard of living. Your children and grandchildren have done nothing to cause this inflation. Your generation and the generation before it are responsible. You do not want to leave the mess to them.

Having decided you want to stop inflation, what do you do next?

Normally when there is a situation that needs attention, Congressmen, Senators, and the Administration are already aware of it and have proposed legislation. They may have heard from one or two percent of their constituents recommending or demanding that legislation be passed on the subject. One or two percent sounds small, but it is still several thousand people per Congressman. Most legislators measure public opinion by the volume of mail, phone calls, telegrams, and personal visits they receive on a subject.

This is why organizations from all points on the political and economic spectrum urge their constituents to contact their legislators whenever critical legislation comes up. Volume is more important than elegance of composition, since Congressmen do not have time to read all their mail. Mail from constituents will practically always get answered, though sometimes with form letters.

The first hurdle is to get legislators to understand the real cause of this prolonged period of inflation. To do so, legislators should read this book. They receive countless books, magazine articles, and newspaper clippings from their constituents and others. They cannot read everything they receive. An assistant may skim through letters, books, etc., and pass along to his boss those he considers important or worth reading.

So the way to start is by writing your legislators a short note. It might say:

> "Inflation will not be stopped by present administration and Federal Reserve policies. Letting people charge more, year after year, for doing the same work or less, or for providing the same services, is the major cause of this 45-year period of inflation. A book, *The Real War On Inflation Has Not Begun* has been sent to you by the author. He analyzes the history of inflation and has developed a sound but difficult to adopt program for stopping inflation permanently. I urge you to read this short book and send me your comments on it."

If you know your legislator your letter can be longer and more personal, but it should contain the above message. You will probably get an acknowledgment of your letter which may say the Congressman has received the book and will read it when he gets time. (I will have sent every Congressman and Senator a copy by the time you receive yours).

If you receive such a letter, wait a month and then write again to find out if he has read it, or to prompt him to read it. If he says he cannot find his copy, let me know. My address is 2982 Brown Road, Ashtabula, Ohio 44004. I would appreciate receiving copies of commenting letters you have received from your legislators.

Congressmen and Senators have in the past generally avoided commenting on the Contax Plan, either pro or con. To favor it would incur the wrath of union officials. Unions make political contributions to Congressmen and Senators of both parties; often their contribution to a Republican incumbent is the largest single contribution received.

Legislators who are union supporters will try to ridicule or suppress the plan. Many others will want to support it but will wait until they see which way the wind blows before taking a public stand. To get the wind blowing in the right direction is up to you. Most legislators will need to receive letters and other contacts from thousands of their constituents to take a stand for the Contax Plan. A one-time flood of letters is not nearly as convincing as a steady flow. You can influence the number of constituents contacting their legislators. Your own contact is important, but getting scores of others to do the same is also a job you can handle.

Explain to your neighbors, friends, and relatives what harm inflation has done to them and to the country, what the eventual outcome of inflation will be, and how the Contax Plan will stop inflation permanently. Get them to read this book. Ask them to write their U.S. legislators and to contact others, both locally and in other Congressional districts and states. Legislators read their local newspapers. You and others can write letters to the editor of your newspaper. You can give talks to local groups, or on the radio and T-V. If you talk to a local group, give the local newspaper a report on your talk promptly. Talk to editors, business and economic reporters and columnists.

You may not feel you have all the data needed or a thorough enough understanding of the Contax Plan to talk and answer questions about it and how it will stop inflation. Write me if you have questions.

If you give a talk, do not be afraid of questions. Most of the audience will be on your side.

Running for local, county, or state office will not give you any power to directly legislate away the cause of this inflation, but if you are elected or make a better-than-expected showing, your U.S. legislators will give more weight to your views. Furthermore, getting elected to an important office can be a step toward becoming a U.S. legislator.

Do not expect everyone to understand the Contax Plan at first and be enthusiastic about it. Gradually people will come around to your way of thinking, but the slowness will be maddening.

An opportunity to show the strength of the Contax Plan concept exists in Congressional districts which have elected strongly pro-union Congressmen term after term. Get nominated by the other party. In the general election incorporate the Contax Plan into your platform. If you receive a larger percentage of votes than previous candidates of your party, it should indicate the Contax Plan has political appeal.

Until the political appeal of the Contax Plan has been proven we cannot expect a candidate in a tightly-contested race to adopt it or even mention it. It is too controversial. The average candidate does not have the time to explain it. The candidate who wins by wide margins probably will not adopt the Contax Plan because he does not need to take stands on controversial subjects to get elected. Some who realize it is the only way to stop inflation will adopt it.

Is it likely that some existing national organization will pick up the Contax Plan and run with it? I doubt it. Several years ago I had two or three meetings with Reed Larson, head of the National-Right-to-Work Committee. He and other members of his staff listened carefully while I presented my story. A director of the N-R-T-W Committee suggested to Larson that I be made a director.

Larson turned the suggestion down. He said I appeared to be very anti-union. His organization maintains it is not anti-union, it is only anti-compulsory unionism. It has been attacked in court many times over the years by union officials. They want to force N-R-T-W to reveal its list of supporters (around 1,500,000 people and firms). They also want the government to cancel its tax exempt status. Larson has successfully defended against these attacks. He probably feels that sponsoring the Contax Plan would increase the risk of unfavorable court action. His organizations are doing an excellent job in a narrow field. I support them but do not expect support from them.

Some conservative organizations might be expected to support the Contax Plan, but there are some aspects of the plan that are anathema to conservatives. They envision National Job Evaluation as creating another huge government bureaucracy. Temporarily it would, but it would eliminate far more government jobs than it would create.

I would welcome inquiries from present reputable national organizations who might be interested in supporting the Contax Plan. I will meet with their officers or boards anywhere to determine if our ideas are compatible and if money donated to them is spent wisely. I am not optimistic.

If there is enough individual interest shown, a national

organization to promote the Contax Plan might be established. This would receive strong financial support from me.

I am not enthusiastic about a national Contax Party with candidates for President and Vice-President. There are now many restrictions which make such an attempt very difficult. In many states a minimum number of registered voters must sign petitions to even get the candidates on the state ballot.

Contax Plan supporters should work within the existing two party system, at least for several years. If a legislator continues to show no inclination for the Contax Plan, an attempt should be made to nominate a Contax Plan supporter in a primary. Each Congressional district is somewhat different than any other, so no fixed program can be applied in all cases. Lots of work and time will be required to make any progress.

Don't be lulled by a slow-down in the rate of inflation. The rate of inflation will vary considerably from month to month, and even from year to year. Bumper crops cause lower food prices, drought the opposite. In a business recession, prices do not go up as fast as when business activity is high—but they still go up, positive proof of compensation–cost–push. Unions and U-groups may not demand as large increases during recessions, but none will give up its power to get more for its members.

It is important that you have studied this book thoroughly enough to be able to explain to others why the other purported remedies for inflation have not, and will not, stop inflation. People will wishfully think that there is some other simpler way to stop inflation. *There is not.* Recent history has proved that.

The Contax Plan, or some similar program, is the only way inflation can be stopped permanently.

The Contax Plan will provide Economic Justice and

a Higher Standard of Living for Everyone. It will not be adopted unless you try to get it adopted. Is this country worth protecting? We spend trillions over a few years to protect it from its external enemies. Protecting it from internal problems which will destroy it is equally important. We do not need bombers, atomic bombs, tanks, submarines, and tremendous taxes to do so. All we need is enough concerned and determined citizens to get the Contax Plan program started and keep it expanding. Millions of Americans have bled and died to provide us this country. We can do a little working and sweating to perpetuate its future, not only in their memory, but also for our own future and the future of our children.

Summary

WHAT WILL THE CONTAX PLAN DO?

WHY IS THE CONTAX PLAN NECESSARY?

WHY DO I HAVE TO GET INVOLVED?

A person attempting to interest others in the Contax Plan needs a concise statement about the Contax Plan to get other people interested in it. Here is such a statement:

What will the Contax Plan do? The Contax Plan will stop inflation, reduce interest rates, help restore business activity and insure economic justice and a gradually improving standard of living for all American consumers and taxpayers.

Why is the Contax Plan necessary? It is necessary because it is the only way inflation can be stopped. If inflation is not stopped it will continue and accelerate until our economic, social, and political system is destroyed. Interest rates will stay high as long as inflation continues.

Why has it not already been adopted? If the Contax Plan will accomplish all this and no other program will, why doesn't the government adopt it and stop inflation once and for all? The Contax Plan requires that groups give up their present powers to force their compensation demands on employers and through them on consumers and taxpayers. Compensation will be determined by the law of supply and demand, with minimum compensation rates for various occupations determined by National Job Evaluation. Legislators do not want to antagonize union bosses by supporting the Contax Plan.

Why do I have to get involved in promoting it? The Contax Plan will be strongly opposed by groups having virtually the power to determine their own compensation. They also have inordinate political power. Most legislators do not want to alienate these groups and will not support the Contax Plan until a large majority of Americans demand that they do so. No present national organization can be expected to support the Contax Plan at this time, so support for it must start in the grass roots, which means you and I must carry the ball to get it started.

Introduction to the Analysis Section

By Angus Ray

This work has been described as "A Book and a Half"; the following section is the "half" portion.

While the main portion of the book traces the development of today's inflation and proposes a viable solution, this section deals with where we are now and postulates procedures that can be useful during the time we victims await the adoption of a permanent cure.

Perhaps you will find yourself in one of the three typical families analyzed in "The Cost of Living—What It Isn't." If not, construct your own econometric model with the worksheet provided.

You might find some useful tips in "Inflation—Can You Fight Back?" In that Great American Institution, the TV Dinner, you pay the equivalent of $10.50 a pound for your cardboard-flavored meat course. There are better ways to go.

You might find hope in the essay on the enormous strides in agricultural research, but frustration in the accounts of pyramiding processing and handling costs standing between the farmer and your table.

There is a note of despair in the account titled, "The Anatomy of a Strike" as well as in the essay on current problems of working people—and what has caused them.

You will find the article by former Congressman Hastings Keith a horror story, but will admire his determination to take steps to change the destructive patterns of the Federal retirement system.

There is something chillingly prophetic in the two articles written by Mr. Morrison in 1965. This time, we had better listen. Not everyone will, of course, as his exchange of correspondence with Douglas Fraser indicates.

Obviously, we have reached a point where others control our destiny. No one can doubt the truism that, "Tyranny begins when good men keep silent."

It is time we raised our voices.

ANALYSIS 7

The Cost of Living . . . What It Isn't

Every month, the Bureau of Labor Statistics of the U.S. Department of Labor publishes an index of retail prices of goods and services. This index is widely reported by the media as the Cost of Living Index. It isn't . . . nor is it intended to be.

The index is officially—and accurately—named the Consumer Price Index. It is described in government publications as measuring, "the price change of a market basket of goods and services over a period of time." The BLS really does a remarkable job of measuring some 382 items that affect all of us, but does not claim to reflect the total "cost of living" change for your family or mine. There is no way it can. There are too many variables.

For example, family expenditures for taxes are not a part of the C.P.I. . . . how could they be? A family with two children and one wage-earner making $15,000 per year pays a completely different percentage of income in taxes than a like family where the wage-earner makes $35,000 per year. Other costs not included in the C.P.I. can differ vastly, too. Suppose the oldest child of each family reaches 18 and graduates from high school. The child of the $15,000 per year family might go to work, while the other family's pride and joy might go to a private college. Net result: the first family loses a tax deduction of $1,000—but has one less person to support. The second keeps the $1,000 deduction but picks up an added expense of some $10,000 a year.

We could cite a host of other variables proving that the Consumer Price Index cannot measure every family's cost-of-living. Does this mean that it is useless to us as individuals? Not at all . . . it can be extremely useful. We just have to adapt it to our own case. This chapter and the next will offer methods you can use to calculate your own cost of living increase as well as ways to ease the pinch of what we must accept as our built-in inflation.

We have discussed what the C.P.I. *is not;* let's talk about what it *is,* where it comes from, and how it is compiled.

TODAY'S CONSUMER PRICE INDEX

The C.P.I. is a statistical average of prices covering items upon which all American families spend money. Prices of some 382 items as divergent as pork chops and tranquilizers, as sport vehicles and toddlers clothing, are monitored in 85 separate areas. Food prices are checked in 2,300 food stores, with total pricings of some 700,000 per year; other retail outlets visited number 19,300, with 675,000 individual pricings per year; some 70,000 rents are checked in 18,000 rental units, and 28,000 property tax quotes are gathered from 18,000 housing units.

These price changes gathered are published monthly for the U.S. as a whole and for the five largest city areas, Chicago, New York City, Detroit, Los Angeles and Philadelphia. Prices (except those of food, fuel and a few other items which are checked monthly) are monitored semi-monthly in smaller cities such as Milwaukee, Scranton, Pa., and Honolulu, as well as in all urban areas with populations of 2,500 or more. The sampling covers some 80% of U.S. families, but omits farm families and those in military service.

The items to be monitored were selected from a Consumer Expenditure Survey conducted in 1972 and 1973, covering about 20,000 families. The particular retail outlets to monitor were picked from a point of purchase survey conducted in 1974, when 23,000 families were asked where they purchased various specific items. The Point of Purchase Survey is being continued by updating the marketplace information for ⅕ of the 85 primary sampling areas each year, so that changes in buying locations nationwide are tracked every five years.

At the time of the last revision in methods of collecting data for the Index, January, 1978, changes in it directly affected the income of some 11 million employees in business and industry, almost 31 million Social Security recipients, about 2½ million retired military and Federal Government employees and survivors, 20 million food stamp recipients as well as a varying number of CETA employees. At that time government statisticians estimated that a rise of 1% in the Index triggered approximately 1 billion dollars in additional payments. The compounding effect of increases over the three years since then has substantially increased this payment level to an almost unbearable burden. The cost to the steel industry alone for the years 1979 and 1980 totalled over 1.3 billion dollars.

How accurate is the C.P.I.? As an index of changes in the cost of living, not very accurate. It is, after all, statistical; it applies to average expenditures on items it *does* cover for a nation of some 220 million people.

Yours would not be an "average" family. In fact there can be no "average" family, except in the realm of the statisticians. This does not mean that we cannot use the concepts upon which the Index is based.

ORIGINS AND CONCEPTS—THE C.P.I.

Federal agencies have published data on prices for almost 100 years. Studies of family expenditures for the years 1888–1890 appeared in the 1890 Annual Report of the Commissioner of Labor. The first C.P.I. was born of a decision by The Shipbuilding Labor Adjustment Board during World War I to attempt to reach a "fair wage scale" in shipyards; a wage scale that would increase as prices rose. During 1918 and 1919 the Board investigated buying habits in 92 shipbuilding and industrial cities and monitored prices of some 145 commodities in 32 cities. In February, 1921, regular publication of the National Consumer Price Index was begun. The collected data were originally—and erroneously called— cost-of-living indexes. In the minds of most people, that name still sticks. Structurally, the concept is easy to understand. It is based on a "market basket" which cost $100 when purchased during a given year, which is known as the "base year." Changes in the cost of this market basket are expressed in dollars. For example, if prices were to increase such that the Index figure for "All Items" (see Table #1 page 286) stood at 110 at the end of the first year following the base year, the increase would be $10, or 10%. If the index stood at 120 at the end of the following year, representing a further $10 increase, the *percentage* increase would be 9.091% for the second-year period.

There have been many revisions over the years, and the base period has changed several times. The present base period is 1967 (1967 = 100); this is due to change in 1982 to a base period of 1977 = 100.

The tables included in this chapter show that the $100.00 1967 market basket of goods and services, labeled "All Items," had increased in cost to $280.70 by November, 1981. A close look shows that the index for nonalcoholic beverages increased from a base of 100 to 411.9, while alcoholic beverages increased only to 195.9. It would be easy to jump to the conclusion that you would save money by drinking more booze and less pop.

"Weighting" in the Index means assigning percentages of relative importance to the items monitored as a percentage of the total cost of the "market basket." Since no family uses all of the 382 items, the Index groups them into seven main categories: food and beverages, housing, apparel and upkeep, transportation, medical care, entertainment, and a miscellany called "other goods and services." For those who enjoy data-wading, all the detail is available. It reminds us though, of the little boy who told the librarian he wanted to learn something about frogs. She found him a book that gave voluminous detail on frogs; the many species with their Latin as well as popular names; the life-cycle and development stages of each type, etc. When he returned the book, the librarian asked him how he liked it. His reply . . . "There's more about frogs in this book than I really want to know."

A quick scan of the detail can have value, however, in assessing our own cost effects. As we will see, we do have some choices that can affect our own *cost* of living without significant changes in our *standard* of living.

YOUR PERSONAL COST OF LIVING

Thus far, we have looked at the C.P.I. as an ongoing statistical study of changes in prices gathered, at no small cost to taxpayers, by an army of investigators, and used principally to adjust wages and benefits being received by some 65 million of our 223 million people. Where does that leave the other 158 million Americans? Frankly . . . in trouble. But how much trouble?

Today's numbers can scare you to death. By the actuaries "Rule of 72," an increase in the *actual* cost of living . . . which the C.P.I. does *not* represent . . . of 10% per year would double this cost in 7 years, 3 months, and 1 week. And 1980's C.P.I. increase was 12.4%. Figures such as these have spawned a number of best-sellers by the "doom and gloom boys" and a new cult called the "survivorists."

Our government, in its various spasms of paternalism, has created a monster in trying to be fair to shipbuilding labor 54 years ago. It is easy to understand why organized labor . . . with its sympathetic stooge, the National Labor Relations Board, interpreting the rules . . . has pushed for inclusion of Cost of Living Adjustments (COLA) in its contracts. Industries, particularly steel, automotive, mining, and trucking, have knuckled under to this coalition of labor and government . . . prices could always be raised to cover COLA cost.

Today, at last, people are beginning to see the end results of riding this wild horse. The steps being proposed in Washington are going to help . . . a little, and slowly. But . . . we are going to be faced with escalating costs, and we need to know what they will be for us personally. Let's look at three sample families:

The Lezaks

John Lezak, age 35, works in a plant as an operator, and earns $15,000 a year. His wife, Mary, is also 35. She keeps house and takes care of their two children, ages 9 and

13. They live in an older 3-bedroom apartment, rent $250 per month, in the city of 25,000 people where John's plant is located. They have two cars, one 2 years old, with payments of $165 per month with two more years to pay, driven 10,000 miles per year; the other a "clunker" that John drives to work, paid for, and driven 2,000 miles per year. Automobile insurance costs $325, with no collision coverage on the "clunker." Heat is furnished for their apartment; water and electricity average $43 per month. Mary picks up beer for John at the grocery, and their total food and beverage cost averages $48 per week.

This amount may seem low to many of today's housewives, but Mary Lezak is an "old country" cook. She uses a minimum of prepared foods, does her own baking, etc. Also, some items such as toilet articles are included in the category of other goods and services. This miscellaneous expense runs $450 per year. Household furnishings and supplies such as cleaning materials, fall into a separate category at $311 for 1980.

John's employer pays for John's medical insurance, and part of that for his family; he pays the difference of $30 per month. Last year, they spent $440 on clothing and dry-cleaning. John and Mary both belong to bowling leagues and John plays golf about once a week at a public course. These expenses, plus an occasional movie and outings for the children, amounted to about $375 last year.

The listing that follows shows how the Lezaks spent their income during 1980. First, we have to boil down the $15,000 that John earns to what economists term "disposable" income by taking out Federal, State and local income taxes of $1,541.00 and FICA (Social Security) withholdings of $997.50. This leaves them with disposable, or spendable, income of $12,461.50. The percentages shown, however, are of their income actually spent.

THE LEZAK'S PERSONAL COST OF LIVING

Category	Relative Importance	Detail	Dollars Expended
Food & Beverages	21.07%		$ 2,496
Housing			
Rent		$3,000	
Tenant's Insurance		125	
			3,125
Fuel & Other Utilities	4.36%		516
Household Furnishings & Supplies	2.62%		311
TOTAL HOUSING	33.36%		$ 3,952
Apparel & Upkeep	3.71%		440
Transportation			
Car Payments		1,980	
Gasoline			
Family Car 10,000 mi.			
× $1.36/gal. = 16 mi./gal.		850	
John's Clunker 2,000 mi.			
× $1.31/gal. = 14 mi./gal.		187	
Auto Insurance		325	
Maintenance and Repairs		210	
TOTAL TRANSPORTATION	29.99%		3,552
Medical Care			
Hospitalization Insurance		360	
Uninsured & Dental Care		220	
TOTAL MEDICAL	4.90%		580
Entertainment	3.17%		375
Other Goods & Services	3.80%		450
TOTAL EXPENDED	100%		$11,845

These basic costs leave the Lezaks $616.50 or about 4.95% of their income for savings or discretionary spending on such items as life insurance, vacations, etc.

The Lezaks were picked . . . or invented . . . as a *typical* blue-collar family. To emphasize the hypothesis that there is no "average" blue-collar family, we can compare the percentage of John's disposable income to the "Relative Importance" column, Table #1 page 286, showing the action of the C.P.I. from February, 1980 to February, 1981.

A look at this comparison shows that the Lezaks "relative importance" differs widely from C.P.I. figures in two principal categories: housing and transportation.

Category	Table #1 Relative Importance	Lezak Family % of Expended Income
Food & Beverages	18.309	21.07
Housing (Shelter)	31.650	33.36
Fuel & Other Utilities	6.550	4.36
Household Furnishings & Operation	7.319	2.62
Apparel & Upkeep	4.854	3.71
Transportation	18.955	29.99
Medical Care	4.717	4.90
Entertainment	3.647	3.17
Other Goods & Services	3.999	3.80

In the above table, the "Housing" category has been broken down into sub-parts from Table #1's total of a relative importance of 45.519, which is the sum of the Tables' "Shelter," "Fuel and Other Utilities" and "Household Furnishings and Operations." In the Lezak's case, total housing costs have a relative importance of 40.34. This difference occurs because the index attempts to factor in home purchase costs as well as rental costs of living. If the Lezaks lived in a large city, their housing costs would probably be greater, but greater availability of public transit facilities could eliminate the need for two cars and lower the miles driven per year on their family car. At today's fuel and replacement costs, this could lower their transportation costs measurably. Figures from the American Automobile Association indicate that the final cost of driving the average late-model car is about 33¢ per mile. Again, "average" would combine a Cadillac and a Chevette, so we have to make our own adjustments. Some averages are like the old French recipe for horse-and-rabbit stew: equal parts . . . 1 horse . . . 1 rabbit.

One minor category, "Household Furnishings and Operation," also shows considerable variation. A glance at the detail in C.P.I. Table #1 page 286 shows that housekeeping *services* comprise almost 2% of this 7.319% expense. Since Mary does her own housecleaning, this frill can be eliminated.

So far, we find that the Lezaks have—like most of us—spent about 95% of their income. Since we are concerned with price changes, which has meant sharp increases in recent years, let's look at the effect of a C.P.I. increase of the same 11.3% for 1981 as that which occurred over the past 12 months, February, 1980 to February, 1981. We will use the C.P.I. percentages where they apply to the Lezak's and footnote any that probably will not apply.

Category	Lezaks' Cost	CPI % Increase	Lezaks' New Cost
Food & Beverages	$ 2,496	10.5%	$ 2,760
Housing	3,125	8.8[1]	3,400
Fuel & Other Utilities	516	15.8	598
Household Furnishings & Operation	311	11.8[2]	348
Apparel & Upkeep	440	5.9	466
Transportation	3,452	$1,037 × 14.9[3] 210 × 10.5	3,628
Medical Care	480	9.6	636
Entertainment	375	9.6	411
Other Goods & Services	450	9.3	492
TOTAL	$11,645		$12,739

[1] Used figure for rental increase
[2] Used figure for household supplies
[3] Used % increases for gasoline and maintenance—payments and insurance will remain the same.

From these figures we find that the Lezak's expenditures would increase by $1,094 over the year, which would result in an actual cost of living increase of 9.39% vs. the 11.3% increase indicated by the index. If John were covered by a typical union contract with a COLA clause offsetting 80 to 90% of the C.P.I. increase, he would get a raise of about $1,500. Even after allowing for taxes, the Lezaks are money ahead, without any lowering of their standard of living. As indicated, the income increase for this family is the result of the COLA factor only. If this happened to be the year in which John's union contract were re-negotiated, he could count on an additional hourly increase of say, 8–10%, which would add about another $1,200 to $1,500 to his gross income, *and* would introduce another level to his COLA-compounded total for future years.

It is easy to see why millions of people in similar income brackets who have had to lower their living standards in these inflationary times resent the fact that union COLA agreements are fueling inflation.

The Haldersons

Tom and Beth Halderson live in the same small Midwestern city as the Lezaks, but in a different econosphere. Tom, 38 years old, is sales manager for a large industrial supply company at a salary of $35,000 per year plus a liberal expense account. Beth, in addition to her housekeeping duties, spends a good part of her time in activities such as Junior League volunteer work and in transporting their two children, ages 12 and 15, to and from school functions, dance and tennis lessons, etc.; in short, being a typical suburban housewife. Their income, though not large by many standards, is considered Upper Middle for their city.

They budget $95 per week for food and beverages, which includes an occasional dinner out and about $15 per week for Tom's lunches that are not covered by his expense account.

They bought their 3 bedroom Colonial-style home six years ago for $60,000 (it would sell for $100,000 now) with a $20,000 downpayment and a $40,000 mortgage at 10% interest. Taxes are $1,050 per year; insurance, including a "valuable objects" rider covering silverware and Beth's jewelry, costs $360 per year. Mortgage payments are $386.40 per month, $4,636.80 per year, of which approximately $3,425 goes for interest and $1,211.60 to principal. At present, they owe $34,793.60, giving them a present-value equity of about $65,206. Maintenance and repairs average $400 per year. Their gas bill, including heat, hot water and a gas clothes dryer, is on a monthly budget billing of $52, totaling $624 per year. The electric bill totals $360 per year; other utilities run $325 per year. Beth's cleaning woman charges $4.50 per hour and comes in for six hours each week, which amounts to an annual cost of $1,482, including Social Security. Cleaning supplies cost $157 for the past year.

In 1980 the family spent $1,080 for apparel and upkeep.

Tom's employer provides him with a company car, one of the most popular "perks" in today's business world. Ostensibly, the car is for making business calls, but as is the case with most company cars, he can use it for personal driving. Operational costs for this car, including gasoline, are paid by the company. The Haldersons replaced "Beth's car" last month, with $8,650 of the purchase price financed over three years at payments of $320.83 per month. This, their family car, is driven about 8,000 miles per year.

Tom's company pays the same percentage of his family's medical insurance as John Lezak's, so his cost is the same; $360 per year. Medical expenses not covered and dental care cost $260 during 1980. (Fortunately, both the children had straight teeth).

Entertainment is a bigger item for the Haldersons than for the Lezaks. The Haldersons' entertain mainly at the local country club. As in most small cities, the club is much less expensive than those in metropolitan areas. Tom's company pays the "men's single" amount of his membership, $1,100, while Tom pays the additional $350 for a full family membership. The family's expenditures at the country club, including occasional meals, parties, golf carts, etc., run about $1,000 per year. The family spends another $400 per year on movies, entertainment items while on vacation trips, and other incidental recreational costs.

Under the C.P.I. category, "Other Goods and Services," the Haldersons spent $1,100 for miscellaneous personal care, toilet goods, tennis lessons, school supplies, etc. Tom also carries life insurance on the balance of his mortgage and a policy on his life to provide for Beth and at least part of the childrens' future college costs, at an added cost of $1,050 per year.

As is apparent from a look at the contrasts between the life-styles of the Haldersons and the Lezaks, there are three basic differences:

1. The Haldersons own their home while the Lezaks rent;
2. The two families travel in different social spheres, with part of the added cost subsidized by Tom's expense account, and;
3. Tom Halderson will not automatically receive a COLA increase.

Housing costs have always been a headache for the Bureau of Labor Statistics. In preparing comparable tables for our two families, the housing category for the Haldersons must contain components not applicable to the Lezaks. It creates a difference in the way the two families file their income taxes as well. John Lezak pays his taxes using the standard deduction tables; Tom Halderson, principally because of the $3,425 he pays this year in mortgage interest, files the long form. Using the standard deduction tables, he would pay a total of $7,691 in Federal, State, and local taxes. When he includes interest and other deductions, this total reduces to $6,865. He pays the maximum FICA (Social Security) of $1,975. His disposable income is reduced from the $35,000 gross to $26,160. This represents a drop of 25.26% compared to John Lezak's tax and FICA bite of 16.92%.

As we can see, Tom starts out at a percentage disadvantage compared with John Lezak, and this in a category not recognized by the C.P.I. Our first table for the Halder-

THE HALDERSON'S PERSONAL COST OF LIVING

Category	Relative Importance	Cost (Detail)	Total Dollars Expended
Food & Beverages	19.76%		$4,940
Housing:			
House Payments		$4,637	
Real Estate Taxes		1,050	
Homeowners Insurance		460	
Gas		624	
Electricity		360	
Other Utilities		325	
Property Maintenance		400	
Cleaning & Supplies		1,639	
TOTAL HOUSING	37.98%		9,495
Apparel & Upkeep	4.32%		1,080
Transportation			
Car Payments		3,850	
Gasoline—8,000 mi.			
× $1.36 per gal. =			
18 mi. per gallon		604	
Car Insurance		370	
Maintenance & Repairs		140	
TOTAL Transportation	19.86%		4,964
Medical Care			
Hospitalization Insurance		360	
Uninsured & Dental Care		260	
TOTAL Medical	2.48%		620
Entertainment	7.00%		1,750
Other Goods & Services	8.60%		2,150
TOTAL Expended	100%		$24,989

sons will show the similarities—and differences—related to the two families.

The final total shows that the Haldersons have $1,271 left after these basic expenditures, or about 4.9% of their disposable income, and out of this must come United Way and church donations, etc. True, they will have reduced the mortgage loan on their house by about $1,200, which increases their equity, but . . . equity in a house does not provide cash income to offset rising costs . . . unless you sell the house. Nor does increased equity due to rising housing prices . . . you still have to live somewhere.

If we compare the Haldersons percentages of disposable income to the Relative Importance figures in the Bureau of Labor Statistics Table #1 page 286, we arrive at this analysis:

Category	Table #1 Relative Importance	Halderson Family % of Expended Income
Food & Beverages	18.309	19.76%
Housing (Total)	45.519	37.98%
Apparel & Upkeep	4.854	4.32%
Transportation	18.955	19.86%
Medical Care	4.717	2.48%
Entertainment	3.647	7.00%
Other Goods & Services	3.999	8.60%

Again, we are looking at a typical "Upper Middle" family. The housing category shows a widely divergent dollar cost. Had the Haldersons bought their house in late 1980 instead of six years before, at the $100,000 appreciated price and at an interest rate on a larger mortgage at 15% interest rather than 10%, the relative importance could easily match that given by the index. The attempt to factor housing purchase costs into the index accounts for one of the largest inaccuracies of the C.P.I.

The variations in expenses for entertainment and other goods and services reflect differences in life style and the fact that the C.P.I. market basket contains no provision for substantial amounts of life insurance.

Since we are analyzing price *changes* for specific family units rather than the static effect of prices, let's see how the Haldersons will fare if the 1981 C.P.I. figures should be comparable to those in the past 12 months.

Category	Halderson's Cost 1980	C.P.I. % Increase	Halderson's New Cost 1981
Food & Beverages	$4,940	10.5%	$ 5,434
Housing:			
House Payments	4,637		4,637
Real Estate Taxes	1,050		1,050
Homeowner's Insurance	460		460
Gas & Electricity	984	15.8	1,139
Other Utilities	325	7.6	350
Property Maintenance	400	10.6	442
Cleaning & Supplies	1,639	8.0	1,770
TOTAL HOUSING	9,495	12.1[1]	9,848
Apparel & Upkeep	1,080	5.9	1,144
Transportation:			
Car Payments	3,850		3,850
Gasoline	604	14.9	694
Insurance	370		370
Maintenance & Repairs	140	10.5	155
TOTAL TRANSPORTATION	4,964	13.1[2]	5,069
Medical Care	620	9.6	680
Entertainment	1,760	9.6	1,929
Other Goods & Services	2,150	9.3	2,252[3]
TOTAL EXPENDED	$25,009		$26,356

[1] Although the cost of housing, the largest category by relative importance in the C.P.I., increased 12.1% in the 1980 period, the Halderson's dollars expended increased only 3.53%.

[2] Halderson's car payments and insurance remained the same.

[3] Increase applies only to miscellaneous amount, $1,100; Tom's life insurance premium remains the same.

We find that the Haldersons spent just over 95% of their disposable income . . . very near the National average. Surprisingly, we find that their basic cost of living increased only 5.31% between the 1980 and 1981 period. How could this be . . . with the C.P.I. up by 11.3%?

The biggest part of the difference lies in the housing category. The C.P.I. attempts to break this category into components that relate to both renters and homeowners, and to factor into their figures widely varying costs for utilities, mortgage interest costs, taxes, insurance, etc. If we check our table comparing the C.P.I.'s relative importance figures with the Halderson's percent of disposable income, the difference is only 9.6%. But . . . we are pinpointing the *changes* in cash expended year-to-year. The largest single increase in the C.P.I. housing category over the past 12 months is in the sub-group, "financing, taxes and insurance," which grew 18.9%. The heaviest component was interest cost. Tom's mortgage loan stays at 10%; his taxes will not increase until his property is reappraised or the voters approve an added levy . . . which is rare in these times, and; his insurance will probably stay the same until he feels the replacement cost of his house merits more coverage.

No wonder the B.L.S. keeps tinkering with the housing component of the index.

It could be argued that, since part of Tom's payments reduce the balance of his mortgage loan, his cost of living is actually decreased by that amount, but it doesn't work that way. He is building his equity and, in the parlance of bank trust officers, "increasing his estate," but; his year-to-year cost of living is a "cash flow" account. No matter how much his house would sell for, he still has to expend cash to live.

A similar argument could be advanced for Beth's new car. At the end of 3 years it will be paid for, but it will have depreciated in value. Perhaps they can get a year or two of payment-free use from it, but in 5 years its replacement cost, if the C.P.I. figures on new cars hold true, could be about 30% more than it cost last month.

Unless Tom gets a raise, they will have to cut back

expenses somewhere or go in the red by a few dollars this year. Tom does not have a COLA agreement that guarantees an increase. If the company is having a good year . . . and a good many are not . . . he may receive the 8% raise being granted by a number of companies. This would add $2,800 to his gross; about $1,680 to his disposable income in his tax bracket. But, his added cost of Social Security payments due to the increase scheduled for 1982 will be $216, up from $1,975 to $2,190.

It is easy to see that, even for a successful young executive receiving a salary increase, Tom must . . . like Lewis Carroll's Alice . . . "run faster and faster just to stay in the same place."

The Edmonds

Joe and Helen Edmond—both 66—have reached the final plateau of The American Dream. Joe worked in the office of the same company that employs Tom Halderson, and rose to the position of office manager the last few years of his employment. Joe retired just over a year ago. He and Helen draw a total of $550 per month, or $6,600 per year, in Social Security benefits.

Benefits from the company pension plan amount to $8,400 per year, giving them a total annual income of $15,000. Income taxes are not much of a problem for the Edmonds; with their double deductions in their over-65 bracket, and the tax-free status of their Social Security benefits, they pay only $158, which leaves them disposable income of $14,842. They have a small savings account for emergencies. They thought their savings would be more of a cushion, but decided to buy a new car when Joe retired. This car, as they say, "must last us 10 years."

Their two children have been self-supporting for some time now.

The Edmonds own a modest house in a neighborhood

halfway between those of the Lezaks and the Haldersons. The house is paid for, and would be valued today at about $40,000. Real estate taxes run $570 per year, and homeowners insurance is $150. Joe does most of his own maintenance, and his cost for materials such as paint, weedkiller, etc., averages $250 per year. They heat with gas and have a gas water heater and clothes dryer, costing, on a monthly budget billing, $44. Their electric bill averages $30 per month, and telephone and water bills total another $25 per month . . . (this includes occasional calls to talk to the grandchildren). Housekeeping supplies amount to about $180 per year.

They drive their new car about 6,000 miles per year, and are disappointed in the 18 miles per gallon they get from it, since the estimated mileage should average 22; but their driving, except for occasional visits to the children, is mostly local. Automobile insurance, with their safe-driving and senior citizens discounts, costs $200 per year, and maintenance costs them $75 per year. This might seem high maintenance for a new car, but they buy all the manufacturer-recommended services . . . it has to last 10 years!

Joe and Helen eat out with friends a couple of times a week. Their meals at home are good but not gourmet, so they usually meet their food and beverage budget of $60 per week.

Wearing apparel is not as big a budget item as it was. Nowadays, its a special occasion when Joe wears a suit and tie. The clothing they replace, together with dry cleaning and incidental costs, averages about $330 per year.

Medical expenses have not changed much since Joe's working days. True, they are *partly* covered by Medicare–Part "A," for catastrophic illness, but they paid $9.60 per month each for Part "B," and this increases in July,

1981, to $11. Also, the Medicare plans do not cover all expenses (i.e.: prescription drugs, dental costs), while Joe's coverage under his company's plan did pay at least a part of these. And there is a deductible amount under Medicare for hospitalization costs, currently $204 for 1981 . . . up from $180 in 1980. This deductible amount will increase as medical costs grow. This is a real worry for the Edmonds. So far, they have been lucky.

For years Joe had played in a company golf league every Wednesday, and with a foursome on Saturday. Helen was a regular member of the ladies day group on Tuesday morning. Since Joe's retirement, they have taken a family membership at a local municipal course, which costs them . . . with a senior citizen's discount . . . $240 for the season. Other entertainment costs, movies, an occasional concert, having friends in for bridge, etc., add another $250 to their "fun" budget.

The Edmonds, after many years of "watching the pennies" while the children were growing up, now allow themselves a 2-week vacation trip to a beach resort in the mid-South during early Spring. Their "efficiency" quarters cost $250 per week at out-of-season rates, and they spend one night on the road each way. Altogether, this vacation costs about $1,000 over and above their normal costs for food, entertainment, etc., and accounts for 1,800 of the 6,000 miles they put on their car each year. This gives them a total in the category of entertainment of $1,490.

For the last of the C.P.I. categories, "Other Goods and Services," Joe and Helen spent $600 for miscellaneous personal goods such as cigarettes, toilet goods and articles, gifts, etc., and another $400 for the premium on a $15,000 "whole life" insurance policy on Joe's life with Helen as beneficiary. This policy is to supplement the 50% survivors benefit Helen will receive from Joe's com-

pany pension if he dies first, and the decreased benefit
she would receive under Social Security.

Let's take a look at the Edmonds' current cost-of-living
as we did for the other families, the Lezaks and the Haldersons, again using percentages of expended income as
"relative importance."

THE EDMONDS' PERSONAL COST OF LIVING

Category	Relative Importance	Cost (Detail)	Total Dollars Expended
Food & Beverages	32.04%		$3,120
Housing			
Taxes		$570	
Homeowner's Insurance		160	
Gas		528	
Electricity		360	
Other Utilities		300	
Property Maintenance		250	
Cleaning & Supplies		180	
TOTAL HOUSING	24.11%		2,348
Apparel & Upkeep	3.39%		330
Transportation			
Gasoline—8,000 miles ×			
1.36 = 18 mi. per gal.		604	
Car Insurance		200	
Maintenance & Repairs		75	
TOTAL TRANSPOR-TATION	9.02%		879
Medical Care			
Medicare–Part "B"			
9.60 × 2 × 12 months		230	
Uninsured & Dental Care		40	
TOTAL MEDICAL CARE	5.86%		570
Entertainment	15.30%		1,490
Other Goods & Services	10.28%		1,000
TOTAL EXPENDED	100%		$9,737

We find that the Edmonds, with the same gross income
as the Lezaks, end up the year with $5,105 unspent, in

contrast with the Lezak's $616.50. What accounts for the difference?

First . . . taxes and FICA costs.

Lezaks	$2,538.50
Edmonds	158.00
DIFFERENCE	$2,380.50

The Edmonds, with $6,600 tax-free, and double deductions totaling $4,000 from their pension benefits, only pay taxes on the remaining $4,400 *after* the standard taxtable deduction allowance.

Next: housing and transportation. The Edmonds are reaping the benefits of home ownership after years of house payments. And they don't have the burden of $1,980 in car payments. True, they might have to replace their car before the ten years they hope it will last, but then, so will the Lezaks. Actually, most American families purchase their automobiles on a "buy as you drive" basis during their earning years, and any equity they accrue in todays car usually becomes at best a down payment on tomorrows.

A look at how the Edmonds percentages of expended income contrasts with the relative importance column of the Index shows how inapplicable it is to the retired couple.

Category	Table #1-pg. 286 Relative Importance	Edmonds Family % of Expended Income
Food & Beverages	18.309	32.04%
Housing (Total)	45.519	24.11%
Apparel & Upkeep	4.854	3.39%
Transportation	18.955	9.02%
Medical Care	4.717	5.86%
Entertainment	3.647	15.30%
Other Goods & Services	3.999	10.28%

Next, let's look at the effect of an increase in the coming 12 months equivalent to the past period on the Edmonds living costs.

Category	Edmond's Cost 1980	C.P.I. % Increase	Edmond's New Cost
Food & Beverages	$3,120	10.5	$ 3,448
Housing			
Taxes	570		570
Homeowner's Insurance	160		160
Gas & Electricity	888	15.8%	1,028
Other Utilities	300	7.6%	323
Property Maintenance	250	10.7%[1]	277
Cleaning & Supplies	180	8.0%	194
TOTAL HOUSING	$2,348	12.1%[2]	$ 2,552
Apparel & Upkeep	330	5.9%	350
Transportation			
Gasoline	604	14.9%	694
Insurance	200		200
Maintenance & Repairs	75	10.5%	83
TOTAL TRANSPORTATION	$ 879	13.1%	$ 977
Medical Care			
Medicare–Part "B"			
2 people at $9.60			
per month—12 months	230		247[3]
Uninsured & Dental	340	9.6%	373
TOTAL MEDICAL CARE	$ 570		$ 620
Entertainment	$1,490	9.6%	$ 1,633
Other Goods & Services	$1,000	9.3%	$ 1,056[4]
TOTAL EXPENDED	9,737		$10,636

[1] Figure used is increase in materials . . . Joe furnishes labor.
[2] Edmonds cost increase is 8.2% since taxes and insurance do not change.
[3] Reflects cost increase from $9.60 to $11.00 for 6 months.
[4] Increase affects only $600 of category. Life insurance premium remains constant.

Apparently, Joe and Helen Edmond are going to do well, even in these inflationary times, with a semi-fixed income. There is a basic difference, however, between their situation and that of the other two families.

For example, John Lezak might become a foreman and move into a higher bracket. Tom Halderson hopes to be named a vice president, which would make him eligible for a bonus in future years. Joe Edmond knows, on the other hand, that his income will increase only by the increment provided by the Social Security C.P.I.-based bonus each year. He cannot count on future raises in pay to replace the family car, or a washing machine that gives out. But . . . their savings, plus any interest those savings earn, appear substantial enough to insure a comfortable future.

Since a chief area of concern about the rising cost of living is its effect upon retired people, let's chart the progress of the Edmonds for the ten years following retirement. To make this meaningful, we will make a series of "worst case" assumptions:

1. The C.P.I. will continue at the same 11.3% level that it shows from February, 1981 to February, 1982;
2. The Edmonds Social Security checks *averaged* $550 per month during 1980;
3. They will receive income on their savings at rates comparable to those available on bank certificates of deposit today, approximately 12%, and; they will not invest their unspent income until the end of each calendar year, starting with the $5,105 they were able to save by the end of 1980.
4. They will experience tax "bracket creep" on their investment income, but the first $400.00 of such income is exempt from the long arm of the IRS, and taxes are calculated using standard Federal tax tables;
5. The last assumptions are that the Social Security COLA percentage continues to follow the present pattern and that income tax rates remain the same as today.

After a cursory look at the figures on the chart of the Edmonds' future, many people would say, "That's impossible!" But it isn't. We might agree that it is *improbable,*

Income

Year	Company Pension	Social Security Jan. thru June	Social Security July thru Dec.	Investment Income	Income Taxes	Net Income	Expended	Saved	Net Financial Position
1980	$8,400	$6,600			$ 158	$14,842	$ 9,737	$5,105	$ 5,105
1981	8,400	$3,300	$3,670	$ 613	188	15,795	10,636	5,159	10,264
1982	8,400	3,670	4,085	1 232	274	17,033	11,621	5,412	15,679
1983	8,400	4,085	4,547	1 882	373	18,541	12,697	5,844	21,529
1984	8,400	4,547	5,061	2 584	486	20,106	13,873[1] / 72	6,161	27,696
1985	8,400	5,061	5,633	3,324	604	21,814	15,230	6,584	34,286
1986	8,400	5,633	6,270	4,115	741	23,677	16,634	7,043	41,335
1987	8,400	6,270	6,979	4,961	893	25,717	18,168[2] / 10,360	(2,799)	38,530
1988	8,400	6,979	7,768	4,624	832	26,939	19,833[3] / 751	6,355	44,891
1989	8,400	7,768	8,646	5,388	970	29,232	21,652	7,580	52,477
1990	8,400	8,646	9,623	6,153	1,108	31,795	23,456[4] / 4,840	3,499	55,982[5]

[1] A reappraisal of the Edmond house increased real estate taxes by $48.00 per year, and they increased insurance coverage at an added cost of $24.00 per year. This is added to their base expenses and is in excess of their 9.26% personal cost of living increase. This will add $72.00 per year to their costs; but; since it does not increase each year, will *not* change their factor, at least until the next reappraisal.

[2] What happened? Things were going along so nicely! Well . . . the car didn't last 10 years. It had cost $7,500 at the beginning of 1980, but eight years price increases at 5.4%, compounded, had increased the selling price of its replacement to $11,422. Sales tax had increased to 8%, adding $913.00, and the dealer's title fee of $25.00 brought the net cost, after a $2,000 trade-in allowance, to $10,360. This expenditure is non-recurring, but we will have to add the higher cost of $112.00 for increased car insurance to each succeeding year.

[3] This year, 1988, Helen spent 15 days in the hospital. The hospital room and services would have cost $200.00 per day in 1981, but the 9.4% annual increase shown in Table #1 for Medical Services had boosted this to $410.25 a day, or a total of $6,153.75. Medicare paid all of this but the deductible portion, which had *also* increased . . . from $204.00 in 1981 to $418.00 in 1988. The doctors bill was $1,200, of which Helen was charged the deductible . . . up from $60.00 to $117.00, and the 20% of costs in excess of the deductible portion, $216.00. This $751.00 is a nonrecurring expense, and shows no effect on future years. (This assumes that their major medical considered the surgeon's charge "usual"; if not, they could have had to pay the difference.)

[4] By 1990, Joe and Helen have been in retirement for 10 years. Their household appliances, all fairly new when Joe retired, are beginning to develop symptoms, even though not subject to the hard wear they would have endured while the children were at home. They decided to replace the washer, dryer, and television set. The three together cost $2,540 at 1990 prices, or about 60% more than in 1980. The refrigerator should be good for at least another five years. Joe also decided that the roof of their house, new 25 years ago, was on borrowed time. The new one, of good quality 235 # asphalt shingles, would have cost $1,000 in 1981. By early 1990, the cost was $2,300.

[5] We have to consider, however, that the purchasing power of the Edmonds' savings would have to be looked at from the 1990 level, rather than from what it represents today.

because of the old axiom, "spending tends to rise to fit income." It is highly probably that Joe and Helen might spend more freely as they saw their financial picture improving, but they might not . . . these are frugal people who have never become accustomed to high-style living.

We have allowed for built-in increases at the annual rate of 9.26% that their Personal Cost of Living tables indicate they would experience. And . . . there are indications that the rate of inflation might be decreasing, viz., 1979 C.P.I. was 14.3%; 1980 was 11.2%; February 1980–February 1981 shows 11.3%. With negotiated labor rates under union contracts running at a 10% increase, however, there is little indication that the C.P.I. will total much less than double-digit during the next few years.

And then, there is Murphy's Law . . . "Whatever can happen . . . *will* happen." (We could add Callahan's Hypothesis . . . "Murphy was an optimist"). Of course, there is always the possibility of a disaster . . . but, we have allowed for one expensive illness, and Medicare parts "A" and "B" have taken much of the financial sting out of it.

The *real* disaster for the Edmonds would be the collapse of the Social Security system. The built-in increases of their benefits . . . all exempt from income taxes . . . are the main factor that contributes to their prosperity, viz.:

By 1983, these tax-exempt payments will have passed the total of Joe's company pension; by the end of 1987, their benefits will have more than doubled;

Two-thirds of the way through 1989, the tax-free portion of their income will exceed the total income they received upon retirement.

The key to all of these rather amazing results is the effect of *compounding,* both in the escalating Social Security payments and the growth of their savings. Compounding is great for the Edmonds, but what of its effect on the Social Security system?

When you consider this carefully, we hope you can still sleep nights.

WHAT HAVE WE LEARNED?

From this look at our three typical families we have found some facts that are surprising, and a number that are revealing. Let's look at these facts:

1. In analyzing the families on a "cash-flow" basis, we find that their actual cost of living increases less than the Consumer Price Index:

Family	Actual % Increase	C.P.I. Increase
Lezaks	8.77%	11.3%
Haldersons	5.27%	11.3%
Edmonds	9.26%	11.3%

2. The Haldersons, with the largest income, can expect the lowest income increase as a percentage of income expended, but are affected less by C.P.I.-category increases as a percentage of disposable income, but more by income tax "bracket-creep."

3. The use of the C.P.I. as a basis for adjustments in union contracts and in Social Security benefits discriminates against those in middle- and upper-middle income positions.

HOW ABOUT *YOUR* COST OF LIVING?

Using the methods we have shown, it is a relatively easy job to calculate your own increase in living costs in comparison to the C.P.I. figure. The steps are: first, calculate your *disposable* income by subtracting income taxes . . . Federal, State and local, and your anticipated Social Security payments from your gross income. (Social Security = 6.65% of income up to $29,700 for 1981; 6.70% of income up to $32,700 for 1982, or 9.30% of first $29,700 if you are self-employed, rising to 9.35% of $32,700 in 1982).

A simplified table, "Your Personal Cost of Living," is included so that you can do your calculations without becoming bogged down with the detail shown in Table

YOUR PERSONAL COST OF LIVING

Group	Your Dollar Cost	C.P.I. % Increase	Your Dollar Increase	Your New Cost
Food at home	$	10.6	$	$
Food away from home		10.2		
Alcoholic beverages	_____	8.6	_____	_____
TOTAL FOOD & BEVERAGES				
Rent		8.8		
House Payments				
Real Estate Taxes				
Insurance				
Maintenance & Repairs		10.6		
Fuel Oil, Coal, Bottled Gas		25.3		
Gas & Electricity		15.8		
Other utilities		7.6		
Household Furnishings and operation	_____	8.0	_____	_____
TOTAL HOUSING		12.1		
APPAREL & UPKEEP		5.9		
Car payments				
Gasoline		14.9		
Car Insurance				
Maintenance & Repair		10.2		
Public Transportation	_____	25.5	_____	_____
TOTAL TRANSPOR-TATION		13.1		
Medical Insurance				
Uncovered Medical & Dental	_____		_____	_____
TOTAL MEDICAL CARE		9.6		
ENTERTAINMENT		9.6		
OTHER GOODS & SERVICES	_____	9.3	_____	_____
TOTAL ALL ITEMS				

#1 page 286. The first group, Food and Beverages, supplies a breakdown of food at home, food away from home, such as lunches and other restaurant meals, and for alcoholic beverages if they are a part of your budget.

Your costs for housing will include *some* of the items under "Housing" in Table #1. Note that there are two sub-groups under "Housing"; the "Shelter" group includes both rental costs and costs for homeowners, while the next group, "Fuel and other Utilities" would apply to either renters or homeowners. For your cash-flow analysis, use only those that apply to your case; our simplified table breaks them out for you. For example, our first family, the Lezaks, had only rent and renters insurance in the first group, while the Haldersons included house payments, taxes, homeowners insurance and maintenance.

Do not become confused with the many categories in "Apparel and Upkeep." The category is divided into groups showing amounts spent upon each, which total the relative importance figure at the top. For most families, just a total of money spent for clothes and that spent for dry cleaning, laundry, and shoe repair will suffice, as our simplified table indicates.

Transportation will be a major factor. For practical purposes, use the same method as that shown in the Lezak or Halderson cases. If you want to accrue the replacement costs of a car, you have to estimate the years you plan to keep your car, what it should be worth as a trade-in, and what a replacement should cost by the time you are ready to switch, and factor in all these estimates. Our table again breaks out the main categories. If you use public transportation and/or instead of, your own car, you can add this into your total transportation costs.

Medical care costs can vary widely, but hospitalization and major medical insurance can help cut down the

TABLE 1

CONSUMER PRICE INDEX FOR ALL URBAN CONSUMERS: U.S. CITY AVERAGE, BY EXPENDITURE CATEGORY AND COMMODITY AND SERVICE GROUP

(1967 = 100)

Group	Relative Importance, December 1980	Unadjusted Indexes		Unadjusted Percent Change to Feb. 1981 from—		Seasonally Adjusted Percent Change from—		
		Jan. 1981	Feb. 1981	Feb. 1980	Jan. 1981	Nov. to Dec.	Dec. to Jan.	Jan. to Feb.
All items	100.000	260.5	263.2	11.3	1.0	1.0	0.7	1.0
All items (1957-59 = 100)	—	303.0	306.1	—	—	—	—	—
Expenditure Category								
Food and beverages	18.309	261.4	263.7	10.5	.9	.9	.0	.3
Food	17.322	268.6	270.8	10.6	.8	1.0	-.1	.3
Food at home	12.003	265.6	267.3	10.8	.6	.9	-.4	.0
Cereals and bakery products[1]	1.507	262.9	265.3	12.0	.9	1.1	1.7	.9
Meats, poultry, fish, and eggs	4.047	255.1	252.5	6.9	-1.0	1.0	-2.4	-2.1
Dairy products	1.603	240.1	242.1	10.3	.8	1.1	.9	.9
Fruits and vegetables	1.682	257.6	267.3	17.1	3.8	.0	-.6	2.3
Sugar and sweets	.505	385.4	385.4	29.5	.0	1.7	-1.2	-.5
Fats and oils	.333	260.4	267.3	13.3	2.6	2.2	3.6	2.9
Nonalcoholic beverages	1.321	409.7	411.9	7.1	.5	.6	.5	-.4
Other prepared foods[1]	1.005	244.9	246.9	11.3	.8	1.0	1.0	.8
Food away from home	5.319	280.9	284.7	10.2	1.4	1.0	.9	1.1
Alcoholic beverages	.987	193.7	195.9	8.6	1.1	.5	1.0	1.0
Housing	45.519	279.1	280.9	12.1	.6	1.2	.8	.6
Shelter	31.650	300.1	300.5	12.5	.1	1.3	.6	.1
Rent, residential[1]	5.120	200.9	201.9	8.8	.5	.7	.7	.5
Other rental costs	.714	273.9	278.5	8.9	1.7	.2	1.1	1.1
Homeownership	25.816	335.8	335.8	13.3	.0	1.5	.5	.0
Home purchase[1]	10.303	266.2	263.0	8.2	-1.2	.0	-.4	-1.2
Financing, taxes, and insurance[1]	11.963	435.2	437.1	18.9	.4	3.0	1.4	.4
Maintenance and repairs	3.550	296.8	302.8	10.6	2.0	1.3	-.1	2.3
Maintenance and repair services	2.737	321.3	328.7	10.6	2.3	1.4	-.2	2.6
Maintenance and repair commodities[1]	.813	239.7	242.4	10.7	1.1	.8	.3	1.1

Fuel and other utilities	6.550	296.7	304.5	15.4	2.6	1.4	2.1	2.6
Fuels	4.796	375.4	387.4	18.4	3.2	1.6	2.7	3.2
Fuel oil, coal, and bottled gas[1]	1.296	625.9	675.6	25.3	7.9	3.2	6.9	7.9
Gas (piped) and electricity	3.500	318.5	322.9	15.8	1.4	1.0	1.0	1.4
Other utilities and public services[1]	1.754	171.9	173.6	7.6	1.0	.9	.8	1.0
Household furnishings and operations	7.319	212.6	214.9	8.0	1.1	.4	.6	1.0
Housefurnishings	3.935	178.7	180.8	6.8	1.2	.4	.4	1.0
Housekeeping supplies[1]	1.460	259.5	262.8	11.8	1.3	.7	.7	1.3
Housekeeping services[1]	1.924	279.6	281.6	7.6	.7	.4	.9	.7
Apparel and upkeep	4.854	181.1	182.0	5.9	.5	.0	-.2	.8
Apparel commodities	4.192	172.6	173.2	4.9	.3	-.1	-.3	.7
Men's and boys' apparel	1.310	171.1	171.6	5.5	.3	.1	.1	.7
Women's and girls' apparel	1.541	152.1	153.4	1.5	.9	-.4	-1.2	1.5
Infants' and toddlers' apparel[1]	.106	249.7	254.3	12.2	1.8	.5	-.2	1.8
Footwear	.635	194.9	194.9	5.6	.0	.5	.1	.0
Other apparel commodities[1]	.600	214.2	212.3	10.9	-.9	-.2	.4	-.9
Apparel services	.662	246.3	249.9	12.1	1.5	.8	.7	1.4

Expenditure Category

Transportation	18.955	264.7	270.9	13.1	2.3	1.0	1.8	2.4
Private transportation	17.763	262.9	269.4	12.3	2.5	1.0	1.7	2.5
New cars	3.566	185.3	184.8	5.4	-.3	-.1	.1	-.1
Used cars	2.986	234.0	234.3	20.0	.1	2.4	1.2	.5
Gasoline	5.947	385.2	410.8	14.9	6.6	1.0	3.8	6.6
Maintenance and repair	1.454	282.7	285.4	10.5	1.0	.8	.8	.6
Other private transportation	3.810	232.4	234.2	10.2	.8	1.0	.6	.5
Other private transportation commodities[1]	.695	203.7	205.8	7.6	1.0	.2	.0	1.0
Other private transportation services	3.115	242.4	244.0	10.7	.7	1.1	.8	.4
Public transportation[1]	1.192	286.4	288.1	25.5	.6	1.1	2.2	.6
Medical care	4.717	279.5	282.6	9.6	1.1	.6	1.1	.9
Medical care commodities	.785	176.7	179.2	10.5	1.4	.7	.9	1.2
Medical care services	3.933	302.1	305.2	9.4	1.0	.6	1.2	.8
Professional services[1]	1.887	264.7	267.2	10.0	.9	.5	1.1	.9
Other medical care services	2.045	347.3	351.1	8.8	1.1	.6	1.1	.7
Entertainment	3.647	214.4	216.7	9.6	1.1	.3	1.0	1.0
Entertainment commodities	2.173	217.1	219.7	9.6	1.2	.3	.7	1.0
Entertainment services[1]	1.474	210.9	213.0	9.5	1.0	.4	1.5	1.0

TABLE 1—(Continued)

Group	Relative Importance, December 1980	Unadjusted Indexes		Unadjusted Percent Change to Feb. 1981 from—		Seasonally Adjusted Percent Change from—		
		Jan. 1981	Feb. 1981	Feb. 1980	Jan. 1981	Nov. to Dec.	Dec. to Jan.	Jan. to Feb.
Other goods and services	3.999	226.2	227.4	9.3	.5	1.0	.6	.6
Tobacco products[1]	1.054	211.9	212.3	7.2	.2	1.7	.5	.2
Personal care[1]	1.581	222.5	224.6	8.8	.9	.9	.7	.9
Toilet goods and personal care appliances[1]	.712	216.9	219.5	10.5	1.2	1.3	.8	1.2
Personal care services[1]	.869	228.3	230.0	7.4	.7	.6	.7	.7
Personal and educational expenses[1]	1.364	253.6	254.4	11.6	.3	.6	.9	.6
School books and supplies	.170	228.6	229.8	11.3	.5	.7	2.0	1.1
Personal and educational services	1.194	259.7	260.4	11.6	.3	.6	.7	.5
Commodity and Service Group								
All items	100.000	260.5	263.2	11.3	1.0	1.0	0.7	1.0
Commodities	58.396	245.4	248.3	10.3	1.2	.7	.6	1.1
Food and beverages	18.309	261.4	263.7	10.5	.9	.9	.0	.3
Commodities less food and beverages	40.087	234.3	237.4	10.2	1.3	.6	1.0	1.4
Nondurables less food and beverages	17.761	250.2	258.6	11.6	3.4	.7	2.2	3.3
Apparel commodities	4.192	172.6	173.2	4.9	.3	-.1	-.3	.7
Nondurables less food, beverages, and apparel[1]	13.569	294.4	306.8	13.6	4.2	1.0	2.4	4.2
Durables	22.327	221.0	220.3	9.0	-.3	.4	.3	-.3
Services	41.604	287.7	290.1	13.0	.8	1.4	.9	.8
Rent, residential[1]	5.120	200.9	201.9	8.8	.5	.7	.7	.5
Household services less rent	22.592	342.3	345.4	15.1	.9	2.0	1.0	.9
Transportation services	5.760	258.7	260.5	13.5	.7	1.0	1.1	.5
Medical care services	3.933	302.1	305.2	9.4	1.0	.6	1.2	.8
Other services	4.200	230.4	232.3	10.0	.8	.6	.9	.8

Special indexes:

All items less food	82.678	257.6	260.4	11.5	1.1	1.0	1.0	1.1
All items less shelter	68.350	247.6	251.2	10.9	1.5	.9	.9	1.3
All items less mortgage interest costs	90.173	247.8	250.6	10.3	1.1	.9	.6	.9
All items less home purchase and mortgage interest costs	80.950	245.8	249.3	10.6	1.4	1.0	.7	1.2
All items less medical care	95.283	259.2	261.9	11.4	1.0	1.0	.7	1.0
Commodities less food	41.074	232.4	235.4	10.1	1.3	.6	1.0	1.4
Nondurables less food	18.747	245.3	253.2	11.4	3.2	.7	2.1	3.2
Nondurables less food and apparel[1]	14.555	281.1	292.4	13.2	4.0	1.0	2.3	4.0
Nondurables	36.069	256.9	262.3	11.0	2.1	.9	1.0	1.4
Services less rent	36.484	304.2	306.9	13.6	.9	1.5	.9	.9
Services less medical care[1]	37.672	284.2	286.5	13.4	.8	1.4	1.1	.8
Energy[1]	10.834	381.7	401.1	16.4	5.1	1.2	3.1	5.1
All items less energy	89.166	251.2	252.5	10.7	.5	1.0	.6	.3
All items less food and energy	71.844	245.7	246.8	10.8	.4	1.1	.6	.4
Commodities less food and energy	33.739	211.5	211.7	8.6	.1	.5	.4	.1
Energy commodities[1]	7.335	420.4	449.0	16.6	6.8	1.2	3.8	6.8
Services less energy	38.104	285.4	287.6	12.7	.8	1.5	.9	.7
Purchasing power of the consumer dollar:								
1967 = $1.00[1]	100.000	$.384	$.380	-10.2	-1.0	-.8	-.8	-1.0
1957–59 = $1.00[1]	—	.330	.327	—	—	—	—	—

[1] Not seasonally adjusted.
Note: Index applies to a month as a whole, not to any specific date.

guesswork. The cost to your family of these insurance policies plus your estimate of uncovered items should put you fairly close.

Entertainment costs are highly personal, and vary from family to family. Remember to include costs for sports activities as well as movies, parties, concerts, etc.

The last category, "Other goods and services," is a catch-all. For this one, you have to look at toothpaste and tobacco, school supplies and Berlitz lessons, life insurance, and anything not covered elsewhere.

After you have compiled and estimated all these expenditures, compare them with the applicable cost increases shown in our simplified table.

Use of the percentage increases supplied in our table should give you your approximate costs for the next 12 months if the inflation rate remains the same. Hopefully, it will be less.

In any event, it is a good bet that your cost of living *increase* will be significantly less than the Consumer Price Index.

Try it and see.

ANALYSIS 8

Inflation—Can You Fight Back?

In the preceding chapter, we found that the Consumer Price Index cannot accurately delineate our own cost changes, but that its concepts can be useful. How can we use what we have found?

Economics is a highly inexact science . . . at one extreme are the Doom and Gloom Boys, selling millions of books and advisory letters warning of the financial Armageddon that is galloping down upon us. At the other end of the spectrum are the members of the Serendipity School, assuring us that tomorrow will be better. (The second group tends to work for the Federal government, and multiplies during Democratic administrations.)

The real truth, of course, lies somewhere in between. Let's look "in between" and consider the pluses and minuses to arrive at a logical range of expectations.

GASOLINE

PLUS: Petroleum supplies are more adequate, largely because we are using less. The increases in gasoline prices should moderate and, in fact, gas could come down slightly. This is probably optimistic since many states are increasing their tax on gasoline, and additional Federal taxes are possible.

MINUS: The Middle East could boil over at any time, disrupting supplies and generating shortages again.

EXPECT: No significant change in our overall expense.

FOOD

PLUS: Food prices in the near term should benefit from bumper crops expected in 1981, after the disastrous effects of drought conditions in the 1980 growing season. This, however, is a year-to-year variable.

MINUS: Labor costs in the food industry will continue to rise, from the costs of "stoop labor" in the produce industry all the way through the chain of service costs necessary to put the finished product in your grocery cart.

EXPECT: A continuing increase similar to the 10.5% of the 12 months we have chosen for our examples, but *less* than the 14.5% predicted by many economists for the year of 1981.

HOUSING

PLUS: It is hard to find any positive signs on housing, except that resale prices of existing housing have decreased in many parts of the country, though certainly not in the booming Sunbelt areas.

MINUS: New construction has almost priced itself out of the market. With the cost of an average 3-bedroom house hovering near $100,000, and financing costs ranging upwards from 16 percent, most families will have to settle for their present quarters.

EXPECT: No relief in shelter costs in the foreseeable future.

PLUS: Improved insulation and more moderate thermostat settings have had some effect on home heating and/or cooling costs.

MINUS: Prices for natural gas, the most widely-used home heating fuel, will escalate with decontrol . . . probably *at least* as much as the 15.8% shown in our sample 12 months. Costs for electricity will be pushed up by the recent inflationary settlement of the soft-coal strike. Expanded use of nuclear power has been sidetracked by both the pressure of protesters and the dubious decision of the Carter administration to block breeder reactor development.

EXPECT: Further increases in home energy costs over the next two-to-three years.

APPAREL

PLUS: Clothing prices, according to Table #1 of The Consumer Price Index, have increased at a rate of less than half that of the Index figure for our sample period of the 12 months ending in February, 1981. Apparel services . . . dry cleaning, laundry, alterations, etc., show a rate of increase of *more* than the overall increase, but they account for only about ⅐ of overall apparel costs.

MINUS: High-style clothing has always escalated faster than "off the rack" items, and imports from low-cost labor areas such as Hong Kong and Taiwan have tended to hold down prices of moderately priced clothing. Price resistance is being felt in the soft goods area, too; "after Christmas sales" have backed up almost to Thanksgiving. Special promotions are becoming a routine part of department store merchandizing.

EXPECT: Increasing price competition in soft goods.

Better buys can be found, but it will take more study to find them.

MEDICAL CARE

PLUS: Improvements in available treatment have been spectacular over the past few years. The killer/crippler, poliomyelitis, once a specter hovering over our children, has been reduced to a nightmare memory. Bypass surgery has made joggers out of yesterdays doomed invalids, and we now take for granted dozens of treatment processes that did not exist a generation ago.

MINUS: The cost increases have also been spectacular. The mystique of medicine has become more mystical. . . . Todays doctor will have batteries of tests run that his patient may never have heard of . . . some, unfortunately, for his *own* protection in this era of malpractice suits. We can be a healthier people physically, if not financially.

EXPECT: A continuing increase, across the board, in the area of some 10% a year for medical commodities and services.

ENTERTAINMENT

PLUS: This is a controllable expense . . . you can spend as much, or as little, as you wish . . . or can afford. The C.P.I., interestingly enough, does not include television in its category for entertainment, TV is included in *Housing,* just as are such items as water heaters and refrigerators. In thirty years, a luxury has become a necessity!

In some areas, entertainment prices seem to have peaked . . . at least for the immediate future. Motion picture theatre operators are finding that increased competition from cable television and its by-product, pay-TV programming, is limiting increases in ticket prices.

MINUS: Sports and recreational equipment will continue to reflect the rising costs of hand labor. Legitimate theatre and musicals are in deep trouble. Rising production costs and limited seating capacity will continue to force ticket prices up, but, even at present prices, only the biggest hits show any profit at all.

EXPECT: Increases slightly less, overall, than in the past few years.

OTHER GOODS AND SERVICES

PLUS: For those families without children in . . . or approaching . . . college, this is a relatively minor category, and is largely controllable.

MINUS: For those with college in the present or future, it becomes gargantuan!

EXPECT: More families to send their children to local or area community colleges for at least the first two years of work toward the baccalaureate degree, with many being content with available associate degree programs. College loans will become rarer and more expensive.

If we consider the preceding items as a rough scenario of tomorrow's inflation, several points become apparent:

1. Inflation is not going to go away, but it might become somewhat more bearable;
2. Prices will not begin to come down so long as labor costs go *up;*
3. Some items are controllable.

What is not as obvious is that *most* items are controllable to some extent; all it takes is what we will call the Incentive to Choose.

We have two ways to save . . . *BIG WAYS* and *little*

ways. Both are important, and though most of us can see the *BIG WAYS,* the *little ways* often slip through the cracks, and missing them can negate the savings accrued by taking care with the *BIG WAYS.* Most of us realize this, but have we taken the time to look at the *little ways?*

This is where incentive comes in. We have to tell ourselves that, if we really want to improve our financial position, we have to plan . . . to look at the way we are handling our expenditures, and to find the ways to get more for our money. This will involve choices . . . macaroni and cheese vs. steak.

Most of us will not make choices that involve self-discipline until circumstances force us to choose. This is a quirk in human nature that carries over even into otherwise well-managed businesses. When business is good, managers tend to overstaff, particularly in clerical and staff positions. When things toughen up, they must cut back on some of the "frill positions" to keep the business operating at a profit. The best managed businesses constantly monitor expenses . . . staff and otherwise . . . and build up a profit cushion that sustains them over the bad periods. We can take this same approach with our personal expenditures . . . it will pay off.

As we go through the various expense groups of the C.P.I., we can find many ways to get more for less . . . and . . . we don't have to do it all on our own. There is a great deal of help available, and whether or not we realize it, we are paying for it. Some examples are:

1. Your local utility companies can supply you with information on the costs of operating various home appliances, both on the cost of energy and on their life expectancy. Most such companies have home economists on their staffs who can show you ways

to save on operating costs, even to the extent of sup-
plying sample menus that can let you prepare an
entire meal with one oven setting.

2. Your local library should have complete files on various consumer periodicals indicating the best buys
in a wide spectrum of products . . . from automobiles to mattresses. Their test results often show that
you get more for your money with an "own brand"
item from a major National retailer than from the
prestige brand-name item on last night's television
commercial.

3. Don't overlook your county Agricultural Extension
Service. This agency's help is in no way limited to
farmers. Your County Agent can supply you with
information about your own area . . . usually as div-
erse as how to care for your shrubbery or what to
plant in a garden, to schedules as to what local produce will be available when, and how to preserve
or freeze it to use during seasons when it would be
expensive in your grocery.

4. Get to know your banker. He, or she, is trained to
help you plan your financial moves; everything from
buying a house or car to investing your bonus, or
even to analyzing your personal financial statement.
Consult your banker before making any significant
financial commitment. If he does not have the information you need, he knows where to get it.

5. And do not overlook Big Brother. The Government
Printing Office can supply you with informative
pamphlets on everything from growing earthworms
to surviving earthquakes. Most cities large enough
to have a Federal Building will have a bookstore
with a good selection of publications for sale, and
a catalog from which one can order . . . literally
. . . thousands of separate pamphlets or books.

Prices are reasonable . . . the Government has not made a profit on anything since Seward bought Alaska from the Russians.

If a visit to an outlet as described above is not practical, information on available publications may be obtained by writing or telephoning:

Washington, D.C. 20402
U.S. Government Printing Office
Telephone: (202) 275-2051

BUT FIRST . . . Check with your County (Agricultural) Service . . . They frequently have some U.S. Department of Agriculture home-advisory pamphlets available free of charge.

Incidentally, the figures used in the preceding chapter, reproduced as Table #1, were from one of the G.P.O. publications, *C.P.I. Detailed Report, February, 1981.* You can obtain the latest monthly copy of this report from the above source; specify Library of Congress Catalog Number 74–647019; price is 75¢ for a single copy. You will find some detail *not* covered in these chapters useful in your planning, viz: seasonal fluctuations in price changes of food products.

In the following section of this chapter, we will examine each group of expenses found in the Consumer Price Index, with suggestions on how to fight back. Much of the data quoted was gleaned from sources such as those listed above.

FOOD AND BEVERAGES

Of the three groups highest in relative importance, this one has the most data available. The U.S. Department of Agriculture, Cooperative Extension Service departments of State universities, and various county Agricultural Extension Services, County Agents, etc., all publish information . . . most of it free . . . and usually accurate.

They all seem to agree on one point: buy a home freezer, and . . . keep it as nearly full as possible.

Home canning of fruits and vegetables is still practiced by many families, but it is losing popularity to the use of a freezer. Canning has the advantage of not requiring electricity to keep the food edible; but it has three disadvantages. Many items are cheapest and plentiful when weather is hottest, and home canning is a miserable job in mid-summer. It is almost useless for keeping meat products. And there is always the danger of botulism if you happen to make a mistake.

The size freezer you buy is important, and depends both on the size of your family and the amount you will use the appliance. While the home photographer might caution you to keep his darkroom door closed or you will "let the dark out," the boss of the home freezer will caution you against "letting the cold out." A well-filled freezer takes less electricity because it has less air to cool . . . and to re-cool each time the lid is opened.

The economic advantages of a freezer are:

1. Food items may be purchased when supplies are heaviest and prices lowest, for example:

MEATS:
Beef—supply heaviest during Fall and Winter, with October usually best for bargains.
Pork—October to December are heaviest months.
Lamb—heaviest supply in Winter.
Veal—supply largest in late Summer and Fall.
Chicken—pretty much year-round . . . watch for special sales.
Turkeys—supply heaviest in July and October–December.
Fish—best supply in early Summer.
Shellfish—supplies good June through October, but wait until September for Oysters.
Eggs—heaviest supplies in Winter and Spring.

FRUITS:
Citrus—best supplies Winter and Spring.
Apples—October through November.
Berries, melons, peaches, plums, apricots, pears—
June through September.
VEGETABLES:
Tomatoes—Summer months.
Locally grown fresh vegetables usually in best supply from July
through September; some available for very short times . . . your
County Extension Service can advise you.

Source: The Cooperative Extension Service, The Ohio State University.

2. Another cost saving feature of a food freezer can be elimination of many trips to the grocery. A two-mile round trip in a 1977 mid-sized car, can consume ¼ of a gallon of gasoline. With unleaded gas at $1.40 per gallon, eliminating three such trips a week can save $1.05 per week, or $54.60 per year.

In addition to the possible savings and convenience of using a freezer for produce items, substantial savings can accrue by buying meat during lower-cost periods, or specific meats that might be on sale as a part of individual promotions put on by grocery stores. For larger families, purchase of a half or a quarter of beef can produce substantial savings. Smaller families can do well by watching for sale specials.

Getting the most for your money in meat purchases can be tricky . . . different cuts can vary widely in cost per serving. The U.S. Department of Agriculture publishes an excellent booklet on the subject, which your County Agent's Office can probably supply you at no cost, or you can order, free of charge, from:

Office of Governmental and Public Affairs
U.S. Department Agriculture
Washington, D.C. 20250

The title is: *Your Money's Worth in Foods*
(Home and Garden Bulletin Number
183)

The same office also furnishes a number of other pamphlets on cost-effective buying of specific food items.

The USDA also publishes pamphlets of instructions for freezing or canning various food products. A few of the titles are:

Home Freezing of Fruits and Vegetables
(Home and Garden Bulletin Number 10)
Freezing Meat and Fish in the Home
(Bulletin G 93)
Freezing Combination Main Dishes
(Bulletin G 40)
Home Care of Purchased Frozen Foods
(Bulletin G 69)

If your county extension service does not have copies, these can be ordered from:

Office of Governmental and Public Afairs
U.S. Department of Agriculture
Washington, D.C. 20250

We have discussed some of the advantages of using a food freezer; how about the costs? Recent selling prices of freezers in the catalog of a major national retailer indicate a cost of about $340 for a unit of about 15 cu. ft., and of $470–$500 for a 23 cu. ft. model. Lifespan of a freezer should be at least 15 to 20 years.

Under present Federal Regulations, major appliances must bear an "Energy-guide" label, showing approximate annual operating costs under varying costs per kilowatt hour of electricity. This cost per kwh varies in different parts of the country, and will generally run higher in summer. Using average costs in the North Central States, a good estimate today would be up to $110 a year for a 15 cu. ft. unit, and up to $150 for a 23 cu. ft. model. In determining whether or not a freezer would save you money, estimate your savings on food and balance against this energy cost . . . don't forget to allow for savings on trips to the grocery.

Whether or not you decide on a freezer, you can save on food costs by employing the information available through your county extension service, from your utility companies, and from Federal Government publications.

There is also the factor of *choice.* We have talked about the "Incentive to Choose"; how much you can save depends upon the strength of your incentive. One of the USDA publications, *Your Money's Worth in Foods,* lists four separate "food plans." Thrifty . . . Low Cost . . . Moderate Cost . . . and Liberal. Among our invented families, the Lezaks come under the "Thrifty" plan, the Haldersons under "Moderate," and the Edmonds under "Liberal."

It is a question of choice, or, if you prefer, selection. A serving of T-bone steak would cost 70% more than the same size serving of pot roast . . . *if the price per pound were the same!* The table of comparative serving costs in the "Money's Worth" booklet can help you make choices that make a lot of sense.

And . . . if you enjoy a drink . . . it makes more difference *where* you drink than how expensive a brand you choose. A highball of medium-priced booze will average from $1.50 to $2.50 in the average bar; the same drink at home will cost about 32¢ . . . or make it 50¢ if you use seltzer instead of water. You won't, of course, have the benefit of counsel from that philosopher/psychiatrist of the brass rail, the bartender, but look at the percentages!

HOUSING

Since this is the major category in relative importance in the C.P.I. and our own studies have shown that it is the largest for two of our three families, it deserves a careful look.

First, let's examine the purely economic aspects of that cornerstone of The American Dream: owning your own home. We will take a family in the same general career path as the Haldersons, only ten years younger, in today's economic climate.

Ron Duncan, 28, is an assistant controller for a local manufacturer and appears to have good job prospects. As the Executive recruiters say, Ron is "earning his age," $28,000 per year. He and Eleanor, his 26-year old wife, have a four-year-old and would like to have one more child. They get along fairly well of Ron's salary, and have been thinking of buying a house. They are presently renting a 3-bedroom, twenty-year-old house in a good neighborhood for $375 per month. The rent will probably go up when their 2-year lease expires in June of 1982, and they feel that they are not "building equity" by renting.

They like some new houses being built in a neighborhood near them. These are not elaborate houses, but are nice . . . not quite as much floor space as their rental house, but probably more energy-efficient. Their selling price is just about the U.S. average for new, 3-bedroom houses . . . $94,000. Since they have had the benefit of an inheritance, and have been able to save some money, they can manage the 20% down-payment of $18,800 plus closing costs of about $800 and the "2 points," or 2% fee of their resulting mortgage loan of $75,200. Their original investment, then, would be $21,104.

Since Ron is an accountant, he wants to know all the details of just what it would cost them to make the move.

On his company's computer, he runs an amortization schedule on the 25-year, 16% mortgage that the financial institution has offered, checks out the anticipated taxes and homeowners insurance, and estimates his maintenance costs at today's rates. He pays for utilities now, so he makes the assumption that they will remain about the same whether he continues to rent or buys the new house.

He also factors in the amount he could earn on the $21,100 he would be investing originally. The results give him quite a shock. For the first year:

Present Dollars Expended		*New House*	
Rent:	$375/mo. × 12 = $4,500	Payments:	
Renters Insurance:	125	$1,021.88/mo. × 12 = $12,262,56	
TOTAL	$4,625	Real Estate Taxes	1,020.00
	Less:	Maintenance	400.00
Income on $21,100 @ 14%	(2,954)	Homeowners Insurance	280.00
	$1,671	TOTAL	$13,962.56

Ron finds that, during the first year of his mortgage, he will be paying just about half of his gross income just to keep up the payments and other direct expenses on the house, and this is *before* allowing anything for utilities, cleaning supplies, etc.

This, when contrasted with the 16.5% in basic rental costs they are paying now look pretty one-sided, even without allowing for the earnings they could get on their $21,100 down payment. (These earnings would be subject to income taxes, but after the $400 exemption, taxes in their income bracket would be fairly low).

But . . . how about the equity they would be building in their own home? Well, let's look at the figures from the amortization schedule:

Amount of Mortgage Loan	$75,200.00
Monthly Payment—25 year basis	1,021.88
Interest Rate	16%

Status at End of:	Mortgage Loan Balance	Amount to Interest	Cumulative Equity Increase
First year:	$74,951.76	$ 12,014.32	$ 248.24
Fifth year:	73,450.91	59,563.71	1,749.09
Tenth year:	69,578.71	117,004.31	5,621.29
Fifteenth year:	61,006.44	169,744.84	16,886.92
Twentieth year:	42,029.15	203,222.05	33,170.85
Twenty-fifth year:	17.07	231,381.00	75,183.00

Ron's figures show that he would have made payments totaling $306,564 over the 25-year period. These payments, plus the amount of his original cash investment of $21,100, would give him a total cost of $327,664 for the new house. This does not take into account reappraisals that would raise real estate taxes or increases in insurance rates if the house appreciates in value.

During the past few years, the meteoric rise in house prices has provided "unearned profits" for thousands of people, but for growing families, the replacement house has usually gone up even more. If Ron and Eleanor Duncan could afford this new house . . . and our figures show that they cannot, at least for the present . . . would it be worth the investment of well over a quarter of a million dollars they would have made? Probably not, but as we have pointed out, they have to live somewhere, and their rent won't stay at $375 a month forever. Over the past 14 years, rental costs have almost exactly doubled. If they continue to increase at the 8.8% rate of the last 12 months, they could double again in just over 8 years.

Well . . . *is there* an answer for the Duncans? There might be. Suppose they offered to buy the house they are renting at the present . . . and asked the owners if they would finance part of the price at, say, 12%? Let's say that they agreed upon a price of $50,000. With $20,000 down, this would leave $30,000 to finance. On a 15-year mortgage, at 12%, the Duncans would pay $360.05; on a 20-year mortgage, $330.33 per month. Even after adding real estate taxes, insurance, and maintenance, the Duncans would have housing costs well within the parameters of their income.

Would this arrangment look good to the present owners? It should. In the first place, they are not charging enough rent. To earn a 12% return on their property, they should get a monthly rental of $500, or 1% of the value per month, *plus* enough to take care of taxes, insurance, and maintenance; say, another $110 per month. This could be difficult . . . in their small city, its hard to find renters who will pay $610 monthly rent. By selling to the Duncans, they would have $20,000 cash that they could invest in a money market fund, and an income of $4,320.60 per year for the next 15 years. They would have capital gains taxes to pay on the profit from the sale, but much of this would be spread over the 15 years they will be receiving payments.

Under this arrangement, the Duncans would not have the brand-new house that they have admired, but there again . . . they would *own* this house . . . the new one would own *them.*

In these days that combine high house prices and prohibitive interest rates, realtors report that something like 80% of used-house sales involve at least some measure of owner financing. It is well worth a look to anyone in the market for housing today.

Energy costs become an enormous factor in their cost of living. Much has been said and written about energy-saving techniques: more, and more effective, insulation; lower thermostat settings, etc., but little has been said about one simple way to increase the level of comfort at lower house temperatures: *proper humidity control.* Home humidifiers are relative inexpensive and can make your house much more comfortable in the colder weather in Northern parts of the country. Some other ways to save and increase comfort are: zone-control thermostat systems in larger and particularly in split-level . . . houses; insulation in the floor for bedrooms over garages in split-level houses; storm windows and doors.

Gas is generally cheaper than electricity for heating, cooking, drying clothes, and hot-water heaters. Gas air conditioning systems are cheaper to operate, too, but have more service problems and higher original installation costs. The old gas pilot lights are becoming a thing of the past with electric spark lighting on new gas ranges and furnaces, which introduces a desirable safety factor as well as providing some fuel savings.

Many other house and household expenses vary widely and involve more of the Incentive to Choose. The couch you might buy for $1,500 might have to be recovered sooner than the one you might buy for $700. The price of upholstery fabrics is always affected by the time it takes to set up the machines for weaving the fabric. On the other hand, your Oriental rug might wear for generations, but its original cost will be many times that of a good-quality rug of one of the durable acrylic fibers.

Your side-by-side refrigerator-freezer is convenient, but will cost more to operate than the same size in a top-freezing compartment model. A dishwasher might be a housewife's (or househusband's) best friend, but you will pay much more per clean dish.

To paraphrase the old pitchman's chant, "You takes your choice, *then* you pays your money!"

APPAREL AND UPKEEP

As mentioned earlier, careful shopping and avoiding high-style clothing are the best ways to fight back against rising clothing costs. Choice of as many permanent-press clothing items as possible can help combat escalating laundry and dry cleaning costs, and following both seasonal and special promotion sales can provide the most for your money.

Style changes have always been the camp-followers of prosperity. During boom periods, when production rises, jobs start looking for people instead of vice-versa, and there is money left on the day-before-payday, style changes flourish. Hemlines soar or plunge, neckties get wider or narrower, and designers are sure that nobody would be caught dead in last year's model.

But . . . when things begin to pinch, "style" becomes less important, and styles tend to become more conservative and change more slowly. One economist—James M. Dawson, Senior Vice President and Economist for The National City Bank of Cleveland—received headlines for his Hemline Theory during the Soaring 60's. He charted the relationship between business conditions and the lengths of skirts for several business cycles, and found that when skirts were shorter, business was better.

Men's clothes avoided radical style pressures for many years until the Age of Television. A plethora of "designer" suits hit the market during the 60's and early 70's, many of them popularized by one or another television star. They sold . . . and sold big, particularly to younger men. After a time, however, these style-oriented men found that last year's suit looked out of place this year. In a few years, their closets were full of suits that "didn't look right." So the trend swung back to the 3-button, natural shoulder, narrower lapel suits that had always been favored by the more conservative, higher quality men's clothiers. A spokesman for Brooks Brothers was quoted last year as saying, "It is nice to know that we have been right all the time."

In men's suits, as much as in anything you can buy, you get what you pay for. A good, all wool business suit might cost twice what a bargain "off the rack" suit will, but it can last three to four times as long and still be worn with confidence. Buy quality.

The same principles apply to women's clothes. If you can live without following every whim of the fashion arbiters, but buy from a "good house," but not an ultra-fashion house, you can be proud of your appearance anywhere.

Did you ever wonder what happened to all those mini-skirts?

TRANSPORTATION

The cost of getting from here to there, like Shakespeare's "gentle rain from heaven," falleth alike on all of us . . . like a ton of bricks. It roughly parallels the cost of food in the Index. Our analysis of a typical blue-collar family indicates that it can exceed food expenditures. Since the base year of 1967, the price of gasoline alone has increased over 300% . . . and we are an automobile-oriented society. We have, in fact, become so dependent upon private cars that, except in our larger metropolitan areas, public transportation is either inadequate or nonexistent.

It is useless to berate ourselves for allowing this dependence on the automobile to develop . . . there are a multitude of reasons . . . our suburban-sprawl lifestyle . . . affluence to live elsewhere than in the shelter of our factories . . . the convenience of close-in parking that has spawned shopping malls while downtown business sections have deteriorated, etc., etc. The fact is that the condition exists, and we have to live with it. Let's look at some ways. SMALLER . . . MORE FUEL EFFICIENT . . . CARS.

In the late 1930's, Adolph Hitler commanded German automakers to develop a "peoples car" so that more Third Reich families could have a car of their own. The resulting Volkswagen was a laughing matter to most Americans. The "bug" or "beetle" was cramped, uncomfortable, and certainly no match for *our* "people's cars," the Fords, Chevrolets, and Plymouths. True, the Volkswagen would run for somewhat over 30 miles on a gallon of gas . . . about a penny a mile . . . but the American cars ran for about 1½ cents a mile in fuel costs, and 6,000 miles a year was about average . . . who wanted to put up with the obvious disadvantages of a VW for $30 a year?

But then came automatic transmissions . . . and lower gas mileage. American cars gained weight, automatic chokes were installed, luxury features such as power steering and air conditioning became available, and fuel consumption went higher. When the fuel crunch hit in 1973–1974, and gasoline prices took off, we started to wonder if, perhaps, we *could* live with a little less luxury.

It took time, though, for us to cool our love affair with the Big Car. When the first significant down-sizing of American cars started in 1977, there was a chorus of complaints. It's hard to abandon an ingrained status symbol.

The transition was painful, but it does make sense. National averages show the average family car is driven about 10,000 miles a year; 6,000 local and 4,000 highway. With $1.40 per gallon gasoline, an overall difference of 3 miles per gallon, city, and 7 miles per gallon, highway, can save about $200 each year, and switching from a 1977 mid-sized car to a 1981 compact can about double this saving.

THINKING BEFORE DRIVING

We are all guilty. It's so easy to jump in the car and drive to the grocery for some minor item we think we need right now. What happens when we do? First, the car's engine is cold, so the automatic choke enriches the fuel mixture, which means you use several times as much gas as normal. And . . . by the time you reach the store, this convenience device is still helping you get smooth operation . . . but you are paying for it.

It is convenient to drive your own car to work, but what does it cost in comparison to pooling your rides with three other people? If you commute 10 miles each way and your car gets about 18 miles per gallon (highway), car-pooling would save you about $350 per year, not counting any cost for parking your car.

There are other ways to save: lower highway speeds, proper tires and tire pressure, a well-tuned car, and . . . if available . . . the use of public transportation. Again, the amount you can reduce your costs will depend on the strength of your incentive to save.

The other obvious way to reduce your transportation cost is to keep your car longer. At today's costs for new cars, the once-popular practice of trading cars every two to three years no longer makes sense. Trade-in values today do not vary much from the "blue book averages" until the car has over 60,000 miles on the odometer. If you drive 10,000 miles a year, why not drive the car for 6 years? Today's engines can last for 100,000 miles without major repairs, and the old problem of "rusting out" can be largely avoided by underseal and innerseal treatments costing an average of about $160. Financing $7,000 of the cost of a $10,000 car for four years at an annual percentage rate of 18% adds $2,869.76 to the cost; the extra two years of use gives you a $1,435 bonus, less the additional maintenance and repair costs expected as the car ages.

There is some hope that *part* of the increase in our transportation costs might be slowing due to resistance of the oil companies to rising crude oil prices. This helps, but the quantum jump in gasoline prices has already occurred, and any reductions thus far have been in the magnitude of pennies, or less, per gallon. Don't count on any substantial *decrease,* though the recent pattern of increases seems to be changing for the better.

MEDICAL CARE

Our C.P.I. Table # 1 page 286 shows us that, of the various categories, medical care cost increases have been exceeded only by fuel costs. We can blame the Arabs for much of one of the latter, but not for the former. There are many things we *can* blame: unionization of hospital personnel; ridiculous settlements in malpractice suits, which have increased doctors' insurance costs from a few hundred to many thousands of dollars per year; sharp increases in fees charged by medical professionals in all disciplines; increased sophistication and costs in drugs, and last but not least; use of hospital beds in cases that could be handled on an outpatient basis.

This last cost typifies the abuse of the intent of both private medical insurance and the Medicare/Medicaid programs that are part of our government's cradle-to-grave "big brotherism."

It makes sound business sense for us to question our physicians as to whether extensive tests are really needed, and whether hospitalization is necessary for procedures that could be performed on an out-patient basis. It also makes sense for us to inquire into surgical costs.

There can be wide differences between what certain surgeons charge and what our insurance considers "usual, customary and reasonable."

Shop for the best deal . . . it's your money.

There is little further we as individuals can do about medical costs except either stay healthy or die a natural death.

ENTERTAINMENT

This is the category over which we have the most measure of control . . . so, of course, it happens to be the smallest in relative importance of the C.P.I. categories.

Entertainment is such a personal-choice category that it is difficult to show specifics of savings. There are a few that are obvious, such as looking for bargain matinee prices at motion pictures, free concerts, off-season vacation rates, etc.

For family vacations at bargain prices, camping is hard to beat . . . that is . . . if you like to camp, and many people do. From tent-camping, the most economical, to rolling in self-propelled recreational vehicles, the most expensive, millions of Americans hit the road for weekends or full vacations.

Perhaps the most important element in enjoyment of a family vacation . . . and thus getting the most for your money from it . . . is attitude. This might be best illustrated by an account of a personal experience from some twenty years ago. We will call it:

THE CAPE COD FUND

It was to be a different vacation. Previously, our vacations had consisted of "visiting the folks" at a cottage on a lake in North Carolina. We had been fortunate to have this option . . . money for vacations was a little scarce.

Our children, Penny, 13, and Duncan, 9, had some idea of money since they had to watch their allowances. But on vacation, Dad paid for things, so money did not matter. As with most children on vacation, they wanted to do everything. Cost was not even considered. "Why can't we go to the amusement park again today?" . . . or, "We haven't been on the cruise boat since Tuesday!" . . . were typical reminders of the self-denial we were forcing upon our progeny.

After one lake vacation, my wife, Ginny, and I decided to hold a family meeting. Penny and Duncan appeared with their usual aggressive-defensive demeanor . . . "Wonder what Dad will be yelling at us about today?"

They perked up, though, when they heard the subject: "how about a different vacation next year?"

The decision to go to Cape Cod was unanimous and enthusiastic—until I brought up the question of how to finance it. This puzzled the children, so we explained to them the realities of payments on our house, the cost of college looming in the future, and such mundane items as insurance, braces for teeth, etc.

The upshot of the meeting was the establishment of the Fund. Penny offered to contribute from her occasional babysitting jobs, and Duncan from his lawn mowing and caddying earnings, while each would put in any Christmas or birthday money. Ginny would watch expenses and squeeze some from her housekeeping funds, and I, as a junior bank officer, would add any money earned from doing estate appraisals for executors or attorneys. By the time we were ready for the trip the following June, the Cape Cod Fund totaled slightly over $300.00.

Since the children were participants in the financing, Ginny and I decided that it would be appropriate for them to handle the money. They shared the job as bursars:

one would be responsible for food and lodging each day; the other for all other expenses, with the assignments rotated daily. We all had input as to what we would like to see and do, and the bursars checked the costs and made the final decisions.

It was a two-day trip from Ashtabula, Ohio, to Cape Cod. We planned to see friends and spend the night in Springfield, Mass. so we asked our friends to make a reservation for us in a local motel, and set out.

Our first day, Penny had "other expenses" and Duncan, food and lodging. Both the children had counted on spending money for lunch, but the first stop at a service station was a revelation. On previous trips, such stops for Penny meant going to the restroom with Ginny, the high point coming when you put a quarter into a machine, pushed a button, and received a squirt of perfume. For both the children, a stop at the vending machines for a soft drink or a candy bar was expected. During these interesting events, Dad said something to the man outside, and when we set off again the gas gauge had moved over to "F." Penny was amazed that it cost about $7.50 to fill up the car ($7.50 . . . remember?). But she was highly indignant when she had to pay $6.15 at the toll-plaza on the New York Thruway, "Just to ride on a road!"

When we arrived in Springfield, I went into the motel office with Duncan to see about our room. The conversation went something like this:

Duncan: "Do you have a reservation for Ray?"
Clerk: "Yes, we do."
Duncan: "How much is it?"
Clerk: "$22.50."
Duncan: "That's too much. I won't pay it."

and with that he turned and walked out, leaving me standing there.

All I could think to say was, "Sorry. Thanks anyway," as I turned and followed him out.

Back in the car, he said, "It's foolish to spend that much just for a place to sleep. We can find a cheaper one."

And we did . . . not very elegant, but it cost only $14.00. Duncan had saved us almost $10.00 . . . real money in those days. He had also taught himself a lesson . . . and reminded the rest of us . . . always ask the price, and do not be afraid to shop around.

When we arrived on the Cape, we started to consolidate our plans. Duncan wanted to go fishing and Penny, having had elementary sailing lessons in the Girl Scouts, wanted to rent a sailboat at Hyannis. The costs were similar, so Ginny and Penny dropped us off at Chatham where we boarded a codfishing boat, then headed for Hyannis for sailing.

Because of our budget limitations, we planned to "eat in" except for a trip to a good restaurant on our last night. This was not too restrictive . . . in those days you could buy "chicken lobsters" weighing just over a pound and freshly boiled to a Chinese red hue, for 95¢.

Our two bursars delighted in being in on all decisions. The time of planning activities was often as much fun as the doing. Duncan and I played golf on a seaside course while the girls went shopping for things such as bayberry candles and cranberry baskets; we spent a day in Provincetown, with the girls buying unbelievable hats from a "hat artist" while Duncan and I admired giant lobsters in a tank on the pier. We were all properly impressed by the Kennedy Compound at Hyannis Port, and froze equally in the chilly June surf.

Finally, the time arrived for our Big Night Out. We selected a quaint . . . and excellent . . . restaurant recommended by several natives. Dinner was great . . . until the waiter presented the check, about $25.00 to Duncan, who slammed his hand down on the table, and said, "This is ridiculous! I won't pay that much!"

"This time," I pointed out, "you have to pay the price. We committed ourselves. And you have to leave a tip for the waiter."

He was still grumbling when we left, "Next time, I'll look at the prices before we pick a restaurant."

All this happened a long time ago. As we look back those 20 years, we can still laugh at some of the details, but we all agree that this week was not only fun, but also a lesson for all of us. The *attitude* was perfect.

For the children, it was part of growing up. Maybe it was for the parents, too.

OTHER GOODS AND SERVICES

This category, like entertainment, varies widely between families: specifics are hard to define.

Two general rules always helpful, however; shop for best values and buy in quantity when you can get a discount. A carton of cigarettes costs less per pack than buying each pack individually. A carton of facial tissues can cost less per unit than you pay when buying one box at a time.

In summary, savings usually come from watching expenditures for the little things. It means taking more time . . . and it is more trouble, but is *is* smart.

Remember . . . if your income is exceeded by your outgo, your upkeep can be your downfall.

Farming: Bright Spot in Productivity

Or: Malthus Revisited

At the turn of the century, one farmer could produce enough food for himself and four other people. During World War II, a farmer in Ohio could feed 20 people. By 1981, one such farmer can feed 56 people besides himself, according to spokesmen for the Ohio Agricultural Research and Development Center.

Chapter 9 of this book discusses the declining rate of productivity increase in manufacturing and reasons for the decline. Obviously, the record of productivity in the farming sector of the economy is much better. It took 13,555,000 farm workers to feed the U.S. in 1910; only 3,774,000 to take care of our needs . . . and those of many other of the world's people . . . in 1979.

The September 28, 1981, edition of Northern Ohio Business Journal gives some interesting statistics.

In 1950, Ohio produced about 150 million bushels of corn. In 1980, on fewer acres, corn production had grown to 417 million bushels.

Wheat production from the same date, has increased

by 50%, and from some ⅔ of the acres planted. This is a net percentage increase of 125%.

Milk production has increased from 7,000 pounds per cow each year to an average of 12,000 with some herds averaging up to 20,000 pounds.

Soybean production in Ohio has grown from 24 million bushels at the end of World War II to 132 million in 1980. Japan, known as the originator of soy sauce and a leader in per-capita soybean consumption, gets some 80% of its supply from the American midwest.

Since the turn of the century, improved feeding practices for cattle and sheep have reduced feed needed to produce a pound of meat by 20% to 30%.

Tomatoes supply a $30 million income to Ohio farmers; $150 million to processors. Researchers in the Ohio Agricultural Research and Development Center (OARDC) are even developing uses for the tomato seeds discarded in processing. High in protein and amino acids, the seeds may prove usable as animal feed supplements or flour extenders.

When Thomas Malthus, in 1798, made his dire prediction of future starvation, he could not have foreseen the effects of research and automation on agricultural productivity. These two factors, research and automation, have changed U.S. farming to an "agribusiness industry," principally since World War II.

Working in cooperation with State universities, commercial seed producers, and the U.S. Department of Agriculture, various State-supported agricultural centers such as the OARDC have sponsored the research that has provided sophisticated breeding, cultivation, and management techniques to agribusiness. High-yield and disease-resistant strains of crops have been developed, plus new varieties of plants suitable for particular soil conditions. The Ohio center, at Wooster, Ohio, employs about 550 people, some part-time from the faculty of Ohio State University. It operates on a budget of some $20 million. Officials of OARDC estimate the value of the State's investment pays an annual dividend of some 50% . . . not a bad investment.

The other key factor in growing agricultural productivity has been automation, with its attendant reduction of labor costs. Huge grain drills have made the sower obsolete; combines that are literally mobile production-lines reap, thrash, and bag grain while binding the straw in neat bundles. The scythe, the thrashing floor, and straw-stacks have gone the way of the buggy whip.

But, farming is still a high-risk business. In addition to its exposure to the vagaries of weather, the oscillations of market prices, and the decisions of politicians about international trade (farm products are America's largest export items), farming is particularly sensitive to inflation and high interest rates. U.S. Department of Agriculture figures show that, with 1977 as the base year of 100, the ratio of *prices received* by farm operators for their products to the *prices they paid* for commodities, interest, wages, etc., has declined from 1.38 to 1 in 1973, to 0.91 to 1 in August, 1981. Even with tremendous gains in productivity, farming feels the pressure of inflation.

Nobody is exempt.

ANALYSIS 10

Business Week Magazine's Index of Business Activity

The accompanying chart and table, showing historical fluctuations in the Business Week Index, were referred to in Chapter 8. The chart shows yearly index figures, the table shows both monthly and yearly figures. The index has been prepared by the staff of Business Week magazine using key indicators of business activity, and is regarded as an accurate indicator of U.S. business activity.

The particular reference in Chapter 8 was to illustrate the drastic downturns that occurred during the depression of the 1930's. Any index that traces the tremendous growth of the U.S. economy will show much larger numbers over the years. So, to gain a clearer perspective of the depression years as compared to other fluctuations in the index, consider the following: between the high point of the Roaring Twenties, July, 1929, and the lowest point in the Great Depression, March, 1933, the index fell 60.5%.

Between July, 1937 and June, 1938 the index dropped 38.3%, the sharpest drop in its entire history before or

CHART XVIII

BUSINESS WEEK MAGAZINE'S
INDEX OF BUSINESS ACTIVITY

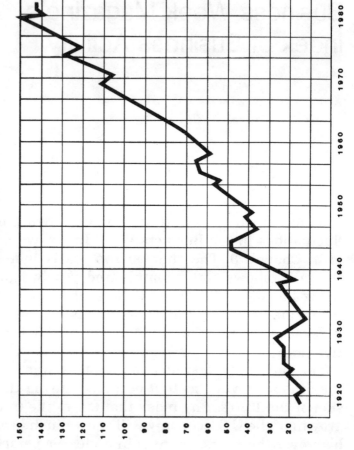

INDEX OF BUSINESS ACTIVITY
(1967 : 100)

BUSINESS WEEK INDEX, MONTHLY AVERAGES OF WEEKLY FIGURES
SEASONALLY ADJUSTED
(Index 1967 = 100)

	1919	1920	1921	1922	1923	1924	1925
JAN	14.9	17.9	13.5	14.0	20.2	20.9	21.5
FEB	14.3	17.4	12.8	14.6	19.8	21.6	21.5
MAR	13.9	17.6	12.4	17.0	20.6	21.3	21.5
APR	14.0	15.7	12.5	15.8	21.4	19.6	21.5
MAY	14.0	17.2	13.0	17.2	21.4	18.4	21.7
JUN	15.9	18.0	13.1	18.4	21.7	17.6	21.8
JUL	17.0	17.7	12.9	18.0	21.7	17.5	22.1
AUG	17.0	17.9	13.2	16.8	20.4	18.6	22.5
SEP	16.5	17.5	13.4	17.4	20.5	19.4	22.7
OCT	15.9	16.7	14.5	20.1	20.4	19.7	23.0
NOV	15.9	16.9	14.3	19.8	20.6	20.9	24.7
DEC	16.4	15.9	14.0	20.6	20.6	21.5	24.8
AVERAGE	15.5	17.2	13.3	17.5	20.8	19.8	22.4

	1926	1927	1928	1929	1930	1931	1932
JAN	23.5	22.7	23.2	26.3	22.7	18.6	14.4
FEB	23.1	23.3	24.0	27.3	23.4	18.9	13.9
MAR	23.4	24.0	24.5	26.8	23.1	19.5	13.3
APR	23.1	23.5	24.5	27.2	24.0	19.5	13.0
MAY	23.4	24.0	24.4	27.5	23.3	18.5	12.5
JUN	23.8	23.4	24.8	27.5	22.8	17.5	12.0
JUL	24.0	22.9	25.5	27.9	21.5	17.2	11.9
AUG	24.6	23.2	25.7	27.3	20.7	16.8	11.5
SEP	24.3	22.5	26.1	27.5	21.2	16.4	11.9
OCT	24.1	22.0	26.3	26.8	20.2	15.9	12.7
NOV	24.0	21.6	25.5	24.5	18.9	15.7	12.7
DEC	22.9	22.2	25.2	22.4	18.6	14.9	12.7
AVERAGE	23.7	22.9	25.0	26.6	21.7	17.5	12.7

	1933	1934	1935	1936	1937	1938	1939
JAN	12.7	14.8	17.3	20.4	23.3	17.1	21.7
FEB	12.3	15.7	17.7	19.9	23.5	17.0	21.1
MAR	11.0	16.6	17.6	19.0	24.5	16.7	20.7
APR	12.1	16.6	17.2	20.5	24.4	16.2	19.7
MAY	13.7	17.1	16.9	21.4	25.4	15.9	19.4
JUN	15.9	17.2	17.2	22.0	24.8	15.8	20.9
JUL	17.5	14.9	16.7	23.1	25.6	17.0	21.4
AUG	16.6	14.2	17.9	23.0	25.2	17.7	22.2
SEP	16.0	14.0	18.0	22.8	24.5	18.8	24.1
OCT	15.7	13.8	18.9	22.7	23.0	20.6	25.3
NOV	14.2	14.1	19.5	23.3	19.5	21.5	25.9
DEC	14.8	15.7	20.2	24.2	17.4	21.8	26.2
AVERAGE	14.4	15.4	17.9	21.9	23.4	18.0	22.4

Business Week Magazine's Index of Business Activity

BUSINESS WEEK INDEX, MONTHLY AVERAGES OF WEEKLY FIGURES
SEASONALLY ADJUSTED
(Index 1967 = 100)

	1940	1941	1942	1943	1944	1945	1946
JAN	25.7	30.4	37.3	46.6	49.9	48.3	34.2
FEB	23.6	31.3	38.8	47.4	50.0	47.9	31.4
MAR	22.4	32.6	39.8	48.1	49.8	48.4	35.3
APR	21.9	31.7	40.8	48.8	50.0	48.3	34.8
MAY	23.4	33.5	40.9	48.9	49.6	47.3	33.5
JUN	25.8	34.7	41.5	48.7	49.1	46.0	35.5
JUL	26.7	35.3	42.1	49.3	49.1	45.0	37.5
AUG	26.8	35.1	43.1	49.7	48.9	40.5	38.3
SEP	27.5	35.3	43.9	49.9	48.3	35.5	38.2
OCT	28.3	35.4	44.7	50.3	48.2	33.3	38.4
NOV	29.5	35.7	45.6	50.4	48.2	34.8	38.7
DEC	29.7	36.2	46.0	49.8	48.3	36.0	38.6
AVERAGE	25.9	33.9	42.0	49.0	49.1	42.6	36.2

	1947	1948	1949	1950	1951	1952	1953
JAN	38.7	40.8	40.5	40.5	49.1	49.6	56.3
FEB	38.7	40.1	39.6	39.0	49.2	49.8	55.4
MAR	40.3	40.4	39.9	40.9	50.3	50.6	56.9
APR	39.8	40.5	40.7	43.1	49.9	50.3	57.6
MAY	39.0	40.8	39.3	44.0	49.9	49.8	57.3
JUN	39.3	41.3	39.2	45.6	50.4	49.3	57.9
JUL	38.8	41.9	38.7	46.4	49.6	49.4	58.9
AUG	39.0	41.9	39.0	47.6	48.3	51.9	58.4
SEP	39.5	40.4	39.2	47.4	48.6	54.5	57.4
OCT	39.5	41.5	39.1	47.7	48.6	54.8	57.1
NOV	39.3	40.5	38.7	46.5	48.6	54.9	54.8
DEC	40.0	40.8	39.5	48.1	49.4	55.8	54.3
AVERAGE	39.3	40.9	39.5	44.7	49.3	51.7	56.9

	1954	1955	1956	1957	1958	1959	1960
JAN	53.9	57.8	62.9	65.4	58.1	64.0	68.8
FEB	52.7	58.1	61.8	64.8	56.5	64.0	67.8
MAR	52.8	59.6	62.2	65.0	55.8	65.4	67.7
APR	52.6	60.3	62.9	64.9	54.6	66.6	67.0
MAY	53.4	61.1	62.8	63.6	55.3	67.2	66.2
JUN	54.3	61.7	62.7	64.3	57.9	68.2	65.7
JUL	54.3	63.1	60.7	65.4	58.6	67.1	66.6
AUG	53.3	62.4	62.2	65.0	59.8	65.6	66.9
SEP	53.6	62.9	63.2	64.1	60.5	64.8	66.9
OCT	53.8	63.3	63.6	62.4	61.3	64.0	66.0
NOV	54.5	63.2	63.1	60.2	61.9	64.3	64.1
DEC	56.8	64.3	64.8	59.6	64.1	68.3	63.8
AVERAGE	53.8	61.5	62.7	63.7	58.7	65.8	66.5

Business Week Magazine's Index of Business Activity

BUSINESS WEEK INDEX, MONTHLY AVERAGES OF WEEKLY FIGURES
SEASONALLY ADJUSTED
(Index 1967 = 100)

	1961	1962	1963	1964	1965	1966	1967
JAN	63.4	72.5	76.0	80.1	86.6	94.9	99.6
FEB	63.2	72.4	75.7	79.7	86.8	95.7	98.3
MAR	63.7	73.2	75.4	80.2	87.4	97.4	97.6
APR	65.5	72.8	75.8	81.6	87.8	97.6	98.7
MAY	66.3	72.3	76.3	81.2	87.7	98.8	99.4
JUN	67.6	71.8	77.8	81.9	88.4	98.6	99.0
JUL	69.8	73.0	77.8	83.0	90.0	99.1	98.6
AUG	70.3	73.6	77.4	83.0	90.1	98.8	100.9
SEP	70.9	74.2	78.5	83.9	89.8	99.8	100.7
OCT	70.0	73.6	79.2	83.0	90.5	100.9	100.8
NOV	71.0	73.2	78.4	84.1	90.8	97.3	102.8
DEC	72.9	74.4	79.2	85.0	92.1	100.5	104.0
AVERAGE	67.9	73.1	77.3	82.2	89.0	98.3	100.0

	1968	1969	1970	1971	1972	1973	1974
JAN	103.8	108.9	108.8	108.0	114.2	126.0	129.3
FEB	104.3	109.3	109.0	107.9	115.0	127.5	129.3
MAR	104.5	110.8	109.3	108.4	116.3	128.3	130.6
APR	105.0	110.7	108.9	108.8	117.6	128.6	130.3
MAY	106.6	110.0	108.8	109.6	118.3	129.7	131.6
JUN	107.1	111.2	108.3	109.7	119.0	129.9	131.6
JUL	107.1	111.2	108.7	109.1	120.0	130.1	131.5
AUG	106.2	112.2	108.8	108.3	120.7	130.1	131.2
SEP	106.3	112.1	106.8	109.7	122.2	130.7	131.6
OCT	106.9	111.9	104.3	110.7	123.8	131.5	130.4
NOV	108.0	111.0	104.2	111.5	124.2	131.8	125.6
DEC	108.4	110.0	106.2	112.4	124.8	130.8	119.6
AVERAGE	106.2	110.8	107.7	109.5	119.7	129.6	129.4

	1975	1976	1977	1978	1979	1980	1981
JAN	115.0	125.2	131.9	139.1	149.2	148.5	143.0
FEB	112.8	126.7	132.5	139.3	150.0	149.1	143.2
MAR	111.3	127.7	134.3	140.9	151.0	148.9	143.7 r
APR	112.0	128.2	135.5	142.3	151.5	145.8	143.6 r
MAY	113.7	129.4	137.2	143.2	151.9	141.0	143.8 r
JUN	116.0	129.6	138.1	143.8	151.8	139.2	143.9
JUL	117.3	130.1	138.9	144.2	151.4	138.1	143.6
AUG	119.8	130.8	138.3	145.1	150.9	137.1	143.3
SEP	121.3	130.6	138.8	145.7	150.9	137.7	142.5
OCT	121.4	130.4	139.1	146.5	151.1	139.1	141.6
NOV	122.7	131.3	139.4	147.3	149.8	140.2	140.3
DEC	123.5	132.4	139.6	148.4	149.2	141.6	138.0
AVERAGE	117.8	129.4	137.0	143.8	150.7	142.2	142.5

since. Several reasons have been ascribed for this drop, but the primary reason was the very sharp increase in prices of automobiles, steel, and construction caused by wage increases. This is discussed more fully in Chapter 8. This was the first example of stagflation.

The next major drop came between the peak of wartime production during World War II, March, 1945, and the post-war letdown trough in February, 1946, for a total of 35.1%. In a normal business climate, a 35% drop would represent at least a minor disaster, but this was "re-tooling time," converting from a wartime economy and preparing to satisfy the tremendous pent-up demand for consumer goods that followed the war.

The index then rose, with few . . . and minor . . . exceptions until the sharp drop at the end of the "O.P.E.C.-induced" inventory run-up in late 1974. The next sharp drop started in late 1979, bottoming out in mid-1980.

Business activity picked up sharply for about a year and then started dropping again to a still lower level in early 1982. At the time of writing this last line, April 24, 1982, it appears that the present recession will become the worst one since World War II. Compensation-cost-push inflation has finally caught up and smothered business activity and employment. Much lower prices for big ticket items, cars, houses, etc., and much lower interest rates are absolutely essential to restore prosperity and jobs.

Anatomy of a Strike

The scene is a small town in a highly-industrialized area in Northwest Pennsylvania. The *dramatis personae* are a small division of an industrial conglomerate and its 400 workers belonging to the International Association of Machinists.

The company manufactures highly specialized valves and control equipment, much of it related to the nuclear power field. Among their principal customers are electric utility companies involved in nuclear power projects, and the U.S. Navy.

This is an area where labor unrest is not uncommon. It is also an area that is hurting, as is most of the Industrial Heartland, with an unemployment rate of about 9%.

This particular company had been, until this year, enjoying a steady improvement in its relations with the union. Grievance filing had declined steadily from between as many as 400 to 500 in 1977 to a heartening 50 or so in 1980. The leadership of the union changed going into 1981, however, and the grievance rate began to approach the level endured in 1977.

On June 3, 1981, contract negotiations began. On June 17, the company offered a package which was rejected by the union two days later, and the workers voted to strike. By October 4, 123 days after the start of negotiations, the strike had stretched out some three months, with the union having rejected two enriched company offers.

On October 4, the company ran a full-page advertisement in the Erie Times-News. The message was directed to the workers and their families, explaining the details of the wage and benefit package the company had offered . . . and the union rejected . . . on August 26.

More and more companies find that their side of the story on negotiations, after being filtered through the union leadership, is not getting through to the workers.

The advertisement included a graph showing its offer of a 12½% raise effective upon strike settlement plus two 8% increases coming at the beginning of the second and third years of the contract. It is not surprising that the advertisement enumerated and explained 15 benefit increases, including a company-paid dental plan, in addition to the wage raises; increasingly fat benefits are prevalent in today's union demands.

The strike lasted almost 17 weeks. A rough calculation of the loss in wages to the workers and to the community comes to about $2.2 million. Obviously, the company has lost many orders as well. In these tenuous times, neither of these losses are affordable.

However, current losses are not the most significant item. The portion of the tendered agreement that is most symptomatic of compensation–cost–push inflation is the pledge of annual increases over the term of the contract. In its message to the workers, the company calls them "Up Front" cost-of-living adjustments.

The strike was finally settled on October 25, 1981, with

the workers accepting the offer the company had made three months earlier.

Who "won" this strike? Certainly not the company— it lost four months production, numerous new orders, and probably customers they will not get back.

The workers? They lost four months' pay and benefits; their union was censured by the area courts; and, when operations resumed, over 100 of them . . . some . . . 30% were not called back.

In the three years preceeding the strike, the company had not laid off any workers. During slack periods they found cleanup or other work to keep their people on the payroll. Chances are that the company will not be so kindly disposed in the future . . . the union has changed the rules of the game.

Strikes do not produce winners and losers . . . only victims.

ANALYSIS 12
Base Plant Pay Levels by Locality

A study published by the Bureau of Labor Statistics of relative base pay levels in 71 city areas reveals some interesting facts, as shown on the accompanying table.

First: of the ten areas with high relative pay levels, six are in the highly union organized Middle West, three are on the West Coast, and the New York City area brings up the rear.

Second: all of the lowest-paid areas are in SunBelt States.

To compile the figures and establish the index, the BLS used average pay levels for the 262 Standard Metropolitan Statistical Areas (SMSA's) it monitors as the index number of 100. The table shows that pay levels run all the way from 69% of this average in San Antonio to almost 50% above average in Saginaw.

One might assume that living costs would correlate with these base pay levels, but such is not always the case. The Bureau's most famous index, the Consumer Price Index, shows that Houston, with a pay-level index only ¾ of the average, showed a C.P.I. figure of 219.7 in

December, 1978; Detroit, at a pay level almost ⅓ more than average, showed 202.2 on the C.P.I. scale on the same date.

Even a quick look at the figures in the table shows a cogent reason for the massive movement of industry to the South in the past few years.

RELATIVE PAY LEVELS, UNSKILLED PLANT WORKERS IN ALL INDUSTRIES, JANUARY— DECEMBER, 1978

(Average pay levels in 262 Standard Metropolitan Statistical Areas = 100)

Highest

Saginaw, Mich.	148
Davenport–Rock Island, Moline, Iowa	133
Detroit, Mich.	131
San Francisco–Oakland, Calif.	131
Toledo, Ohio–Mich.	125
Seattle–Everett, Wash.	124
Akron, Ohio	124
Chicago, Ill.	121
Portland, Oregon–Wash.	121
New York, N.Y.–N.J.	118

Lowest

San Antonio, Texas	69
Birmingham, Ala.	71
Jackson, Miss.	71
New Orleans, LA	72
Huntsville, Ala.	72
Greenville–Spartanburg, S.C.	74
Jacksonville, Fla.	74
Miami, Fla.	74
Houston, Texas	75

Source: Bureau of Labor Statistics

ANALYSIS 13

A Letter to My Grandchildren

By Robert S. Morrison

In 1965–66, I wrote a series of sixty weekly articles for the local newspaper. One was entitled, "A Letter to My Grandchildren." I believe you will find it interesting, shocking, and frighteningly accurate in its predictions. What amazes me now is how fast these predictions have come true. Here it is.

"Dear Grandchildren: August 21, 1965

"You have been, or likely will be, born into a social and economic group that has become second-rate American citizens. What do I mean by second-rate? Second-rate citizens are those who support, through their earnings and their savings, the first-rate U.S. citizens. First-rate citizens are those who do not support themselves entirely from their own earnings and savings, but are supported by earnings taken away from you second-rate citizens, primarily through taxes or through being able to charge monopolistic prices for their services, far in excess of the value rendered, with such monopolies being

332

sponsored or permitted by the government, usually for political reasons. First-rate citizens also have been granted special privileges which you and other second-rate citizens do not have.

"You, if you follow the paths taken by your parents, your grandparents, and generations before them, will be in the great American middle class socially and economically, a class that has no political power to protect its members, an amorphous class that has no coherence, no single goal, no ethnic, political, geographic, or economic boundaries. As a member of this class, you will be expected to get a good education, usually provided for you by the savings and earnings of your parents and you. Your future will depend almost entirely on your own efforts; you will not only be self-supporting, but you will give freely of your time and money for many worthy but innocuous causes, church, school, college, community funds, and other charities; but you and most of your group will voluntarily devote little time and money to, but a lot of talk and complaining about, your government and the "dirty business" of politics.

"You will, like the generations before you, let government and politics be taken over by people who either represent the entire cross-section of first-rate citizens or one or more of the minority groups composed of first-rate citizens. These politicians, legislators, administrators, judges, and union bosses will give more and more of your time (earnings) and money to their first-rate citizen constituents who will hold, and over the years have held, the balance of power to swing an election. Politicians of any party will cater and have catered to the balance of power minorities because the big, jelly fish American middle-class members are too busy seeking either money or pleasure to take an active strong position in politics. So, the country in which you will probably grow up will either be what we in 1965 would call completely socialistic, or it even may be Communistic through internal or external revolution and/or aggression.

"For tens of centuries older people have complained that the younger generation has "gone to the dogs" and they expect all sorts of economic, social, and physical calamities to happen when the younger generation takes over the reins, but somehow the younger generation learns rapidly and conditions improve economically. Today, 1965—the older generation has failed the younger generation. Now the younger generation of sensible, well-educated, reasonably disciplined American kids have to face and solve some very serious and difficult problems, problems created by the greed, short-sightedness, and self-interest of the older generation and the lack of courage and far-sightedness of our legislators, government leaders, and judges.

"What are these major problems, all resulting from pressure from and giving in to selfish minorities?

"1. Bankruptcy of the Social Security Fund. Young income earners are now being taxed more and more to support older people, most of whom had the opportunity but not the will power and foresight to provide for their older years. This taxation will get greater, far beyond present projected schedules.

"2. Constant inflation. At the past rate of inflation, your dollar will lose 75% of its value over your lifetime. This is one of the major causes for the bankruptcy of Social Security. Our legislators, union bosses, and big businessmen, any two of whom could stop this ridiculous round after round of wage increases in excess of productivity increases, are so shortsighted and so interested in getting re-elected to office next time that they refuse to face the problem squarely. With every round of wage increases and advance in the cost of living, hundreds of thousands of jobs are eliminated and people living on fixed dollar incomes sink further into the pit of poverty, to be supported by you, the new second-rate citizens.

"3. Militant minorities who disregard law and order, private property and private life rights, who make mockery of government and hoodlums and criminals of their members, and who demand, and so far are getting, far more economic and social privilege than their contribution to the economic and social welfare of the country justifies. Unless birth control is universally approved, adopted, and practiced, these minorities can become controlling majorities, and the present great American middle class, the backbone of the nation's intelligence, ability, economic strength, productivity and creativeness, will suffer the same fate as did the upper class in the French Revolution or the Jews in Hitler's Germany. I believe there are fine people of every race, religion, and nationality, but some groups in general do not assume the responsibilities that should go hand-in-hand with the privileges thcy arc demanding.

"4. Universal suffrage. Frankly, I do not believe that a person who cannot read or write English and/or has not generally produced enough products or services to keep from being a public charge and/or is now and will be drawing 65% or more of his income for the rest of his life from funds obtained from others by direct or indirect taxation should be permitted to vote. The power to vote is the power to tax. The power to tax is the power to destroy.

"5. The practically unlimited power of the federal government to tax, to usurp state and local authority, to pass legislation and interpret existing laws in new ways to favor one minority group at the expense of all the people, or to reduce private freedom and private rights, to perpetuate themselves in office, and to increase the scope and cost of federal operations. The present method of selecting and electing government officials from the President on down has resulted in getting mediocre officials and political hacks in office at all levels of government. With the seniority system determining who has control of federal legislation, it is unlikely that needed reforms can be made without a tremendous wave of public resistance and indignation. Democracy is a costly, wasteful luxury with its faults difficult to correct, but it is still the best form of government yet devised.

"6. The last serious problem I shall list—but there are hundreds more—is the grave possibility of the loss of the two-party system. Without two strong political parties, each one capable of winning any election, government will become more and more unresponsive to the will of the people and more and more dictatorial.

"These are the problems which the adults of 1965 and before have permitted to arise, have even encouraged, and have failed to solve. As far as I can see, we have not even tried to solve them. I am trying, in a futile, little way, to make our little area of the country aware of the problems, but that is all I have done so far.

"Next to good health and a sound, active mind, the greatest asset any of you can have is a feeling of insecurity. Security is a dangerous opiate that prevents anyone from doing his best."

Lovingly,

Bob Morrison

Your Grandfather

1965 Analysis of Social Security

This letter appeared as an article in the Ashtabula Star-Beacon

Dear Readers: March 13, 1965

I had already assembled many facts and planned a letter to you on the problems, and possible solutions, in our local government, but a Sylvia Porter article appeared recently in the Star Beacon that made some statements that must be true, but if true, are so shocking when examined closely that I felt I should discuss them immediately.

First, let me say that the original concept of Social Security, with 1% of the first $3,000 of annual earnings paid into the fund by both the individual and his employer, was an excellent idea. What are Social Security tax rates now and what are they scheduled to increase to, even before Medicare or some similar scheme is adopted?

Year	Total Rate	Earnings Ceiling	Total Tax
1965	7.25%	$4,800	$348
1966	8.25%	$4,800	$396
1967	8.25%	$4,800	$396
1968	9.25%	$4,800	$444

Congress has voted increase after increase in benefits, every election year, to be paid to people whose total contributions, including employer, could not even justify the original benefit schedule. On an actuarial basis, the Social Security fund is bankrupt by several hundred billion dollars, yet our Congressmen plan more raids on the fund, but dare not increase the tax rates to a point where the fund could get back on a sound basis in 20 years.

Sylvia Porter's article stated: "If you're a middle-aged worker who will have paid taxes (S.S.) over your full working lifetime of 45 years before you retire, you can look forward to benefits amounting to more than double your contributions."

This sounds not so bad until we remember that for every dollar you paid, your employer paid a dollar, so on that basis you are getting back just about what was paid into your account. However, over 45 years, your payments should have earned compound interest. At 4% compound interest the amount credited to your total account should have increased to about 273% of the amount paid in during your 45 years of working life. If between you and your employers you had paid in $444 a year for 45 years, (a total of $19,980) this sum, with compound interest, should have increased to $54,811. Yet, according to Sylvia, you will get somewhat over $19,980. Congressmen, buying votes for themselves now, will have given away over $34,000 of money that is rightfully yours.

Now, this is not all of your loss. At the present rate of erosion of the value of the dollar, the $19,980 you will receive during your period of retirement will buy less than $10,000 would have bought, on an average, during your 45 years of working. During the thirty years Social Security has been in existence, the purchasing power of the dollar has dropped almost 65%, but it may not drop quite as fast in the future. So you will be short, on your Social Security, almost $44,000, the biggest nest-egg most people will ever have.

If you had, at age 20, placed $444 a year into buying an annuity from an insurance company, you would receive, during your period of retirement after 65, total payments of $39,620 if you live till age 80, the average life expectancy of a 65-year-old person, plus having $25,000 life insurance all the time from age 20 to 65. With $5,000 life insurance, your annuity would pay you $55,520.

If you put $444 each year for 45 years into common stocks listed on the New York Exchange, and reinvested your dividends after current income tax, you would have stocks worth somewhere around $150,000, if inflation continues as it has in the past. Common stocks increase in dollar value as the cost of living goes up. Of course, you would have to select the stocks, and these stocks could have increased far more than that, or could be worth far less than that. A reputable investment trust would be the best way for the small investor to buy common stocks.

So, the Great White Fathers in Washington are doing a lousy job providing for the old age of people who will work many years before retirement. Any insurance company that did such a lousy job would find its executives all in jail.

For a person just starting to work, Sylvia reports: "You can anticipate total retirement benefits nearly half again as big as your own contributions. . . ." She calls this "reassuring." I call it legalized robbery and the biggest swindle yet perpetrated in the entire world at any time in history. What does this swindle amount to in dollars? Now 63,000,000 people are paying Social Security taxes. If we figure this as a swindle just on them and not a continuing swindle, and each of them and their employers pay in $19,980, over their working lives, and they receive back only 75% of $19,980, which at the time they receive it will be worth only $9,990, they will get $7,498 in equivalent dollars as compared to $54,545 they should receive. So the total amount they are swindled is $2,980,719,000,000. No one now collecting Social Security or starting to collect it in the next few years will get swindled, because present benefits far exceed the contributions and accrued interest made by the recipients.

How much is almost three trillion dollars? It is greater than the net value of all the physical assets in the U.S. at present. It is almost six times our present Gross National Product, and ten times the present annual income of all individuals in the U.S. put together.

Congress has approved paying out to Social Security recipients many times the total amount that should be paid them based on what has been paid in and accumulated earnings. Sylvia says: "If you are now a retired person, you can expect benefits—of more than ten times your contributions." The Federal Civil Service Pension Fund is overdrawn $34,500,000,000 because payments have exceeded contributions.

The way the government is running the Social Security Fund is just like the old chain-letter racket. As long as many times as many people are working and paying into the fund as are getting payments from the fund, the fund will be able to meet payments, and by swindling younger people out of what is rightfully theirs, it could become solvent again in about 40 years if benefits are held at the present levels, which, of course, they will not be. Congressmen should never be allowed to buy votes with money put in trust for you and me. They buy votes with our tax money, but we are used to this type of hooking.

I really do not think Sylvia Porter is naive enough to believe the Social Security situation is reassuring.

Sincerely yours,
/s/Bob Morrison

P.S. On August 14, 1970, the 35th Anniversary of Social Security was noted. The publicity release bragged that Social Security provided over a trillion dollars in life insurance for its participants, more than all the private life insurance companies put together. However, the assets behind this life insurance are so small that future pay-offs will be made from future taxes.

ANALYSIS 15

Why Exempt Federal Pensions from the Anti-Inflation Drive?

*By Hastings Keith**

President Reagan's budget revisions of March 10 indicated for the first time that his budget analysts were beginning to comprehend the potentially disastrous nature of cost-of-living adjustments (COLA) for federal retirees.

Administration officials are now asking Congress to replace the twice-a-year COLA for civil service and other federal pension beneficiaries with a single annual adjustment, at a savings approximating a whopping $900 million in 1982.

But Office of Management and Budget (OMB) Director David Stockman's budgeteers have thus far only scratched the surface of the federal pay problem. They have yet to confront the totality of the extraordinarily costly and exorbitantly generous federal pension systems. The long-range implications of these pensions may portend for the nation what New York's financial crisis was

---

* Keith, a former U.S. congressman from Massachusetts, 1959–73, has served as vice chairman of the Defense Manpower Commission and as project manager for the Aspen Institute's workshop on public pensions.

to that city and what Studebaker's and now Chrysler's crises are to the auto industry.

The federal pension systems are unique when contrasted with retirement systems for the rest of the nation's work force. We federal retirees are treated as sacred cows—protected by the same safety net that, properly for the most part, shelters Social Security beneficiaries.

FROM ONE WHO KNOWS

I am a prime example. I am one of more than 2.5 million federal retirees whose benefits have been increased as the result of cost-of-living adjustments. My federal pensions now total $1,000 a week.

Specifically, my pension as a retired congressman with both civil and military service has gone from $1,560 a month in 1973 to $3,420 as of March 1, 1981. I also get a military (reservist) pension which has gone up from about $600 per month in 1975 to $900 as of March 1, 1981. And, as of my 65th birthday, I am eligible for a tax-free Social Security check of about $600 per month. Because my military time counts twice—for both military and civil service pensions—I am what is known as a "double dipper." My pensions may not be typical but they are illustrative of flaws in the benefit formulas that are widespread in the civil service. They also reflect some of the logic behind the conclusions I have reached.

Frankly, my conscience troubles me. It troubles me because, as George Will implied in a recent syndicated column, we in the Congress, in voting for unlimited indexation of pensions—and then passing these costs on to future generations—have, in effect, been "mugging" our children and our grandchildren. Most of us did this innocently, thinking that our 7 or 8 percent contribution, when matched by the government, would be sufficient to support the benefits we would eventually get. This is not the case. Few members of Congress have such a sweet arrangement as I do. Reform could be helpful to those who will be bypassed by the present rules of eligibility, specifically five years of service.

The civil service retirement plan started off as a good plan but the increasingly liberal benefit formula ruined it. The early retirements, the double-dipper credits for military service in both military and civil service retirements, the liberal definition of disability (accounting for more than 30 percent of all civil service retirements), the twice-a-year indexation of the total annuity to the cost of living—all of these things, together with the unanticipated high rates of inflation, have had an explosive impact on costs. At the same time, the generous benefits are actually inducing civil servants to leave government early and take jobs in the private sector, thereby becoming eligible for Social Security benefits and often another pension as well.

Civil service pensions alone take from the taxpayer $4.50 for every dollar the civil servant puts in. Even so, the contributions from these two sources fall far short of funding the eventual benefits that the plan promises.

The unfunded liabilities for the civil service, according to the working papers of the President's Commission on Pension Policy, published in January 1981, were $403.1 billion as of Sept. 30, 1979. For the foreign service they were an additional $3.8 billion and for the military $444.6 billion. All three bring the total federal liability to close to a trillion dollars—in effect almost doubling the national debt! (These projections reflect the cost of pensions for those already retired and for the service to date of present employees.)

Another way to look at it is that for *each* participant,

active and retired, there are unfunded liabilities of $237,000 for the foreign service, $103,000 for the military and $89,000 for the civil service.

And so I am extremely concerned that our economic recovery efforts will be flawed unless and until this most important issue of federal employee pensions is confronted.

SAVINGS IN THE BILLIONS

Modest reforms in the federal pension benefit formula—in addition to the once-a-year COLA—could, by the end of President Reagan's first term, save the nation's taxpayers as much as several billions of dollars a year. Such reforms would: (1) establish a ceiling beyond which the pension would not be indexed; (2) change the definition of civil service disability to conform to that of Social Security; (3) cut out from the civil service benefit formula all credit for years of service in the military; (4) provide, in the case of military retirees, a retirement supplement until Social Security begins, as is the case with many private plans (military retirees now get gratuitous add-ons to their regular pensions); and (5) remove the "socially-weighted" benefit portion of any Social Security pension paid to federal retirees whose pensions are above a specified minimum.

The federal employee with a relatively short Social Security earnings record gets a "socially weighted" benefit that was intended to take care of the poorer segments of our society. If the Social Security pension were actuarially computed, one would find many federal employees' contributions would be minimal, providing in most cases only a very small percentage of the funds required.

But major restructuring—integrating the three largest federal pension systems with Social Security—would lift many more billions from the backs of taxpayers of today and for generations yet unborn.

Fortunately, there are several federal systems that have gone this route. One, the Tennessee Valley Authority (TVA), is an excellent model in that its total benefits— except for early retirements—are quite comparable with those of the civil service. One difference is that, because of a belief that there should be an "incentive for continued work and contribution to society," the plan does permit long-service retirees to receive benefits that amount to more than 100 percent of final pay.

The TVA plan is unique among federal plans in that it funds benefits as they are earned. Also, its disability provisions, following the pattern imposed by the Social Security Administration, are more strictly administered. It gives no credit for military service; it discourages early retirements; and its pension plan costs only 11.5 percent of payroll. (To comply with the Employee Retirement Income Security Act—ERISA—would require 14.7 percent of payroll.) Adding the cost to the government of the Social Security pension benefit increases these totals another 5.35 percent.

What a difference it would make in the 1985 federal budget if the Congress would agree with the concept of the TVA plan and would require the civil service to integrate with Social Security. With a projected payroll of $74.4 billion in 1985, the savings in pension costs for the civil service alone would be $12.239 billion.

But that is not all. Rita Ricardo-Campbell, chairman of President Reagan's Task Force on Social Security, testified in February before the House Ways and Means Committee that mandatory coverage of all federal employees would yield an additional $11 billion for the Social Security funds next year and progressively higher amounts each successive year.

It is no surprise to me that Reps. J. J. Pickle (D.-Tex.) and Barber Conable (R.-N.Y.) have put these facts together, have seen the savings to the taxpayer of $25 billion, and are sponsoring bills calling for Social Security coverage for members of Congress and their staff and, in the case of Conable, all federal employees. They know that universal coverage must come, and that the question of the solvency of Social Security will loom as a big issue and come up for resolution perhaps later this year. They want their constituents and their colleagues to be thinking about it and be ready for it.

NO WAY TO MATCH

There is no way that private sector retirement plans can be brought up to the levels of the civil service pensions— it's just too costly. Adding the cost of such pensions to the cost of production would price us out of the world market and subject us to a flood of imports. As a matter of fact, if one considers that taxes are part of the cost of doing business in this country, we have already, in the civil service pension programs alone, an overhead that is bound to adversely affect our ability to compete on the world scene.

And so reform of the civil service, foreign service and military pension systems is imperative if we are to save the entire nation from a fate similar to that which befell New York City. The essential difference between the situation in New York City in 1975 and the federal government's problems in 1981, of course, is that New York City had to balance its budget whereas the federal government, in effect, prints more money. It's a classic case of more money chasing fewer goods.

Although the president did not directly state or suggest that he had such reforms in mind, he did set the stage for pension reform when he said that the nation would no longer continue to subsidize individuals where real need could not be demonstrated, adding that only programs for the highly deserving would remain untouched. In all logic, I believe that the president should not ignore the clear evidence that the pension benefits of most federal employees far exceed the norm of private sector pension plans and that large numbers of public employees are getting what amounts to transfer payments. There is every reason for OMB's Stockman to set his budgeteers to researching this area. It is, as I have said, fertile ground.

Only a handful of members of Congress—or industry or labor leaders for that matter—are prepared to get out in front on this issue. Congressmen often find it difficult to vote for something that might appear to affect the federal pension systems adversely. But we know that the vast majority of the members of Congress and the civil service place the public interest above personal interest and would support pension reform if they *and* their constituents had the facts.

In the final analysis, of course, it is the president who must take the lead in federal pension reform. My basic feeling is that Ronald Reagan was elected because the American people felt he stood for basic values, including the value of a healthy, stable currency. The best way to safeguard the dollar is to attack the psychology that breeds inflation, a psychology nurtured by the present federal pensions situation.

CAUSE TO RENEGE

President Reagan may feel constrained by campaign statements that indicated his administration would not tamper with federal pensions, especially as regards the twice-a-year indexing. However, new evidence has come to light which, in my view, frees the administration from any "commitment" not to act.

Included in this new evidence is a study by the Joint Economic Committee of Congress which warned that, based on 1975–78 projected inflationary growth rates, federal costs of the civil service pensions alone could reach a mind-boggling $80 billion a year by 1990, less than nine years away. Other evidence was provided by the President's Commission on Pension Policy. The commission noted that expected 1980 federal contributions were 30.8 percent of payroll for the civil service pension system and 83.5 percent for the foreign service systems. It went on to say that if these systems were funded on the same basis as private pension plans (according to ERISA minimum standards), costs last year would have been 79.8 percent and 107.1 percent of payroll respectively!

As these costs sink into the consciousness of those who only have Social Security, there will be strong public support for pension reform for the federal work force. This will be particularly true as arguments are advanced to have these taxpayers postpone their retirement to age 68 to allow the average civil servant to retire at 55.

Fresh data such as this has prompted distinguished citizens to organize for action. John Macy, the former Civil Service Commission chairman, and I are recruiting other former civil servants to rally around a "common sense in public compensation" banner that could lead to effective reforms. Former Undersecretary of Commerce Joseph Bartlett, who served as chairman of the Universal Social Security Study Group, strongly endorses Social Security for federal employees and joins Macy and me in this effort.

A similar response by the Reagan administration to the overwhelming and increasingly obvious case for federal pension reform would be a clear signal that the federal government is determined to put its own house in order and thereby honor commitments implied in the election sweep of last November. As longtime U.S. Comptroller General Elmer Staats wrote in a letter to the president, "Although congressional action will be required to effect most of the needed reforms, strong presidential support will be needed to bring them to fruition."

When the president acts, he will find many allies across the country, including rank-and-file federal civil servants, who will support the effort to restore common sense in public compensation through responsible reform of the present extravagant and inflation-fueling federal pensions system.

ANALYSIS 16

Douglas Fraser Letters

In the mid-1970's Douglas Fraser, then Vice President of the United Auto Workers, and I appeared on a Lou Gordon TV show telecast in Detroit and Cleveland. We reached absolutely no points of mutual agreement. The accompanying letters are self-explanatory.

As this is written, October, 1981, it appears that the suggestion I made last December, that the United Auto Workers cut their wages and fringes by 20% to get the auto industry reestablished and also lead in the drive to stop inflation, was an excellent one. Fraser's replies to my letters indicate how difficult it would be to get union officials to accept such a program willingly.

In January and February, 1982, both General Motors and Ford negotiated with the U.A.W. to reduce labor costs per unit produced. As this later comment is written, no changes have been accepted by the union.

For later developments, see page xiv.

December 23, 1980

Douglas Fraser, President
United Auto Workers of America
Solidarity House
8000 East Jefferson
Detroit, Michigan 48214

Dear Mr. Fraser:

About six or seven years ago I appeared with you on the Lou Gordon television show. Our views on the economic situation were diametrically opposed, so we did not become acquainted.

At that time I told you that the policies of the U.A.W. and other labor unions would lead to pricing themselves and their products out of the market. I further said that productivity increases, if and when they occurred, should be passed along to all the buyers or users of the product or service being produced by the union members rather than be absorbed in increases solely for the union members. I further pointed out that increases in excess of productivity increases were inflationary.

I appreciated then—and I still do—that the heads of unions have to attempt to get more and more for their members or their members become quite vociferous. Under the circumstances, it is difficult for a union executive to take a long-range, sound view of wage policies and the pricing of the products being produced by the company that employs the union members.

It is a great disgrace that Japanese cars can be produced in Japan, which has no basic raw materials, and shipped all the way to the United States and distributed at prices as low as or lower than comparable American cars. Setting high tariffs is not the answer, because the tariffs protect only the inefficient producers and overpaid workers at the expense of the rest of the American public.

I was an auto dealer for over ten years and have sold to the auto industry for thirty years. I have also been an amateur economist and a writer of books on the subject. You had a copy of my book with page after page underlined by people who did not agree with me and did not realize the soundness of my views.

It is unlikely that Chrysler can be rescued with anything but a very massive cut in compensation costs. These massive cuts would trickle through to Chrysler suppliers and gradually throughout the entire U.S. economy. A 20% cut in compensation would, over a period of time, result in close to a 20% cut in prices, which would make American products not only competitive in their own market but competitive in some foreign markets.

I felt I should pass along these truths to you even though I doubt if you are in a position to implement them even if you agreed with me. I will be happy to sit down and discuss the subject with you if you wish.

Very truly yours,

Robert S. Morrison

RSM:ec

January 8, 1981

Mr. Robert S. Morrison
Chairman and C.E.O.
Molded Fiber Glass Companies
1315 W. 47th Street
P. O. Box 675
Ashtabula, OH 44004

Dear Mr. Morrison:

I have your letter of December 23, and I don't think any constructive purpose would be served by you and I sitting down and discussing economics.

I do very well recall your book, and you are right that I had underlined all of the passages that contained gross inaccuracies. As you may recall, there were many.

We have always bargained based upon the realities at the bargaining table, and evidently the following situations have escaped your attention: UAW accepted reductions in pay in White Motor, in Massey-Ferguson, and, coincidentally, we are now negotiating with the Chrysler Corporation and the result of these negotiations will be a paycut for the Chrysler workers, although I am not prepared to say, at this point, how much. The United Rubber Workers took wage cuts in both Goodyear and Goodrich. The United Steelworkers, in a couple of locations, accepted wage freezes and wage cuts. So you see, Mr. Morrison, again you want to have a discussion based upon a completely and totally inaccurate premise. As I stated, based upon such inaccuracies, a discussion would serve no useful purpose.

Sincerely,

Douglas A. Fraser
President

DAF:mw
opeiu-494

January 14, 1981

Douglas A. Fraser, President
United Auto Workers of America
8000 East Jefferson Avenue
Detroit, Michigan 48214

Dear Mr. Fraser:

I was pleased to receive your letter of January 8. I can see no justification for further correspondence, but I feel I should comment on two points brought up in your letter:

You spoke of my book containing "gross inaccuracies." There were no gross inaccuracies in it. There were gross differences between your people's view of certain subjects and my views, but there were no statements of fact that were inaccurate. If anybody wishes to point out what they think are inaccuracies in it, I will be glad to study their claims.

The U.A.W. accepted reductions in pay at White Motor and Massey-Ferguson because they had no choice. The companies were bankrupt. You accepted elimination of costly future fringes with Chrysler but until this time have not actually reduced compensation rates at Chrysler. In all of these cases you were forced into it, and you did not make any adjustments of your own free will.

As far as the rubber workers and steel workers are concerned, any reductions in pay they were forced to accept were to keep from losing jobs completely by the shutting down of plants.

How you can claim that the unions, of their own volition, accepted these pay cuts is beyond me. All of these companies were put into the condition they are currently in by excessive wage and fringe demands and by work policies that prevented the plants becoming as efficient as they should be to become competitive with foreign companies. If you had had any foresight, you would have realized this several years ago and adjusted your demands to where the American auto companies, steel companies, and rubber companies could be healthy and stay in operation. It does your people no good to work for unhealthy, weak companies, which eventually go bankrupt.

I doubt if your union will have enough self-discipline and foresight to keep Ford Motor Company from following the path of Chrysler. Even General Motors cannot continue to operate at its present volume level and pay the fabulous and completely unjustified wages and fringes to your people. The American public just will not stand for it. The way the American public registers its complaint is to buy foreign cars or not to buy any cars. You have no monopoly on the American public's dollar, although you may have a monopoly on the sick American auto industry.

You could do a great service to the country's economy

and to mankind in general if you set an example of self-control and long-range appreciation of the problems of American industry by reducing the tremendous amount of money these companies are forced to pay you.

Possibly you saw Peter Drucker's article in The Wall Street Journal recently. In case you did not, I am sending you a copy of it. It illustrates the difficult situation in which your union and many other similar powerful unions have been trapped by their own greed.

Very truly yours,

Robert S. Morrison

RSM:ec
Enc. Drucker article

January 19, 1981

Mr. Robert S. Morrison
Chairman and C.E.O.
Molded Fiber Glass Companies
1315 W. 47th Street
P. O. Box 675
Ashtabula, Ohio 44004

Dear Mr. Morrison:

You are wrong again. Not only did we freeze future wage increases in Chrysler, but we took a $1.15 an hour absolute reduction in wages.

Yours truly,

Douglas A. Fraser
President

DAF:aeb
opeiu494

January 26, 1981

Douglas A. Fraser, President
United Auto Workers of America
8000 East Jefferson Ave.
Detroit, Michigan 48214

Dear Mr. Fraser:

I have your letter of January 19, which puzzles me. On January 14 I wrote you "You accepted elimination of costly future fringes with Chrysler, but until this time"

(January 14) "have not actually reduced compensation rates at Chrysler. In all of these cases you were forced into it, and you did not make any adjustments of your own free will."

All I know is what I read in the papers, and I feel certain that your agreement to accept the elimination of $1.15 an hour was made after my letter of January 14; consequently, I am, as usual, not "wrong again."

Regardless of semantics, a reduction in current payroll costs will be a big help to Chrysler but still may not be enough to solve their problems. Chrysler has, as you know, difficulties beyond those of total labor costs and productivity.

There are two other companies that are suffering very badly from cash flow problems: Ford Motor Company and International Harvester. Why the union refused to accept from International Harvester the same contract terms that they had with John Deere and other farm implement manufacturers is beyond me. We do very little business in the automotive field, but we do quite a bit of business with farm implement manufacturers. My men report to me that productivity and morale in the International Harvester plants are much lower than in John Deere and other plants.

It is difficult to believe that a company as strong and previously as prosperous as Ford Motor Company could, within reasonably short order, be unable to pay its bills. I doubt if the government could come to the rescue of Ford Motor Company at that time.

You, personally, could do a lot to help Ford Motor Company out of their problem. No doubt they will be asking you to make the same reductions in their total compensation package as you made to Chrysler. They need it now and not when they are unable to continue or to borrow money from the banks. Ford's credit is still fairly good, but it will not stay that way very long with these tremendous losses.

You probably can do more than any other single individual to help U.S. industry out of its troubles. U.S. industry must regain its competitiveness, its productivity, and its ability to make products at prices that the American public will and can pay.

In my letters to you, I am trying to encourage you to take these stands. I am not trying to continue our debate or to tell you that you are wrong and I am right. I am just hoping that you have enough power and long-range foresight to eliminate some of the problems that U.S. industry now has.

Very truly yours,

Bob Morrison

Robert S. Morrison

RSM:ec

February 2, 1981

Mr. Robert S. Morrison
Chairman and C.E.O.
Molded Fiber Glass Companies
1315 W. 47th Street
P. O. Box 675
Ashtabula, OH 44004

Dear Mr. Morrison:

I have your latest communication, dated January 26.

This is beginning to sound redundant, but when you state that we "did not make any adjustments of your own free will" you are wrong once more. The first of the three agreements we reached with Chrysler, in the last 15 months, was arrived at in October 1979. This was before the loan guarantee legislation was enacted and, without any outside interference, that agreement with Chrysler resulted in economic concessions in the amount of $202 million over the life of the agreement.

You state in the second paragraph of your letter, "All I know is what I read in the papers," and perhaps, Mr. Morrison, therein lies the problem.

Sincerely,

Douglas A. Fraser
President

DAF:mw
opeiu-494

Index

Index

Index

French & Indian War, 98
Furnace, Bessemer, 93

Garibaldi, 90
Gasoline, 14
General Motors, xli
General practitioner, xvi
George III, 99
Germany, 33
Gin, cotton, 94
God, 106
Gold, 30, 100
Gold standard, 185
Gompers, Samuel, 103
Gottlieb, William, xviii
Government, securities, 28, 31, 32
Government, securities, ownership of, 40
Government, securities, purchases of, 58
Government, U.S., xxii, 27, 31
Grants and Estates, Federal, 97, 98
Greenbacks, 34
Gross National Product, xxi, 171
G.N.P., government's share of, 62

Hamilton, Alexander, 99
Handbook for Manufacturing
   Entrepreneurs, xxxvi
Harvard Business School, xxxi
History of Industrial Employment, 89
Hobbs Act, xxxiii
Housing, 303
Human nature, 131

Immigration, 100
Implicit Price Deflator, xxii, 67
Imports, U.S., 69, 70
Inclosures, 92
Income, corporate share, 109
Income, subsistence, 91
Indentured servant, 90, 97
Independent Workers of the World, 103
Industrial development, xxxi
Industrial Revolution, 89, 93, 101, 105
Industries, auto, steel, construction,
   mining, 111
Inelastic demand, 14, 26
Inelastic supply, 14

Infant mortality, 95
Inflation, xix, xlii
Inflation, anticipation of, 79
Inflation Can Be Stopped, xxxix
Inflation, compensation-cost-push, 107
Inflation, demand-pull, 38
Inflation, hedge against, 232
Inflation, validating, 40
Israel, 73
Institutions, financial, 53
Institutions, savings, 42
Institutions, tax-exempt, 46
Interest rates, 14, 51, 86
International pressures, 85
Investment, 14
Investment, capital, 18
Iran, 70

Jackson, Andrew, 100
Japanese currency, 70
Jefferson, Thomas, 99
Job Evaluation, National, 203–204, 206–207
Justice, Chief, Warren Burger, 215

Kay, John, 93
King Henry V, 5
King Henry VIII, 5
Kings, 90
Kirkland, Lane, xxxiii
Knights of Labor, 101

Labour Party, 95
Landlords, 87
Land prices, 232
Laws, Corn, 95
Laws, poor, 92
Lawyers, Association of Trial, 79
Leasing, 50
Legislation, Social, 106
Lewis, John L., 104, 164
Liabilities, 30
Liability, product, 78
"Little Steel" case, 148
Loans, long-term, 45, 46
Loans, short-term, 45
Loom, power, 93
Loopholes, 76
Lord North, 99

Index

Index